Ex Líbrís

THE
CIVIL WAR

THE
CIVIL WAR

Edited and with an introduction by Stephen W. Sears

Houghton Mifflin Company
Boston
1991

PRINTED IN THE UNITED STATES

CIP data is available.
ISBN 0-395-61905-X

10 9 8 7 6 5 4 3 2 1

CONTENTS

INTRODUCTION

The Civil War has always occupied an important place in the pages of *American Heritage*. In part, of course, this is because of the war's surpassingly important place in the nation's history, that history being the magazine's beat. As Oliver Jensen, one of the magazine's editors once put it, the Civil War is "America's most monumental drama and morality tale." A second reason for the war's treatment in the magazine is that beginning in 1954, when *American Heritage* began appearing in its present form, Bruce Catton was the editor—and in later years the senior editor and editor emeritus.

As one of the best historians the Civil War has ever had, Catton naturally attracted other writers to the magazine who believed they had something important to say about the war, and they were made welcome. Catton, and now the Catton legacy, have much to do with the shape and range of the selections that follow. I know that in the many years I worked for and with editor Catton, enough of his interest in the war's history rubbed off that it is now my chief interest as well.

The range of these pieces is as wide as the war itself. The first one, appropriately enough, is by Bruce Catton, who offers cogent observations on the writing of Civil War history, which is what he did best. What he said in 1966 is no less true today: "To understand that part of our past we need to understand the present, because today we are grappling with the commitment that was made for us a century ago." James M. McPherson, whose Civil War writings are as widely known today as Catton's were in his day, is interested in the same theme. In "A War That Never Goes Away" he analyzes Americans' continuing and unceasing fascination with a conflict whose last witnesses have been gone now for some four decades.

Major themes woven together make up the tapestry of the Civil War, and three such themes are examined in these pages.

The eminent historian Allan Nevins takes an unsparing look at the weakling Buchanan's role in the coming of the war. The equally eminent Carl N. Degler examines the surprisingly broad range of opinions throughout the old South on the burning issues of that day. No theme of the war is more significant than that of emancipation. Stephen B. Oates traces the long and tortuous road that led to freedom for the slaves.

The fate of all these themes of war came down at last to the battlefield. They rested, as James McPherson tells us, "on the shoulders of those weary men in blue and gray who fought it out during four years of ferocity unmatched in the Western world between the Napoleonic Wars and World War I." The men and the battlefields receive their due here. No American general has so captured our national imagination—in the North as well as in the South—as Robert E. Lee, whom Stephen Vincent Benét called "the marble man." Far less famous, but crucial to the Union's final victory, was George Thomas, "The Rock of Chickamauga" and crafter of Northern victories in the Western theater. Here too is the story of a general's courage when the fighting was done—"General Grant's Gallant Last Battle." Stories of the less famous are no less compelling. Belle Boyd was a Confederate spy who, paradoxically, became known for spying. A black sergeant named William Walker whom hardly anyone knew demonstrated that he was willing to die for a principle.

Two battles great in dimension are examined in detail. In "Crisis at the Antietam" Bruce Catton looks at the fateful day in September of 1862—the bloodiest single day in our national history—on which so much depended. In a purely military sense, the most remarkable single battle of the war was Chancellorsville, detailed by Robert K. Krick, that marked the peak of Robert E. Lee's genius.

Seen in tight focus are the stories of the two vitally important but utterly contrasting warships, the Yankees' *Monitor* and the Rebels' *Alabama*. There is high adventure in two stories geographically far apart—"The Great Locomotive Chase" that coursed through the state of Georgia, and one of the weirdest bank robberies in American history in far-off Vermont. By contrast, there was nothing romantic about that day in Pennsylvania when the town of Chambersburg was burned to the ground. When finally the four years of war were over, it was celebrated with a spectacular parade in which two great armies marched through the capital of the reunited nation.

These are stories of large scale and of the tightly focused incident, in the same way that the war itself was a mosaic of the large and small. They add in an important way to our understanding of that prodigious conflict, for all are stories of people—Americans who lived in a time when (in Oliver Wendell Holmes's phrase) their lives were "touched with fire."

—*Stephen W. Sears*
May 1991

ON WRITING ABOUT THE CIVIL WAR

by BRUCE CATTON

How it should be done, by a master of the craft.

I t seems like a long time ago as I write this, and as a matter of fact it really was—sixteen years, roughly, which make up a fair fraction of any man's life—but somewhere around 1950 I got into the Civil War, and now it seems time to talk about it.

Getting into a war that ended almost ninety years earlier and that has no living survivors is a good deal different from getting into a real live war that is being fought by contemporaries who would like to become living survivors but have no assurance that that will happen; and the veteran of a war that was fought a generation before he was born must walk softly and speak humbly when he tells about what happened to him. But even though death and horror and tragedy have muted echoes when they were actually experienced by someone else, they nevertheless have their effect.

In the beginning, of course—and this was true of most of the actual participants, North and South alike—there was a blind and uncritical enthusiasm. In 1950 the Civil War looked much as it did in the very early part of 1861: full of color, romance, and the glint of high adventure. Jeb Stuart and his plumed hat had something to do with this, and so did General Lee and his gray coat, General McClellan and his great black horse, Phil Sheridan and his furious temper, and the young men in blue and gray who sat around campfires singing the inexpressibly mournful little songs that still send moving harmonies down the years. Part of it came from books read in youth and part of it from the remembered procession of gray-bearded veterans standing bowed in a village cemetery on Memorial Day; part of it, too, from some quirk in the national

memory that inexplicably recalls the bright and shining moments and manages to forget the dark and bloody ones. At the
start it was all swords and roses.

It began, really, with a great desire to get acquainted with
the private soldier of the Civil War. Too many books have
discussed that war strictly in terms of the generals: Sherman
did this, Hancock did that, and Johnston did some other
thing; this general made a heroic assault and that one made a
heroic defense; and the men who fought and died at their
bidding are simply counters that move from this square to that
on an elaborate chessboard and finally are dropped into a box.
It seemed important to get at the man who paid for those
heroic assaults and defenses and to see what the war looked
and smelled and felt like to him.

So my part in the Civil War began, and continued for
quite a while, as an attempt to explain it all in terms of the man
whom we would now call the G.I. Joe. It turned out that
although he was out of reach—on the far side of the river that
Stonewall Jackson saw in his dying moments—the Civil War
enlisted man was easy to get acquainted with. He was most
articulate, he left many letters, diaries, and reminiscences,
preserved in every imaginable depository from university libraries to someone's attic, and he spoke his mind freely. He
talked about his officers and about his food, about the irritat-
ing absurdities of army life and its deadly monotony, and
about the evils of making forced marches across country. (He
had a hard time making up his mind whether marching in the
rain and mud was worse than marching in heat and ankle-deep
dust; the consensus seems to have been that whichever you
were actually doing was worse.) He was usually a bit reserved
when it came to describing the reality of combat. He was
willing enough to tell where his regiment went and what it
did, but when it came to saying what fighting was really like,
he generally picked his words carefully, apparently on the
theory that the man who had been there did not need to be
told about it, while the man who had not been there would
not understand it anyway.

In any case the Civil War soldier is still around, to be
listened to if not to be cross-examined, and he makes good
company. Rather surprisingly, he turns out to be almost
exactly like the young American of today; less sophisticated,
perhaps, a good bit more countrified, but still perfectly recog-

nizable, and a very solid sort of citizen to boot. And for quite a time it seemed that no writer could ask for anything better than the privilege of living with this man and describing him.

Taken by itself, however, this was not good enough. The Civil War soldier had many words to describe his participation in that war, and he used all of them at one time or another, often with some heat; but "privilege" was not one of them, and to feel privileged is to be an outsider. So it seemed advisable to go a little farther and to set up shop as an expert on strategy, tactics, weaponry, and the art of handling men; to analyze campaigns and battles, exercising the power of the second guess to show what went wrong with McClellan on the Peninsula, with Grant at Shiloh, and with Lee at Gettysburg. This can be quite stimulating—being a general is easy if you exercise your generalship after all the facts are in, sitting in a good armchair with books piled all around—and it does no harm to anyone provided you do not begin to take yourself too seriously. To be sure, the writer may occasionally get confused as to whether he himself is the general officer commanding or the high private in the rear rank getting ready to take what the general officer has fixed up for him, but aging veterans often do get confused. I heard not long ago about one ancient Civil War soldier who used to entertain his grandchildren with fascinating tales about his part in the Battle of Gettysburg. After he died some of his descendants, in idle curiosity, examined his service record. He had been a good soldier, but he had never been within 300 miles of Gettysburg.

But even when the confusion is discounted, there is still something lacking. It can be both useful and entertaining to provide an authentic picture of the enlisted in the Northern or Southern armies, and to go on from there to study the way he was used and the reasons why those armies succeeded or failed; to examine, that is, both the chessboard and the pieces that are moved about on it, shedding whatever light one can bring to bear. Yet this sort of thing has been done before, the study of war and warriors is after all pretty specialized, and the analogy of the chessboard is a bad one: it makes a game out of the war, and neither this war nor any other was any part of a game. A latter-day recruit justifies his existence only if he manages to get out of his experience something that justifies his temerity in getting into it. He is compelled, in short, to try to determine what the war meant.

As this point I began to reflect on who it is that rushes in where angels fear to tread. What did the war mean? Well, what does America mean? What does life itself mean—the way it is lived and the terms on which, at last, it must be surrendered? This war killed as many Americans as all of our other wars put together; did those men die to some purpose, or were they all wasted? These are questions amidst which one can hardly hope to do more than grope for an answer; yet it seemed to me that anyone who volunteers for the Civil War at this late date is somehow obliged to make the attempt.

He has to do it because otherwise he has simply been amusing himself, using a tragic and agonizing national experience to provide roaming-space for his imagination and his emotions, and also to provide grist for his typewriter. To show why the war took place, how it was fought, and why it ended as it did is not quite enough. Eventually you come to the baffling riddle: What was it really all about?

It is clear enough that the Civil War was a watershed experience for America. What we have and are today grow out of it, and what makes the fundamental question so unanswerable is that what we have and are now are not yet finished. To understand that part of our past we need to understand the present, because today we are grappling with the commitment that was made for us a century ago. The ultimate meaning of that war depends on what we do now. We are still involved in it. When we move to make a living reality out of the great ideal of the equality of all Americans; when we take our stand anywhere in the world for freedom, and for just dealing between all races and conditions of man; when we work for an enduring unity among human beings, whether at home or abroad—when we do any of these things we are simply trying to meet the obligation that was laid upon us a century ago at a price higher than any other price we ever paid.

So the fundamental question has to wait a while for a complete answer. The Civil War is unfinished business. It is still with us, and whether it was worth its dreadful cost depends on what we do rather than on what we say. Enlist in it now and you are apt to find that you are in for the duration.

Or so, at least, it seems to me.

—April 1966

A WAR THAT
NEVER GOES AWAY

by JAMES M. MCPHERSON

More than the Revolution, more than the Constitutional Convention, it was the crucial test of the American nation.

Americans just can't get enough of the Civil War." So says a man who should know, Terry Winschel, historian of the Vicksburg National Military Park. Millions of visitors come to Vicksburg and to more than a dozen other Civil War national battlefield and military parks every year. More than forty thousand Civil War reenactors spend hundreds of dollars each on replica weapons, uniforms, and equipment; many of them travel thousands of miles to help restage Civil War battles. Another two hundred and fifty thousand Americans describe themselves as Civil War buffs or "hobbyists" and belong to one of the hundreds of Civil War round tables or societies, subscribe to at least one of the half-dozen magazines devoted to Civil War history, or buy and sell Civil War memorabilia.

Above all, Americans buy books on the Civil War. This has always been true. More than fifty thousand separate books or pamphlets on the war have been published since the guns ceased firing a century and a quarter ago. In recent years some eight hundred titles, many of them reprints of out-of-print works, have come off the presses annually. Nearly every month a new Civil War book is offered by the History Book Club or the Book-of-the-Month Club, often as the main selection. Many bookstore owners echo the words of Jim Lawson, general manager of the Book 'N Card shop in Falls Church, Virginia. "For the last two years," he said in 1988, "Civil War books have been flying out of here. It's not [just] the buffs who buy; it's the general public, from high school kids to retired people."

Although we have reached the end of the 125th-anniversary commemorations of Civil War events, the boom shows no signs of fading. As a beneficiary of this popular interest in the Civil War, I am often asked to explain what accounts for it—in particular, to explain why my own recent contribution to the literature on the war and its causes, *Battle Cry of Freedom*, was on national best-seller lists for several months as a hardcover book in 1988 and again as a paperback in 1989. I have a few answers.

First, for Americans, the human cost of the Civil War was by far the most devastating in our history. The 620,000 Union and Confederate soldiers who lost their lives almost equaled the 680,000 American soldiers who died in all the other wars this country has fought combined. When we add the unknown but probably substantial number of civilian deaths—from disease, malnutrition, exposure, or injury—among the hundreds of thousands of refugees in the Confederacy, the toll of Civil War dead may exceed war deaths in all the rest of American history. Consider two sobering facts about the Battle of Antietam, America's single bloodiest day. The 25,000 casualties there were nearly four times the number of American casualties on D-day, June 6, 1944. The 6,500 men killed and mortally wounded in one day near Sharpsburg were nearly double the number of Americans killed and mortally wounded in combat in all the rest of the country's nineteenth-century wars combined—the War of 1812, the Mexican War, and the Spanish-American War.

This ghastly toll gives the Civil War a kind of horrifying but hypnotic fascination. As Thomas Hardy once put it, "War makes rattling good history; but Peace is poor reading." The sound of drum and trumpet, the call to arms, the clashing of armies have stirred the blood of nations throughout history. As the horrors and the seamy side of a war recede into the misty past, the romance and honor and glory forge into the foreground. Of no war has this been more true than of the Civil War, with its dashing cavaliers, its generals leading infantry charges, its diamond-stacked locomotives and paddle-wheeled steamboats, its larger-than-life figures like Lincoln, Lee, Jackson, Grant, and Sherman, its heroic and romantic women like Clara Barton and "Mother" Bickerdyke and Rose O'Neal Greenhow, its countless real-life heroines and knaves and heroes capable of transmutation into a Scarlett O'Hara, Rhett Butler, or Ashley Wilkes. If romance is the other face of horror in our perception of the Civil War, the poignancy of a brothers' war is the other face of the tragedy of a civil war. In hundreds of individual cases the war did pit brother against brother, cousin against cousin, even father against son. This was especially true in border states like Kentucky, where the war divided such famous families as the Clays, Crittendens, and Breckinridges and where seven brothers and brothers-in-law of the wife of the United States President fought for the Confederate States. But it was also true of states like Virginia, where Jeb Stuart's father-in-law commanded Union cavalry, and even of South Carolina, where Thomas F. Drayton became a brigadier general in the Confederate army and fought against his brother Percival, a captain in the Union navy, at the Battle of Port Royal. Who can resist the painful human interest of stories like these—particularly when they are recounted in the letters and diaries of Civil War protagonists, preserved through generations and published for all to read as a part of the unending stream of Civil War books?

Indeed, the uncensored contemporary descriptions of that war by participants help explain its appeal to modern readers. There is nothing else in history to equal it. Civil War armies were the most literate that ever fought a war up to that time, and twentieth-century armies censored soldiers' mail and discouraged diary keeping. Thus we have an unparalleled view of the Civil War by the people who experienced it. This has kept the image of the war alive in the families of millions of Americans whose ancestors fought in it. When speaking to audiences as diverse as Civil War buffs, Princeton students and alumni, and local literary clubs, I have sometimes asked how many of them are aware of forebears who fought in the Civil War. I have been surprised by the large response, which demonstrates not only a great number of such people but also their consciousness of events that happened so long ago yet seem part of their family lore today.

This consciousness of the war, of the past as part of the present, continues to be more intense in the South than elsewhere. William Faulkner said of his native section that the past isn't dead; it isn't even past. As any reader of Faulkner's novels knows, the Civil War is central to that past that is present; it is the great watershed of Southern history; it is, as Mark Twain put it a century ago after a tour through the South, "what A.D. is elsewhere; they date from it." The symbols of that past-in-present surround Southerners as they grow up, from the Robert E. Lee Elementary School or Jefferson Davis High School they attend and the Confederate battle flag that flies over their statehouse to the Confederate soldier enshrined in bronze or granite on the town square and the family folklore about victimization by Sherman's bummers. Some of those symbols remain highly controversial and provoke as much passion today as in 1863: the song "Dixie," for example, and the Confederate flag, which for many Southern whites continue to represent courage, honor, or defiance while to blacks they represent racism and oppression.

This suggests the most important reason for the enduring fascination with the Civil War among professional historians as well as the general public: Great issues were at stake, issues about which Americans were willing to fight and die, issues whose resolution profoundly transformed and redefined the United States. The Civil War was a total war in three senses: It mobilized the total human and material resources of both sides; it ended not in a negotiated peace but in total victory by one side and unconditional surrender by the other; it destroyed the economy and social system of the loser and established those of the winner as the norm for the future.

The Civil War was fought mainly by volunteer soldiers who joined the colors before conscription went into effect. In fact, the Union and Confederate armies mobilized as volunteers a larger percentage of their societies' manpower than any other war in American history—probably in world history, with the possible exception of the French Revolution. And Civil War armies, like those of the French Revolution, were highly ideological in motivation. Most of the volunteers knew what they were fighting for, and why. What were they fighting for? If asked to define it in a single word, many soldiers on both sides would have answered: liberty. They fought for the heritage of freedom bequeathed to them by the Founding Fathers. North and South alike wrapped themselves in the mantle of 1776. But the two sides interpreted that heritage in opposite ways, and at first neither side included the slaves in the vision of liberty for which it fought. The slaves did, however, and by the time of Lincoln's Gettysburg Address in 1863, the North also fought for "a new birth of freedom. . . ." These multiple meanings of freedom, and how they dissolved and re-formed in kaleidoscopic patterns during the war, provide the central meaning of the war for the American experience.

When the "Black Republican" Abraham Lincoln won the Presidency in 1860 on a platform of excluding slavery from the territories, Southerners compared him to George III and declared their independence from "oppressive Yankee rule." "The same spirit of freedom and independence that impelled our Fathers to the separation from the British Government," proclaimed secessionists, would impel the "liberty loving people of the South" to separation from the United States government. A Georgia secessionist declared that Southerners would be "either *slaves in the Union or freemen out of it*." Young men from Texas to Virginia rushed to enlist in this "Holy Cause of Liberty and Independence" and to raise "the standard of Liberty and Equality for white men" against "our Abolition enemies who are pledged to prostrate the white freemen of the South down to equality with negroes." From "the high and solemn motive of defending and protecting the rights which our fathers bequeathed to us," declared Jefferson Davis at the outset of war, let us "renew such sacrifices as our fathers made to the holy cause of constitutional liberty."

But most Northerners ridiculed these Southern professions to be fighting for the ideals of 1776. That was "a libel upon the whole character and conduct of the men of '76," said the antislavery poet and journalist William Cullen Bryant. The Founding Fathers had fought "to establish the rights of man . . . and principles of universal liberty." The South, insisted Bryant, had seceded "not in the interest of general humanity, but of a domestic despotism. . . . Their motto is not liberty, but slavery." Northerners did not deny the right of revolution in principle; after all, the United States was founded on that right. But "the right of revolution," wrote Lincoln in 1861, "is never a legal right. . . . At most, it is but a moral right, when exercised for a morally justifiable cause. When exercised without such a cause revolution is no right, but simply a wicked exercise of physical power." In Lincoln's judgment secession was just such a wicked exercise. The event that precipitated it was Lincoln's election by a constitutional majority. As Northerners saw it, the Southern states, having controlled the national government for most of the previous two generations through their domination of the Democratic party, now decided to leave the Union just because they had lost an election.

For Lincoln and the Northern people, it was the Union that represented the ideals of 1776. The republic established by the Founding Fathers as a bulwark of liberty was a fragile experiment in a nineteenth-century world bestridden by kings, emperors, czars, and dictators. Most republics through history had eventually been overthrown. Some Americans still alive in 1861 had seen French republics succumb twice to emperors and once to the restoration of the Bourbon monarchy. Republics in Latin America came and went with bewildering rapidity. The United States in 1861 represented, in Lincoln's words, "the last, best hope" for the survival of republican liberties in the world. Would that hope also collapse? "Our popular government has often been called an experiment," Lincoln told Congress on July 4, 1861. But if the Confederacy succeeded in splitting the country in two, it would set a fatal precedent that would destroy the experiment. By invoking this precedent, a minority in the future might secede from the Union whenever it did not like what the majority stood for, until the United States fragmented into a multitude of petty, squabbling autocracies. "The central idea pervading this struggle," said Lincoln, "is the necessity . . . of proving that popular government is not an absurdity. We must settle this question now, whether, in a free government, the minority have the right to break up the government whenever they choose."

Many soldiers who enlisted in the Union army felt the same way. A Missourian joined up as "a duty I owe my country and to my children to do what I can to preserve this government as I shudder to think what is ahead of them if this government should be overthrown." A New England soldier wrote to his wife on the eve of the First Battle of Bull Run: "I know . . . how great a debt we owe to those who went before us through the blood and sufferings of the Revolution. And I am willing—perfectly willing—to lay down all my joys in this life, to help maintain this government, and to pay that debt."

Freedom for the slaves was not part of the liberty for

which the North fought in 1861. That was not because the Lincoln administration supported slavery; quite the contrary. Slavery was "an unqualified evil to the negro, to the white man . . . and to the State," said Lincoln on many occasions in words that expressed the sentiments of a Northern majority. "The monstrous injustice of slavery . . . deprives our republican example of its just influence in the world—enables the enemies of free institutions, with plausibility, to taunt us as hypocrites. . . ." Yet in his first inaugural address, Lincoln declared that he had "no purpose, directly or indirectly, to interfere with . . . slavery in the States where it exists." He reiterated this pledge in his first message to Congress, on July 4, 1861, when the Civil War was nearly three months old.

What explains this apparent inconsistency? The answer lies in the Constitution and in the Northern polity of 1861. Lincoln was bound by a constitution that protected slavery in any state where citizens wanted it. The republic of liberty for whose preservation the North was fighting had been a republic in which slavery was legal everywhere in 1776. That was the great American paradox—a land of freedom based on slavery. Even in 1861 four states that remained loyal to the Union were slave states, and the Democratic minority in free states opposed any move to make the war for the Union a war against slavery.

But as the war went on, the slaves themselves took the first step toward making it a war against slavery. Coming into Union lines by the thousands, they voted with their feet for freedom. As enemy property they could be confiscated by Union forces as "contraband of war." This was the thin edge of the wedge that finally broke apart the American paradox. By 1863 a series of congressional acts plus Lincoln's Emancipation Proclamation had radically enlarged Union war aims. The North henceforth fought not just to restore the old Union, not just to ensure that the nation born in 1776 "shall not perish from the earth," but to give that nation "a new birth of freedom."

Northern victory in the Civil War resolved two fundamental, festering issues left unresolved by the Revolution of 1776: whether this fragile republican experiment called the United States would survive and whether the house divided would continue to endure half slave and half free. Both these issues remained open questions until 1865. Many Americans doubted the Republic's survival; many European conservatives predicted its demise; some Americans advocated the right of secession and periodically threatened to invoke it; eleven states did invoke it in 1860 and 1861. But since 1865 no state or region has seriously threatened secession, not even during the "massive resistance" to desegregation from 1954 to 1964. Before 1865 the United States, land of liberty, was the largest slaveholding country in the world. Since 1865 that particular "monstrous injustice" and "hypocrisy" has existed no more.

In the process of preserving the Union of 1776 while purging it of slavery, the Civil War also transformed it. Before 1861 the words *United States* were a plural noun: "The United States *are* a large country." Since 1865 *United States* has been a singular noun. The North went to war to preserve the *Union*; it ended by creating a *nation*. This transformation can be traced in Lincoln's most important wartime addresses. The first inaugural address contained the word *Union* twenty times and the word *nation* not once. In Lincoln's first message to Congress, on July 4, 1861, he used *Union* forty-nine times and *nation* only three times. In his famous public letter to Horace Greeley of August 22, 1862, concerning slavery and the war, Lincoln spoke of the Union nine times and the nation not at all. But in the Gettysburg Address fifteen months later, he did not refer to the Union at all but used the word *nation* five times. And in the second inaugural address, looking back over the past four years, Lincoln spoke of one side's seeking to dissolve the Union in 1861 and the other side's accepting the challenge of war to preserve the nation. The old decentralized Republic, in which the post office was the only agency of national government that touched the average citizen, was transformed by the crucible of war into a centralized polity that taxed people directly and created an internal revenue bureau to collect the taxes, expanded the jurisdiction of federal courts, created a national currency and a federally chartered banking system, drafted men into the Army, and created the Freedman's Bureau as the first national agency for social welfare. Eleven of the first twelve amendments to the Constitution had limited the powers of the national government; six of the next seven, starting with the Thirteenth Amendment in 1865, radically expanded those powers at the expense of the states. The first three of these amendments converted four million slaves into citizens and voters within five years, the most rapid and fundamental social transformation in American history—even if the nation did backslide on part of this commitment for three generations after 1877.

From 1789 to 1861 a Southern slaveholder was President of the United States two-thirds of the time, and two-thirds of the Speakers of the House and presidents pro tem of the Senate had also been Southerners. Twenty of the thirty-five Supreme Court justices during that period were from the South, which always had a majority on the Court before 1861. After the Civil War a century passed before another resident of a Southern state was elected President. For half a century after the war hardly any Southerners served as Speaker of the House or president pro tem of the Senate, and only nine of the thirty Supreme Court justices appointed during that half-century were Southerners. The institutions and ideology of a plantation society and a caste system that had dominated half of the country before 1861 and sought to dominate more went down with a great crash in 1865 and were replaced by the institutions and ideology of free-labor entrepreneurial capitalism. For better or for worse, the flames of Civil War forged the framework of modern America.

So even if the veneer of romance and myth that has attracted so many of the current Civil War camp followers were stripped away, leaving only the trauma of violence and suffering, the Civil War would remain the most dramatic and crucial experience in American history. That fact will ensure the persistence of its popularity and its importance as a historical subject so long as there is a United States.

—March 1990

THE NEEDLESS CONFLICT

by ALLAN NEVINS

If Buchanan had met the Kansas problem firmly, we might have avoid civil war.

When James Buchanan, standing in a homespun suit before cheering crowds, took the oath of office on March 4, 1857, he seemed confident that the issues before the nation could be readily settled. He spoke about an army road to California, use of the Treasury surplus to pay all the national debt, and proper guardianship of the public lands. In Kansas, he declared, the path ahead was clear. The simple logical rule that the will of the people should determine the institutions of a territory had brought in sight a happy settlement. The inhabitants would declare for or against slavery as they pleased. Opinions differed as to the proper time for making such a decision; but Buchanan thought that "the appropriate period will be when the number of actual residents in the Territory shall justify the formation of a constitution with a view to its admission as a State." He trusted that the long strife between North and South was nearing its end, and that the sectional party which had almost elected Frémont would die a natural death.

Two days after the inaugural Buchanan took deep satisfaction in a decision by the Supreme Court of which he had improper foreknowledge: the Dred Scott decision handed down by Chief Justice Taney. Its vital element, so far as the nation's destiny was concerned, was the ruling that the Missouri Compromise restriction, by which slavery had been excluded north of the 36°30′ line, was void; that on the contrary, every territory was open to slavery. Not merely was Congress without power to legislate *against* slavery, but by implication it should act to protect it. Much of the Northern press denounced the decision fervently. But the country was prosperous; it was clear that time and political action might change the Supreme Court, bringing a new decision; and the explosion of wrath proved brief.

Buchanan had seen his view sustained; slavery might freely enter any territory, the inhabitants of which could not decide whether to keep it or drop it until they wrote their first constitution. In theory, the highway to national peace was as traversable as the Lancaster turnpike. To be sure, Kansas was rent between two bitter parties, proslavery and antislavery; from the moment Stephen A. Douglas's Kansas-Nebraska Act had thrown open the West to popular sovereignty three years earlier, it had been a theater of unrelenting conflict. Popular sovereignty had simply failed to work. In the spring of 1855 about five thousand invading Missourians, swamping the polls, had given Kansas a fanatically proslavery legislature which the free-soil settlers flatly refused to recognize. That fall a free-soil convention in Topeka had adopted a constitution which the slavery men in turn flatly rejected. Some bloody fighting had ensued. But could not all this be thrust into the past?

In theory, the President might now send out an impartial new governor; and if the people wanted statehood, an election might be held for a new constitutional convention. Then the voters could give the nation its sixteenth slave state or its seventeenth free state—everybody behaving quietly and reasonably. Serenity would prevail. Actually, the idea that the people of Kansas, so violently aroused, would show quiet reason, was about as tenable as the idea that Europeans would begin settling boundary quarrels by a quiet game of chess. Behind the two Kansas parties were grim Southerners and determined Northerners. "Slavery will now yield a greater profit in Kansas," trumpeted a Southern propagandist in *De Bow's Review,* "either to hire out or cultivate the soil, than any other place." He wanted proslavery squatters. Meanwhile, Yankees were subsidizing their own settlers. "I know people," said Emerson in a speech, "who are making haste to reduce their expenses and pay their debts . . . to save and earn for the benefit of Kansas emigrants."

Nor was reason in Kansas the only need. Impartiality in Congress, courage in the presidential chair, were also required. The stage was dressed for a brief, fateful melodrama, which more than anything else was to fix the position of James Buchanan and Stephen A. Douglas in history, was to shape the circumstances under which Lincoln made his first national reputation, and was to have more potency than any other single event in deciding whether North and South should remain brothers or fly at each other's throats. That melodrama was entitled "Lecompton." Douglas was to go to his grave believing that, had Buchanan played an honest, resolute part in it, rebellion would have been killed in its incipiency. The role that Buchanan did play may be counted one of the signal failures of American statesmanship.

To hold that the Civil War could not have been averted by wise, firm, and timely action is to concede too much to determinism in history. Winston Churchill said that the Second World War should be called "The Unnecessary War"; the same term might as justly be applied to our Civil War. Passionate unreason among large sections of the population was one ingredient in the broth of conflict. Accident, fortuity, fate, or sheer bad luck (these terms are interchangeable) was another: John Brown's raid, so malign in its effects on opinion, North and South, might justly be termed an accident. Nothing in the logic of forces or events required so crazy an act. But beyond these ingredients lies the further element of wretched leadership. Had the United States possessed three farseeing, imaginative, and resolute Presidents instead of Fillmore, Pierce, and Buchanan, the war might have been postponed until time and economic forces killed its roots. Buchanan was the weakest of the three, and the Lecompton affair lights up his incompetence like a play of lightning across a nocturnal storm front.

The melodrama had two stages, one in faraway, thinly settled Kansas, burning hot in summer, bitter cold in winter, and, though reputedly rich, really so poor that settlers were soon on the brink of starvation. Here the most curious fact was the disparity between the mean actors and the great results they effected. A handful of ignorant, reckless, semidrunken settlers on the Southern side, led by a few desperadoes of politics—the delegates of the Lecompton Constitutional Convention—actually had the power to make or mar the nation.

The other stage was Washington. The participants here, representing great interests and ideas, had at least a dignity worthy of the scene and the consequences of their action. James Buchanan faced three main groups holding three divergent views of the sectional problem.

The proslavery group (that is, Robert Toombs, Alexander H. Stephens, Jefferson Davis, John Slidell, David Atchison, and many more) demanded that slavery be allowed to expand freely within the territories; soon they were asking also that such expansion be given federal protection against any hostile local action. This stand involved the principle that slavery was morally right, and socially and economically a positive good. Reverdy Johnson of Maryland, in the Dred Scott case, had vehemently argued the beneficence of slavery.

The popular sovereignty group, led by Douglas and particularly strong among northwestern Democrats, maintained that in any territory the issue of slavery or free soil should be determined *at all times* by the settlers therein. Douglas modified the Dred Scott doctrine: local police legislation and action, he said, could exclude slavery even before state-making took place. He sternly rejected the demand for federal protection against such action. His popular sovereignty view implied indifference to or rejection of any moral test of slavery. Whether the institution was socially and economically good or bad depended mainly on climate and soil, and moral ideas were irrelevant. He did not care whether slavery was voted up or voted down: the right to a fair vote was the all-important matter.

The free-soil group, led by Seward and Chase, but soon to find its best voice in Lincoln, held that slavery should be excluded from all territories present or future. They insisted that slavery was morally wrong, had been condemned as such by the Fathers, and was increasingly outlawed by the march of world civilization. It might be argued that the free-soil contention was superfluous, in that climate and aridity forbade a further extension of slavery anyhow. But in Lincoln's eyes this did not touch the heart of the matter. It might or might not be expansible. (Already it existed in Delaware and Missouri, and Cuba and Mexico might be conquered for it.) What was important was for America to accept the fact that, being morally wrong and socially an anachronism, it *ought* not to expand; it *ought* to be put in the way of ultimate eradication.

Lincoln was a planner. Once the country accepted nonexpansion, it would thereby accept the idea of ultimate extinction. This crisis met and passed, it could sit down and decide when and how, in God's good time and with suitable compensation to slaveholders, it might be ended.

The Buchanan who faced these three warring groups was victim of the mistaken belief among American politicians (like Pierce, Benjamin Harrison, and Warren G. Harding, for example) that it is better to be a poor President than to stick to honorable but lesser posts. He would have made a respectable diplomat or decent Cabinet officer under a really strong President. Sixty-six in 1857, the obese bachelor felt all his years. He had wound his devious way up through a succession of offices without once showing a flash of inspiration or an ounce of grim courage. James K. Polk had accurately characterized him as an old woman—"It is one of his weaknesses that he takes on and magnifies small matters into great and undeserved importance." His principal characteristic was irresolution. "Even among close friends," remarked a Southern senator, "he very rarely expressed his opinions at all upon disputed questions, except in language especially marked with a cautious circumspection almost amounting to timidity."

He was industrious, capable, and tactful, a well-read Christian gentleman; he had acquired from forty years of public life a rich fund of experience. But he was pedestrian, humorless, calculating, and pliable. He never made a witty remark, never wrote a memorable sentence, and never showed a touch of distinction. Above all (and this was the source of his irresolution) he had no strong convictions. Associating all his life with Southern leaders in Washington, this Pennsylvanian leaned toward their views, but he never disclosed a deep adherence to any principle. Like other weak men, he could be stubborn; still oftener, he could show a petulant irascibility when events pushed him into a corner. And like other timid men, he would sometimes flare out in a sudden burst of anger, directed not against enemies who could hurt him but against friends or neutrals who would not. As the sectional crisis deepened, it became his dominant hope to stumble through it, somehow, and anyhow, so as to leave office with the Union yet intact. His successor could bear the storm.

This was the President who had to deal, in Kansas and Washington, with men of fierce conviction, stern courage and, all too often, ruthless methods.

In Kansas the proslavery leaders were determined to strike boldly and unscrupulously for a slave state. They maintained close communications with such Southern chieftains in Washington as Senator Slidell, Speaker James L. Orr, and Howell Cobb and Jacob Thompson, Buchanan's secretaries of the Treasury and the Interior. Having gained control of the territorial legislature, they meant to keep and use this mastery. Just before Buchanan became President they passed a bill for a constitutional convention—and a more unfair measure was never put on paper. Nearly all country officers, selected not by popular vote but by the dishonestly chosen legislature, were proslavery men. The bill provided that the sheriffs and their deputies should in March 1857 register the white residents; that the probate judges should then take from the sheriffs complete lists of qualified voters; and that the country commissioners should finally choose election judges.

Everyone knew that a heavy majority of the Kansas settlers were antislavery. Many, even of the Southerners, who had migrated thither opposed the "peculiar institution" as retrogressive and crippling in character. Everybody also knew that Kansas, with hardly thirty thousand people, burdened with debts, and unsupplied with fit roads, schools, or courthouses, was not yet ready for statehood; it still needed the federal government's care. Most Kansans refused to recognize the "bogus" legislature. Yet this legislature was forcing a premature convention, and taking steps to see that the election of delegates was controlled by sheriffs, judges, and county commissioners who were mainly proslavery Democrats. Governor John W. Geary, himself a Democrat appointed by Pierce, indignantly vetoed the bill. But the legislature immediately repassed it over Geary's veto; and when threats against his life increased until citizens laid bets that he would be assassinated within forty days, he resigned in alarm and posted east to apprise the country of imminent perils.

Along the way to Washington, Geary paused to warn the press that a packed convention was about to drag fettered Kansas before Congress with a slavery constitution. This convention would have a free hand, for the bill just passed made no provision for a popular vote on the instrument. Indeed, one legislator admitted that the plan was to avoid popular submission, for he proposed inserting a clause to guard against the possibility that Congress might return the constitution for a referendum. Thus, commented the *Missouri Democrat*, "the felon legislature has provided as effectually for getting the desired result as Louis Napoleon did for getting himself elected Emperor." All this was an ironic commentary on Douglas's maxim: "Let the voice of the people rule."

And Douglas, watching the reckless course of the Kansas legislators with alarm, saw that his principles and his political future were at stake. When his Kansas-Nebraska Act was passed, he had given the North his solemn promise that a free, full, and fair election would decide the future of the two territories. No fraud, no sharp practice, no browbeating would be sanctioned: every male white citizen should have use of the ballot box. He had notified the South that Kansas was almost certain to be free soil. Now he professed confidence that President Buchanan would never permit a breach of fair procedure. He joined Buchanan in persuading one of the nation's ablest men, former Secretary of the Treasury Robert J. Walker, to go out to Kansas in Geary's place as governor. Douglas knew that if he consented to a betrayal of popular sovereignty he would be ruined forever politically in his own state of Illinois.

For a brief space in the spring of 1857 Buchanan seemed to stand firm. In his instructions to Governor Walker he engaged that the new constitution would be laid before the people; and "they must be protected in the exercise of their right of voting for or against that instrument, and the fair expression of the popular will must not be interrupted by fraud or violence."

It is not strange that the rash proslavery gamesters in Kansas prosecuted their designs despite all Buchanan's fair words and Walker's desperate efforts to stay them. They knew that with four-fifths of the people already against them, and the odds growing greater every year, only brazen trickery could effect their end. They were aware that the South, which believed that a fair division would give Kansas to slavery and Nebraska to freedom, expected them to stand firm. They were egged on by the two reckless Southern Cabinet members, Howell Cobb and Thompson, who sent an agent, H. L. Martin of Mississippi, out to the Kansas convention. This gathering in Lecompton, with 48 of the 60 members hailing from slave states, was the shabbiest conclave of its kind ever held on American soil. One of Buchanan's Kansas correspondents wrote that he had not supposed such a wild set could be found. The *Kansas News* termed them a body of "broken-down political hacks, demagogues, fire-eaters, perjurers, ruffians, ballot-box stuffers, and loafers." But before it broke up with the shout, "Now, boys, let's come and take a drink!" it had written a constitution.

This constitution, the work of a totally unrepresentative body, was a devious repudiation of all the principles Buchanan and Douglas had laid down. Although it contained numerous controversial provisions, such as a limitation of banking to one institution and a bar against free Negroes, the main document was not to be submitted to a general vote at all. A nominal reference of the great cardinal question was indeed provided. Voters might cast their ballots for the "constitution with slavery" or the "constitution without slavery." But when closely examined this was seen to be actually a piece of chicanery. Whichever form was adopted, the 200 slaves in Kansas would remain, with a constitutional guarantee against interference. Whenever the proslavery part in Kansas could get control of the legislature, they might open the door wide for more slaves. The rigged convention had put its handiwork before the people with a rigged choice: "Heads I win, tails you lose."

Would Buchanan lay this impudent contrivance before Congress, and ask it to vote the admission of Kansas as a state? Or would he contemptuously spurn it? An intrepid man would not have hesitated an instant to take the honest course; he would not have needed the indignant outcry of the Northern press, the outraged roar of Douglas, to inspire him. But Buchanan quailed before the storm of passion into which proslavery extremists had worked themselves.

The hot blood of the South was now up. That section, grossly misinformed upon events in Kansas, believed that *it* was being cheated. The Northern free-soilers had vowed that no new slave state (save by a partition by Texas) should ever be admitted. Southerners thought that in pursuance of this resolve, the Yankees had made unscrupulous use of their wealth and numbers to lay hands on Kansas. Did the North think itself entitled to every piece on the board—to take Kansas as well as California, Minnesota, Iowa, Nebraska, Oregon—to give Southerners nothing? The Lecompton delegates, from this point of view, were dauntless champions of a wronged section. What if they did use sharp tactics? That was but a necessary response to Northern arrogance. Jefferson Davis declared that his section trembled under a sense of insecurity. "You have made it a political war. We are on the defensive. How far are you to push us?" Sharp threats of secession and battle mingled with the Southern denunciations. "Sir," Senator Alfred Iverson of Georgia was soon to assert, "I believe that the time will come when the slave States will be compelled, in vindication of their rights, interests, and honor, to separate from the free States, and erect an independent confederacy; and I am not sure, sir, that the time is not at hand."

Three Southern members of the Cabinet, Cobb, Thompson, and John B. Floyd, had taken the measure of Buchanan's pusillanimity. They, with one Northern sympathizer, Jeremiah Black, and several White House habitués like John Slidell of Louisiana, constituted a virtual Directory exercising control over the tremulous President. They played on Buchanan's fierce partisan hatred of Republicans, and his jealous dislike of Douglas. They played also on his legalistic cast of mind; after all, the Lecompton constitution was a legal instrument by a legal convention—outwardly. Above all, they played on his fears, his morbid sensitiveness, and his responsiveness to immediate pressures. They could do this the more easily because the threats of disruption and violence were real. Henry S. Foote, a former senator from Mississippi and an enemy of Jefferson Davis, who saw Lecompton in the true light and hurried to Washington to advise the President, writes: "It was unfortunately of no avail that these efforts to reassure Mr. Buchanan were at that time essayed by myself and others; he had already become thoroughly *panic-stricken*; the howlings of the bulldog of secession had fairly frightened him out of his wits, and he ingloriously resolved to yield without further resistance to the decrial and vilification to which he had been so acrimoniously subjected."

And the well-informed Washington correspondent of the New Orleans *Picayune* a little later told just how aggressively the Chief Executive was bludgeoned into submission: "The President was informed in November, 1857, that the States of Alabama, Mississippi, and South Carolina, and perhaps others, would hold conventions and secede from the Union if the

Lecompton Constitution, which established slavery, should not be accepted by Congress. The reason was that these States, supposing that the South had been cheated out of Kansas, were, whether right or wrong, determined to revolt. The President believed this. Senator Hunter, of Virginia, to my knowledge, believed it. Many other eminent men did, and perhaps not without reason."

Buchanan, without imagination as without nerve, began to yield to this Southern storm in midsummer, and by November 1857, he was surrendering completely. When Congress met in December his message upheld the Lecompton Constitution with a tissue of false and evasive statements. Seldom in American history has a chief magistrate made a greater error, or missed a larger opportunity. The astute secretary of his predecessor, Franklin Pierce, wrote: "I had considerable hopes of Mr. Buchanan—I really thought he was a statesman—but I have now come to the settled conclusion that he is just the damndest old fool that has ever occupied the presidential chair. He has deliberately walked overboard with his eyes open—let him drown, for he must."

As Buchanan shrank from the lists, Douglas entered them with that *gaudium certaminis* which was one of his greatest qualities. The finest chapters of his life, his last great contests for the Union, were opening. Obviously he would have had to act under political necessity even if deaf to principle, for had he let popular sovereignty be torn to pieces, Illinois would not have sent him back to the Senate the following year; but he was not the man to turn his back on principle. His struggle against Lecompton was an exhibition of iron determination. The drama of that battle has given it an almost unique place in the record of our party controversies.

"By God, sir!" he exclaimed, "I made James Buchanan, and by God, sir, I will unmake him!" Friends told him that the Southern Democrats meant to ruin him. "I have taken a through ticket," rejoined Douglas, "and checked my baggage." He lost no time in facing Buchanan in the White House and denouncing the Lecompton policy. When the President reminded him how Jackson had crushed two party rebels, he was ready with a stinging retort. Douglas was not to be overawed by a man he despised as a weakling. "Mr. President," he snorted, "I wish you to remember that General Jackson is dead."

As for the Southern leaders, Douglas's scorn for the extremists who had coerced Buchanan was unbounded. He told the Washington correspondent of the Chicago *Journal* that he had begun his fight as a contest against a single bad measure. But his blow at Lecompton was a blow against slavery extension, and he at once had the whole "slave power" down on him like a pack of wolves. He added: "In making the fight against this power, I was enabled to stand off and view the men with whom I had been acting; I was ashamed I had ever been caught in such company; they are a set of unprincipled demagogues, bent upon perpetuating slavery, and by the exercise of that unequal and unfair power, to control the government or break up the Union; and I intend to prevent their doing either."

After a long, close, and acrid contest, on April 1, 1858, Lecompton was defeated. A coalition of Republicans, Douglasite Democrats, and Know-Nothings struck down the fraudulent constitution in the House, 120 to 112. When the vote was announced, a wild cheer rolled through the galleries. Old Francis P. Blair, Jackson's friend, carried the news to the dying Thomas Hart Benton, who had been intensely aroused by the crisis. Benton could barely speak, but his exultation was unbounded. "In energetic whispers," records Blair, "he told his visitor that the same men who had sought to destroy the republic in 1850 were at the bottom of this accursed Lecompton business. Among the greatest of his consolations in dying was the consciousness that the House of Representatives had baffled these treasonable schemes and put the heels of the people on the necks of the traitors."

The Administration covered its retreat by a hastily concocted measure, the English Bill, under which Kansas was kept waiting on the doorstep—sure in the end to enter a free state. The Kansas plotters, the Cobb-Thompson-Floyd clique in the Cabinet, and Buchanan had all been worsted. But the damage had been done. Southern secessionists had gained fresh strength and greater boldness from their success in coercing the Administration.

The Lecompton struggle left a varied and interesting set of aftereffects. It lifted Stephen A. Douglas to a new plane; he had been a fighting Democratic strategist, but now he became a true national leader, thinking far less of party and more of country. It sharpened the issues which that summer and fall were to form the staple of the memorable Lincoln-Douglas debates in Illinois. At the same time, it deepened the schism which had been growing for some years between Southern Democrats and northwestern Democrats, and helped pave the way to that disruption of the party which preceded and facilitated the disruption of the nation. It planted new seeds of dissension in Kansas—seeds which resulted in fresh conflicts between Kansas free-soilers or jayhawkers on one side and Missouri invaders or border ruffians on the other, and in a spirit of border lawlessness which was to give the Civil War some of its darkest pages. The Lecompton battle discredited Buchanan in the eyes of most decent Northerners, strengthened Southern conviction of his weakness, and left the Administration materially and morally weaker in dealing with the problems of the next two and a half critical years.

For the full measure of Buchanan's failure, however, we must go deeper. Had he shown the courage that to an Adams, a Jackson, a Polk, or a Cleveland would have been second nature, the courage that springs from a deep integrity, he might have done the republic an immeasurable service by grappling with disunion when it was yet weak and unprepared. Ex-Senator Foote wrote later that he knew well that a scheme for destroying the Union "had long been on foot in the South." He knew that its leaders "were only waiting for the enfeebling of the Democratic Party in the North, and the general triumph of Free-soilism as a consequence thereof, to alarm the whole South into acquiescence in their policy." Buchanan's support of the unwise and corrupt Lecompton constitution thus played into the plotters' hands.

The same view was taken yet more emphatically by Douglas. He had inside information in 1857, he later told the Senate, that four states were threatening Buchanan with secession. Had that threat been met in the right Jacksonian spirit, had the bluff been called—for the four states were unprepared for secession and war—the leaders of the movement would have been utterly discredited. Their conspiracy would have collapsed, and they would have been so routed and humiliated in 1857 that the Democratic party schism in 1860 might never have taken place, and if it had, secession in 1861 would have been impossible.

The roots of the Civil War of course go deep; they go back beyond Douglas's impetuous Kansas-Nebraska Bill, back beyond the Mexican War, back beyond the Missouri Compromise. But the last good chance of averting secession and civil strife was perhaps lost in 1857. Even Zachary Taylor in 1850 had made it plain before his sudden death that he would use force, if necessary, to crush the secessionist tendencies which that year became so dangerous. A similar display of principle and resolution seven years later might well have left the disunionist chieftains of the Deep South so weakened in prestige that Yancey and his fellow plotters would have been helpless. The lessons of this failure in statesmanship, so plain to Douglas, ought not to be forgotten. The greatest mistake a nation can make is to put at its helm a man so pliable and unprincipled that he will palter with a clean-cut and momentous issue.

—August 1956

THERE WAS ANOTHER SOUTH

by CARL N. DEGLER

Was the South solidly for slavery and secession? An eminent historian disputes a long-cherished view of that region's history.

T he stereotype of the South is as tenacious as it is familiar: a traditionally rebellious region which has made a dogma of states' rights and a religious order of the Democratic party. Here indeed is a monotonous and unchanging tapestry, with a pattern of magnolia blossoms, Spanish moss, and the inevitable old plantations running ceaselessly from border to border. To this depiction of almost willful backwardness, add the dark motif of the Negro problem, a few threads of poor white, and the picture is complete.

Such is the mythical image, and a highly inaccurate one it is, for the South is a region of immense variety. Its sprawling landscape ranges from the startlingly red soil of Virginia and North Carolina to the black, sticky clay of the Delta; from the wild and primitive mountain forests of eastern Kentucky to the lush, junglelike swamps of southern Louisiana; from the high, dry, wind-swept plains of the Texas Panhandle to the humid tidelands of the South Carolina coast. An environment so diverse can be expected to produce social and political differences to match, and in fact, it always has.

Today we have come to recognize increasingly the wide variety of attitudes that exist in the region. But this denial of the Southern stereotype is a relatively new development, even among historians. For too long the history of the region has been regarded as a kind of unbroken plain of uniform opinion. This is especially true of what has been written about the years before the Civil War; a belief in states' rights, the legality of secession, and the rightfulness of slavery has been accepted almost without question as typical of Southern thought. In a sense, such catch phrases do represent what many Southerners have believed; but at the same time there were many others who both denied the legality of secession and denounced slavery. It is time this "Other South" was better known.

Let us begin with the story of these Southerners who so cherished the Union that they refused to accept the doctrine of nullification and secession. They included not only humble farmers and remote mountain men, but some of the greatest names in the history of the South; their devotion to the Union was tested in several bitter clashes with states' righters during the antebellum decades. The first of these contests came over the question of the high protective tariffs which many Southerners felt would hurt the cotton trade; the arguments advanced at the beginning set forth the basic lines of debate that were followed thereafter. South Carolina's *Exposition and Protest* of 1828, which John C. Calhoun wrote secretly in opposition to the tariff passed that year, embodied the classic defense of state sovereignty. In the *Exposition*, Calhoun contended that nullification of federal legislation by a state and even secession were constitutional—a doctrine rejected by many prominent Southerners in 1828 and after.

Foremost among them was former President James Madison, the reputed "father of the Constitution." As a Jeffersonian in politics and a Virginian by birth and heritage, Madison was no friend of the protective tariff, and certainly not of the monstrous one of 1828, which had been promulgated by the Jacksonian faction in Congress in an effort to discredit the Adams administration. But he could not accept even that politically inspired tariff as sufficient reason for nullification. Indeed, he could not accept the constitutional doctrine of nullification on any grounds. It is worthwhile to consider briefly Madison's views on nullification, because virtually all subsequent Southern defenses of the Union followed his line of thought; at the time, no man in the South carried more authority on the meaning and interpretation of the Constitution than the venerable Virginian, who celebrated his eightieth birthday in 1830, and was the last surviving signer of that document.

Many political leaders sought his views all through the

tariff crisis of 1828-33, and to all of them Madison reiterated the same conclusions. The United States was a "mixed government" in which the states were supreme in some areas and the federal government in others. In the event of conflict between them, the Supreme Court was the intended arbiter under the Constitution; the Court, Madison wrote, was "so constituted as to be impartial as it could be made by the mode of appointment and responsibility of the judges."

If confidence were lacking in the objectivity of the judges, Madison continued, then there were further remedies: the impeachment of offending officials, election of a new government, or amendments to the Constitution. But neither nullification nor secession was legal, he tirelessly pointed out. Of course, if tyrannized sufficiently, a state could invoke its natural right to overthrow its oppressor; but that was a right of revolution, and not a constitutional right as Calhoun and his followers maintained.

As a Southern Unionist, Madison did not stand alone, either at the time of the nullification crisis or later. In Calhoun's own state, in fact, the Unionists were a powerful and eloquent minority. Hugh S. Legare (pronounced Legree, curiously enough), Charleston aristocrat, intellectual, and one-time editor of the *Southern Review*, distinguished himself in defense of the Union, vigorously opposing Calhoun during the heated debates in Charleston in 1832. (Eleven years later, as United States Attorney General, Legare again differed with the majority of Southerners when he offered the official opinion that free Negroes in the United States enjoyed the same civil rights as white men.)

James Petigru and Joel Poinsett (who, as minister to Mexico, gave his name to the Poinsettia) were two other prominent Charlestonians who would not accept the doctrine that a state could constitutionally withdraw from the Union. Unlike Legare and Poinsett, Petigru lived long enough to fight nullification and secession in South Carolina until that state left the Union. (When asked by a stranger in December 1860, where the insane asylum was, he contemptuously pointed to the building where the secession convention was meeting.)

Andrew Jackson is often ignored by those who conceive of the South as a monolith of states' rights and secession. A Carolinian by birth and a Tennessean by choice, Jackson acted as an outspoken advocate of the Union when he threatened South Carolina with overwhelming force in the crisis of 1832-33. Jackson's fervently nationalistic proclamation to the people of the dissident state was at once a closely reasoned restatement of the Madisonian view that the United States was a "mixed government," and a highly emotional panegyric to the Union. Though there can be no question of Jackson's wholehearted acceptance of every patriotic syllable in that proclamation, it comes as no surprise to those acquainted with the limited literary abilities of Old Hickory that its composition was the work of an adviser. The adviser, it is worth noting, was a Southerner, Secretary of State Edward Livingston of Louisiana.

There were few things on which Henry Clay of Kentucky and Andrew Jackson could agree, but the indissolubility of the Union was one of them. Clay never concurred with those Southern leaders who accepted Calhoun's position that a state could nullify national legislation or secede from the Union. As a matter of fact, Henry Clay's Whig party was probably the most important stronghold of pro-Union sentiment in the antebellum South. Unlike the Democratic party, the Whigs never succumbed, in defending slavery to the all-encompassing states' rights doctrine. Instead, they identified themselves with the national bank, internal improvements, the tariff, and opposition to the "tyranny" of Andrew Jackson. Despite the "unsouthern" sound of these principles to modern ears, the Whig party was both powerful and popular, capable of winning elections in any Southern state. In the heyday of the Whigs, a solidly Democratic South was still unimaginable.

In 1846 the attempt of antislavery forces to prohibit slavery in the vast areas about to be acquired as a result of the Mexican War precipitated another bitter sectional struggle. But as much as they might support the "peculiar institution," the Southern Whigs stood firm against Calhoun's efforts to commit the whole South to a states' rights position that once more threatened the existence of the Union. When, in 1849, Calhoun invited Southern congressmen to join his Southern Rights movement in order to strengthen resistance against Northern demands, forty of the eighty-eight he approached refused to sign the call. Almost all of them were Whigs.

Throughout the Deep South in the state elections of 1851, Unionist Democrats and Whigs combined to stop the incipient secessionist movement in its tracks. In Georgia, Howell Cobb, the Unionist candidate for governor, received 56,261 votes to 37,172 for his opponent, a prominent Southern Rights man; in the legislature the Unionists captured 101 of the 127 seats. After the same election the congressional delegation of Alabama consisted of two secessionists and five Union supporters. In the Calhoun stronghold of Mississippi, where Jefferson Davis was the best-known spokesman for the Southern Rights movement, Davis was defeated for the governorship, 28,738 to 27,729, by his Unionist opponent, Henry S. Foote. Even in fire-eating South Carolina itself, the anti-Calhoun forces won overwhelmingly, 25,045 to 17,710.

By the time of the Kansas-Nebraska Act of 1854, the Whig party had all but disappeared, the victim of a widening sectional schism. Bereft of its traditional political organization, Southern Unionism was, for the time, almost voiceless, but it was not dead. In the election of 1860, it reappeared in the shape of the Constitutional Union party. Its candidate was John Bell of Tennessee, an old-line Whig and staunch Unionist who, in order to prevent disruption of the nation, made his platform the Union itself. That year, in a four-party race, the Constitutional Unionists were the effective second party to the Southern Democrats; for Stephen A. Douglas, the candidate of the Northern Democrats, received few votes outside the border states, and Lincoln was not even on a ballot in ten of the fifteen slave states.

The Constitutional Unionists gave the dominant Democratic party a hot fight in every Southern state. Of the upper Southern states, Virginia, Kentucky, and Tennessee went to Bell outright, while Maryland gave him 45 percent and North Carolina 47 percent of their votes.

Bell's showing in the Deep South was not as strong as in the upper South, but it nonetheless demonstrated that those Southerners still willing to be counted for the Union were a large minority in almost all of the states. From the whole South, Bell received 40 percent of the popular vote to Southern Democrat Breckinridge's 45.

A clear indication of the continuity of Unionism from the days of the Whigs to the election of 1860 is that Bell's support in the Deep South centered in the same general areas where the Whigs had been most powerful in the 1840s. Many of the Delta counties along the Mississippi River—in Arkansas, Mississippi, and Louisiana—which were always strongholds of Whiggery, went for Bell. Whig votes had always been conspicuous in the black belt counties of central Alabama and Georgia, and so were Bell's in 1860.

Surprisingly enough, the wealthy, slaveholding counties of the South were more often Whig than Democratic in the years before the war. Ever since the days of Jackson, the Democracy had been predominantly the party of the small planter and nonslaveholder. Regardless of the serious threat to slavery posed by the Republican party in 1860, many slaveholders could still not bring themselves to violate their traditional political allegiances and vote for a Democratic candidate identified with states' rights.

A further test of Southern Unionism was provided in the election of delegates to the state secession conventions in the winter of 1860–61. Unfortunately, the voting figures do not tell us as much as we would like to know. To most Southerners at the time, the issue was not simply the Union versus the right of a state to secede; more often it was whether secession was expedient, with little thought about its constitutionality. Therefore, those delegates who favored a course other than immediate secession did not necessarily support the Union under all and every circumstance.

Nevertheless, these voting returns make clear that even on the verge of secession, tens of thousands in all the states of the Deep South were still opposed to a break with the Union. In Alabama, for example, 28,200 voted against immediate secession to 35,700 for; furthermore, one-third of the delegates to the convention refused to sign the secession ordinance because it would not be submitted to the people. In Georgia, 37,123 were against secession to 50,243 in favor; in Louisiana the Unionists were an even larger minority: 17,296 against secession, 20,448 for. In Texas, despite much intimidation of Unionists, 22 percent of the voters still opposed secession.

Before Sumter was fired upon and Lincoln called for volunteers, the states of the upper South refused to join the seceding states. Early in 1861 the people of Tennessee voted against having a secession convention, 68,282 to 59,449; the vote of the people of Arkansas against secession in February 1861 was 22,000 to 17,000. North Carolina, in a popular vote, also turned down a call for a secession convention. As late as April 4, the Virginia convention voted down a proposal to draw up an ordinance of secession by an almost two-to-one majority. Even after Sumter, when the upper South states did secede, it is clear that loyalty to the Union was still a powerful sentiment.

Throughout the war Southern Unionists were active in opposition to the Confederacy. Areas of strong Unionist feeling, like eastern Tennessee, western Virginia, northern Alabama, and the mountain counties of Arkansas, quickly come to mind. In eastern Tennessee, for example, Unionist sentiment was so widespread and deep-felt that for a large part of the war, the courts of the Confederacy in that area could not function without military support and not always even then. After the war broke out, Charles Galloway, a staunch Unionist who had opposed secession in Arkansas, led two companies of his fellow Southerners to Springfield, Missouri, where they were mustered into the Union Army. Galloway then led his men back to Arkansas to fight the Confederates. Some 48,000 white Southern Unionists, it has been estimated, served voluntarily in the Army of the United States. In northern Alabama and Georgia in 1863 and after, peace societies, replete with secret grips, passwords, and elaborate security precautions, worked to encourage desertion from the Confederate army.

A recent study of the Southern Claims Commission provides the most explicit and detailed evidence of the character of Southern Unionism during the war. The commission was set up by the United States government at the end of hostilities in order to reimburse those Southerners who had sustained certain kinds of property losses because of their loyalty to the Union. (Only actual material losses incurred by loyal Southerners in behalf of the Union armies were to be honored; acts of charity or mercy, or losses occasioned by Confederate action, for example, were not included.) Since all claimants first had to offer ironclad proof of loyalty before their losses could even be considered, those who did file claims may well be taken as the hard core of Southern Unionism. There must have been thousands more who, because they lacked the opportunity or the substance to help the Union armies, went uncounted. Still others may not have been able to meet the high standards set for proof of loyalty, though their devotion to the Union was unquestioned. Under these circumstances, 22,298 claimants is an impressive number.

One of the striking facts that emerges from a study of the records of the commission is the great number of Southern Unionists who were people of substance. The total amount of the claims was $22.5 million, and 701 claims were for losses of $10,000 or more—a very substantial sum in the 1860s. The wealthy claimants were mainly planters, owners of great plantations and large numbers of slaves. Despite their wealth, or perhaps because of it, they stood with the Union when the storm of secession broke upon them—though to do so often meant obloquy and harassment at the very least, and not infrequently confiscation of property and personal danger.

Southern Unionism also played its part in the complicated history of Reconstruction. Tennessee, for example, probably escaped radical congressional Reconstruction because of the large number of Unionists in the state. William "Parson" Brownlow, an old Whig and Unionist turned Republican, was able to gain control of the state after the war, and under his leadership Tennessee managed to avoid the military occupation that was the retribution visited upon its more recalcitrant neighbors.

In Louisiana, the first Republican governor, Michael Hahn, was also a lifelong Unionist, though originally a Democrat; he had opposed secession and during the war had refused to take a pledge of loyalty to the Confederacy. About a third of the members of the Mississippi legislature during Reconstruction were so-called scalawags; but far from being the disreputable persons usually associated with that label, most of them were actually respectable former Whig Unionists turned Republican.

This shift in allegiance from Whig to Republican—by no means a rarity in the Reconstruction South—is not so strange when it is recalled that Lincoln, the first Republican President, was once a confirmed Whig. Indeed, to many former Southern Whigs it must have seemed that the Republican party—the party of business, national authority, sound money, and internal improvements—was a most fortunate reincarnation of Henry Clay's old organization. And now that slavery was no more, it seemed that Southerners could once again divide politically as their interests dictated.

The opportunity, however, proved to be short-lived, for to resist effectively the excesses of the Radicals during Reconstruction, all Southerners of consequence became Democrats as a matter of necessity. But though they may have been Democrats in name, in principles they were Whigs, and as such worked quite easily with Northern Republicans to end Reconstruction and to bring new railroads and industry to the South in the 1880s.

Most Americans assume that between 1830 and 1860 all Southerners favored slavery. This is not so. In the earlier years of the Republic, the great Virginians had not defended the institution but only excused it as an undeniable evil that was exceptionally difficult to eradicate. It was not until the 1830s that it began to be widely upheld as something to be proud of, a positive good. Here too, as in the nullification controversy, Calhoun's thought dominated the Southern mind. He had been among the first prominent Southerners to shake off the sense of guilt over slavery and to proclaim it a "great moral revolution." At the same time, however, many men and women in the South continued to doubt the utility, the wisdom, and the justice of slavery. These, too, constituted another South.

Although there were some Southerners who opposed slavery for reasons of Christian ethics, many more decried it for economic and political reasons. Cassius Marcellus Clay of Kentucky, a cousin of the more famous Henry, was prominent among those who abominated slavery because it retarded the economic growth of the South. The son of a wealthy slaveholder, Clay was educated at Yale, where his future is supposed to have been decided by hearing William Lloyd Garrison present an abolitionist lecture. Regardless of the cause for Clay's subsequent antislavery views, he emancipated his slaves in 1833, soon after his graduation, and devoted himself to the task of ridding his state of slavery. Despite his proclaimed hostile sentiments on the subject, Clay gained a large following in state and national politics.

The nature of Clay's objections to slavery were made clear in a speech he delivered before the Kentucky legislature in 1841: "Gentlemen would import slaves 'to clear up the forests of the Green River country.' Take one day's ride from this capital and then go and tell them what you have seen. Tell them that you have looked upon the once most lovely and fertile lands that nature ever formed; and have seen it in fifty years worn to the rock . . . tell them of the depopulation of the country and the consequent ruin of the towns and villages; tell them that the white Kentuckian has been driven out by slaves, by the unequal competition of unpaid labor; tell them that the mass of our people are uneducated; tell them that you have heard the children of white Kentuckians crying for bread, whilst the children of the African was [sic] clothed, and fed, and laughed! And then ask them if they will have blacks to fell their forests."

The troublesome race question effectively prevented some antislavery Southerners from taking any concrete steps to end slavery; others saw a threat in the possibility of a large free Negro population. To many, the return of former slaves to Africa seemed the necessary first step in any movement toward emancipation. Cassius Clay was both more radical and more realistic. He recognized that colonization was as illusory a solution to the evils of slavery and the Negro problem as it actually proved to be; many more Negroes were born each year than could possibly be sent to Liberia in a generation. Instead, Clay boldly advocated gradual emancipation, with the owners of the slaves being compensated by the state.

Hinton Rowan Helper is better known today as an antislavery Southerner than Clay, though the latter was certainly the more prominent at the time. Helper was the son of a poor North Carolina farmer; with the publication of his book, *The Impending Crisis of the South*, in 1857, he became a nationally known figure. In an effort to demonstrate the material and cultural backwardness of the slave states, Helper brought together statistics from the Census of 1850—compiled by that most indefatigable Southern publicist, J. D. B. De Bow, and therefore unimpeachable in Southern eyes—to show that in number of libraries, newspapers, and schools, as well as in wealth, manufactures, population, and commerce, the North far outdistanced the South. Helper pointed out that even in agriculture, the vaunted speciality of Dixie, Northern production exceeded Southern. Almost contemptuously, he observed that the value of the Cotton Kingdom's chief staple was surpassed by that of the North's lowly hay crop. The cause for all these discrepancies, Helper contended, was slavery.

Helper's indictment of slavery was sufficiently telling to arouse violent Southern attacks. He also serves to illustrate the variety of motives underlying the Southern antislavery movement. He was more disturbed about what slavery did to the poor while man than about what it did to the Negro. Many antislavery men felt the same, but Helper went further, his concern for the white man was coupled with an almost pathological hatred of the black.

Not its economic disadvantages, but its essential incompatibility with the genius of America, was the more compelling argument against slavery for some Southerners. The great Virginians of the eighteenth century—men like Washington, Marshall, Patrick Henry, Madison, Jefferson, and Monroe—all felt that it somehow contradicted their ideal of a new republic of freemen. Echoes of this view were heard by Frederick Law Olmsted when he traveled through the back country of the South in the 1850s. One mountain dweller told Olmsted that he "was afraid that there was many a man who had gone to the bad world, who wouldn't have gone if he hadn't had any slaves."

Though less moralistic in his conclusions, Henry Clay was of much the same opinion. "I am no friend to slavery," he wrote to an Alabaman in 1838. "I think it is an evil; but I believe it better that slaves should remain slaves than to be set loose as free men among us. . . ." For Clay, as for many antislavery Southerners, it was difficult to believe that emancipated Negroes and whites could live together peacefully in the same country. This deep-seated belief in the incompatibility of the two races constituted the great dilemma in the minds of antislavery Southerners; often it paralyzed all action.

The effects of this dilemma were certainly evident in the course of the remarkable debate on slavery in the Virginia legislature in 1832.

The event which precipitated it was a brief but violent uprising of slaves in Southampton County on August 21, 1831. Led by Nat Turner, a slave preacher given to visions and prophecies, the insurrectionists deliberately killed some sixty white people, mainly women and children. But even the rapidity and efficiency with which the might of the white man had been mobilized against the runaway slaves did not assuage the fear that surged through the minds of Southerners everywhere. And so it was that on January 11, 1832, there began one of the most searching debates on slavery ever held by the elected representatives of a slaveholding people. For two weeks the venerable institution was subjected to the frankest kind of criticism.

Three-quarters of the members of the House of Delegates held slaves, yet more than half of that body spoke out against the institution in one fashion or another. In analyzing the statements and the notes of the members, one historian concluded that 60 of the 134 delegates were consistently antislavery, working for legislation that would eventually terminate Negro bondage in Virginia. Twelve more, whom he calls the compromisers, were antislavery in belief, but were not prepared to vote for any measure which would, at that time, commit the state to emancipation. It was this latter group, in league with the sixty or so defenders of the status quo, who defeated the efforts to initiate gradual emancipation in 1832.

Though individual opponents of slavery remained in the South right up to the Civil War, it is impossible to ascertain their numbers. However, a glimpse into the mind of one such Southerner had been afforded by the publication of the diary of Mary Minor Blackford. Mrs. Blackford lived in Fredericksburg, Virginia, across the street from a slave trader's house, a location which permitted her to see slavery at its worst. And it was slavery as a moral evil rather than as an economic fallacy which troubled her: how could people otherwise good and humane, kind and Christian, hold fellow human beings in bondage? For unlike some Northern abolitionists, she knew slave owners too well to think them innately evil. Her answer was not surprising: material self-interest morally blinded them.

The tragedy of the South's history was woven into the fabric of Mary Minor Blackford's life. Despite her long opposition to slavery, she proudly saw five of her sons serve in the Confederate Army. Yet with its defeat, she could still write early in 1866: "A New Era has dawned since I last wrote in this book. Slavery has been abolished!!!"

Other individual opponents of slavery in the South could be cited, but perhaps it would be best to close by mentioning an antislavery organization. The American Colonization Society, founded in 1817 by Southern and Northern antislavery men, always included prominent Southerners among its leaders. In the course of its half century of operations, the society managed to send more than six thousand Negroes to its African colony in Liberia.

The society was strongest in the South; indeed, it was anathema to the New England and middle western abolitionists. Though it is true that antislavery was never a popular cause in the South, it was never a dead one, either, so long as thousands of Southerners refused to view slavery as anything but an evil for their region.

As we have seen, the South was even less united on nullification and secession than it was on the question of slavery. In fact, it is now clear that if a majority of Southerners ever did support secession—and there is real doubt on this—it was never a big majority, and it was not achieved until the very eve of the Civil War. In short, the South, rather than being a monolith of undivided opinion, was not even of one mind on the two most vital issues of the thirty years that led up to the war.

—August 1960

GETTING RIGHT WITH ROBERT E. LEE

by STEPHEN W. SEARS

How to know the unknowable man.

In 1905, on a visit to Richmond, the noted man of letters Henry James was struck by the sight of the equestrian statue of Robert E. Lee high atop its pedestal overlooking Monument Avenue. There was about it, James thought, "a strange eloquence . . . a kind of melancholy nobleness." Something in the figure suggested "a quite sublime effort to ignore, to sit, as it were, superior and indifferent . . . so that the vast association of the futile for the moment drops away from it." Several decades later Lee's biographer Douglas Southall Freeman passed the Lee statue in Richmond daily and invariably saluted it. "I shall not fail to do that as long as I live," Freeman said. Lee has that effect on people. For almost a century and a third, Americans, Northerners and Southerners, have been trying to get right with Robert E. Lee.

Such is the paradox of the man that today both those who consider General Lee a detriment to the Confederacy and those who consider him an undefiled military genius reach the same conclusion: The South would have been better off without him. The detractor says Lee squandered the South's slim resources of men and matériel, destroying any chance for ultimate Confederate victory; the admirer says that without Lee the Confederacy would have crumbled early, thus saving numerous Southern lives and much Southern suffering. It is at least safe to say that the course of the Civil War as we know it would have been very different without this one man.

Getting right with Lee has never been a simple task. Mary

Chesnut, who observed him carefully during the war, wondered if anyone could really know him: "He looks so cold and quiet and grand." When Lee took command of the Army of Northern Virginia in 1862, writes Bruce Catton, "This gray man in gray rode his dappled gray horse into legend almost at once, and like all legendary figures he came before long to seem almost supernatural, a man of profound mystery." To the poet Stephen Vincent Benét, Lee was:

> *A figure lost to flesh and blood and bones,*
> *Frozen into a legend out of life,*
> *A blank-verse statue— . . .*
> *For here was someone who lived all his life*
> *In the most fierce and open light of the sun*
> *And kept his heart a secret to the end*
> *From all the picklocks of biographers.*

Benét called him "the marble man."

In the aftershock of Appomattox most Southerners were not immediately drawn to idolizing their generals. The war, after all, had been lost on the battlefields, and now there was nothing at all to celebrate except the end to the killing. To be sure, of all the South's generals Lee was even then the most respected, for back in the days when there had been victories to celebrate, most of them were his. In the years after the war, first in Richmond and then as president of little Washington College in Lexington, Lee was quietly honored by his fellow Virginians whenever they had the opportunity. At his death in Lexington in 1870 there was a modest military cortege and bells tolled and a battery from the Virginia Military Institute fired minute guns. The general's last words had been "Strike the tent," and that seemed to sound the proper final note for the old soldier's passing.

But of course that was not the end of it. The tent was never struck. Creating the mythic Robert E. Lee began only after his death, for in life he would never have permitted it. In life Lee was not without ambition, nor was he self-effacing to the point of false modesty, and he harbored pride in what he had accomplished in the war. "There is nothing left me to do but to go and see General Grant," he had said on the day he surrendered his army at Appomattox, "and I would rather die a thousand deaths." But the process whereby he was canonized to secular sainthood would have triggered in him that icy anger that withered anyone at whom it was aimed. Those who created him the marble man, however, were out of his reach from beyond the grave. The marbling process, writes the historian C. Vann Woodward, "was the work of many hands, not all of them pious, the product of mixed motives, not all of them worthy."

In *The Marble Man: Robert E. Lee and His Image in American Society*, Thomas L. Connelly chronicles the rise of what he terms the Lee cult. Two initially rival Lee cliques, in Lexington and Richmond, coalesced and within a decade, by the end of the 1870s, were hard at work. Theirs was an all-Virginian operation—States' Rights energized the cult as well as the Confederacy—spearheaded by the former Army of Northern Virginia generals Jubal Early, William N. Pendleton, Fitzhugh Lee (General Lee's nephew), Lee's former staff members Walter Taylor and Charles Marshall, and J. William Jones, a Baptist minister. The cult's mission, Connelly writes, was to appropriate Robert E. Lee "as a balm to soothe defeat" and as the paladin of the lost cause. "To justify Lee was to justify the Southern cause."

Through speeches, articles, biographies, campaign narratives, and the editorship of the *Papers* of the Southern Historical Society, cult members seized control of Confederate historiography and turned it to their own purposes, which was the production of Lee hagiography. This veneration, explains the Lee biographer Marshall Fishwick, resulted in a St. George of Virginia, a remarkable phenomenon in white Southern Protestantism. To a beaten South, suffering under the lash of Reconstruction, this sainted Lee, so without blemish of character that his defense of the cause and his ultimate failure could only be examples of God's will, was truly a figure of worship.

Lee's elevation was necessarily accomplished at the expense of other Confederate generals, and here the mixed motives of the Lee cult became apparent. Such rivals for military eminence as P. G. T. Beauregard and Joseph E. Johnston were systematically diminished in the pages of the Southern Historical Society *Papers*, which its editor, the Reverend Jones, turned into a showcase for General Lee and his Army of Northern Virginia. Even the heroic Stonewall Jackson, struck down at his moment of victory at Chancellorsville, was carefully reduced to simply Lee's lieutenant, his triumphs gained under the all-seeing direction of the general commanding. But these various demotions pale next to what Connelly terms the "crucifixion" of Lt. Gen. James Longstreet.

The assault on Longstreet was tied directly to the most difficult task the cult faced in its burnishing of Lee's military reputation: explaining the Battle of Gettysburg. Lee partisans would not admit that Gettysburg was an outright Confederate defeat—it was merely a check—yet there was no way they could transmute it into any semblance of a victory either. The greatest single battle of the war could not be reshaped into anything much better than a failure to achieve Lee's goals.

It could be reshaped into someone else's failure instead of Lee's, however, and Jubal Early took charge of that effort. Early was a grouchy, disagreeable sort with an undistinguished war record. He had actually been relieved of his last command, in the Shenandoah Valley, by Lee, who normally juggled subordinates without resorting to dismissal. Furthermore, at Gettysburg it was Early's failure to press an attack on July 1, the first day of the battle, that was widely regarded as a main reason the Federals retained their hold on Cemetery Ridge, from which they repelled the later Confederate attacks. By directing fire at Longstreet, Early was intent on diverting fire from himself.

Longstreet made an easy target. Not only had his second-day attack at Gettysburg failed (albeit narrowly), but in the years after the war he dared to criticize Lee's conduct of the battle. To compound his felony, during Reconstruction Longstreet embraced Republicanism. A barrage of articles on Gettysburg in the Southern Historical Society *Papers*, heavily freighted with innuendo and unsubstantiated charges, locked Longstreet into the scapegoat's role. Jubal Early put the matter with perfect clarity. "Either General Lee or General Longstreet was responsible for the remarkable delay that took place in making the attack," Early wrote of the fighting on July 2. "I choose to believe that it was not General Lee." In that kind of contest Longstreet had no chance.

By the turn of the century the heroic, saintly Lee was no longer being seen merely as a Virginian or a Southerner but instead as a national hero. In a series of influential addresses and essays, Charles Francis Adams, Jr., grandson and great-grandson of Presidents, firmly ensconced Lee in this new role.

Adams spoke of "the debt of gratitude this reunited country of ours—Union and Confederate, North and South—owes to Robert E. Lee of Virginia." Journalists linked Lee with Washington and Lincoln as the "first triumvirate of greatness." When the Hall of Fame was established at New York University in 1901, Lee was one of the first welcomed into the pantheon. Gamaliel Bradford's wide-selling 1912 biography was called simply *Lee the American*. A Southerner nicely summed up the enhanced stature of the foremost soldier of the Confederacy: "Whatever else we may have lost in that struggle, we gave the world Robert E. Lee."

While Lincoln remains unchallenged as the Civil War's most written-about figure, the volume of words expended on Lee, especially when Lee-related accounts of Gettysburg are included, holds second place. Heading the vast Lee literature is Douglas Southall Freeman's monumental four-volume biography, published in 1934 and 1935. With literary mastery and eminent scholarship Freeman firmly fixed greatness on Lee. In his hands Lee the general was certainly not above criticism, but it was never diminishing criticism. Freeman saw Lee's military failings as both few and proper. In Lee the man, Freeman found no contradictions, no secret self that was proof against the picklocks of biographers. "Robert Lee," he wrote, "was one of the small company of great men in whom there is no inconsistency to be explained, no enigma to be solved. What he seemed, he was—a wholly human gentleman, the essential elements of whose positive character were two and only two, simplicity and spirituality."

Thomas Connelly sees considerable irony in the hagiographical efforts of the Lee cult. The general's "military greatness alone would have assured his niche as a major national figure," he writes, without all the manipulation that went into creating the marble man. Perhaps in reaction to the image of the marble man, and certainly in challenge to it, historians in recent years (including especially Connelly) have sifted through everything Lee wrote to uncover the real man behind the improbable mask of the demigod. At the same time, Lee's military thought, his wartime strategy and tactics, have been plumbed anew in efforts to reinterpret his role in Confederate history. These efforts constitute one more attempt to get right with Robert E. Lee.

The Lee who emerges from these investigations is marked

by more humanity and affected by more normal emotions than the demigod Lee. There can be little doubt, for example, that his youthful ambition to succeed and his awesome sense of duty were goaded by the cautionary tale of his father, Light-Horse Harry Lee, the Revolutionary War hero but a ne'er-do-well who deserted his family when Lee was just six years old. No doubt, too, the slack pace of promotion in the antebellum Army caused Lee frequently to question the worth of a career that brought him a colonelcy only after thirty-two years of service. Whether his marriage was less than a success, as has been argued, is not something that can be clearly settled at this distance, but it is clear that Lee complained about the seemingly endless separations from wife and family during his service in the old Army. And it is hardly surprising that amid the uncertainties of war he would fall back increasingly on the rationalization that God ruled all human affairs, the outcome of which were beyond earthly control.

At the same time, it must be said that Lee was hardly singular in his musings about the unfairness of life and in questioning his choice of the Army as a career. There cannot have been a single officer in the 1850s who expressed himself satisfied with his lot in that bureaucracy-ridden, glacier-paced antebellum army. The only surprise is that Lee did not resign to pursue a civilian career, as many others did. As for his religious fatalism, that too was common enough among Civil War generals. It was, after all, the duty of a field commander in wartime to organize and make efficient the mass killing of human beings, and anyone at all sensitive to the paradox of that was likely to seek reassurance that what he was doing was God's will.

Connelly offers the speculation that these various background pressures on Lee's psyche produced in him a repressed personality, turning him overly audacious and aggressive when in command on the battlefield. Lee's penchant for attack was in the end more than the Confederacy could afford, he writes; the Army of Northern Virginia "was bled to death by Lee's offensive tactics."

Such an explanation for Lee's military persona seems unduly complicated. In December 1862, watching a series of doomed Yankee attacks smash against his line at Fredericksburg, Lee remarked, "It is well that war is so terrible—we should grow too fond of it." That thought lends weight to an observation by Paul C. Nagel, the biographer of the Lees of Virginia. "At two points in his life," Nagel writes of the general, "he showed daring and imagination. These were on the battlefields of the Mexican War and the Civil War. But across the longer stretches of time, he seemed lethargic and inclined to stick with what was familiar and at hand." It was the opportunity for leadership and command in battle that raised Lee's consciousness and energized him; possibly his trust in himself did wane at other times, but never in war. It was this supreme confidence in his own generalship that enabled Lee to face down every general he met in the war but the last one, U. S. Grant, who possessed equal confidence in himself as a commander.

The corollary to this battlefield self-confidence is equally important to any understanding of Robert E. Lee the soldier: He invariably fought to *win*. Not every Civil War general fought that way. The Federals' Henry W. Halleck, for example, was primarily interested in gaining territory when in field command. General McClellan was notorious for fighting, when he did fight, so as not to lose. Joseph E. Johnston, when he opposed McClellan in Virginia and later Sherman in Georgia and the Carolinas, constantly retreated in order to avoid defeat. Lee's critics T. Harry Williams and the Englishman J. F. C. Fuller charge him with being both overly aggressive and strategically parochial, interested only in the Virginia theater of war. Williams terms him un-modern, "the last of the great old-fashioned generals." In fact Lee was neither parochial nor old-fashioned. He understood exactly where the South might win this war and what was required to win it, and he single-mindedly bent every effort to that victory. It was a decidedly modern concept.

Southerners might win the war through foreign intervention, as their forefathers had won the Revolution, or they might win on the battlefield and so force the North to the peace table. Militarily the best the Confederacy could hope from any Western victories was simply to arrest the Federal advance there and gain a stalemate. On the other hand, the Confederacy could win its independence at a stroke by winning victories, or just one great victory, in the East. The destruction of the Union's principal army and guardian of Washington, the Army of the Potomac, at a Sharpsburg or a Gettysburg or perhaps at Washington itself, offered the best chance to force the Lincoln administration to sue for peace. Even achieving a bloody stalemate against that army, as Lee nearly accomplished in the summer campaign of 1864, might go far toward gaining at least a negotiated peace and status quo antebellum—the South's return to the Union with its "rights" and its peculiar institution intact.

While Lee did not discount the possibility of British and French intervention, he was realistic in warning against relying on it. "We must make up our minds to fight our battles ourselves," he wrote in December 1861. "Expect to receive aid from no one. . . . The cry is too much for help." There was nothing at all parochial in his outlook. One of his staff recorded his observation that "since the whole duty of the nation would be war until independence should be secured, the whole nation should for the time be converted into an army, the producers to feed and the soldiers to fight." Toward this end Lee strongly endorsed a Confederacy-wide manpower draft, and the conscription bill that passed the Confederate Congress in Richmond in April 1862 was largely of his making.

That Lee frequently acted very aggressively in his strategy and often in his tactics is beyond dispute. That he often had no other practical choice is not always appreciated by those critics who, viewing Civil War battles through the lens of hindsight, rule them inherently indecisive because of the new weaponry and the old tactics of that day. It is true that Lee never gained the great war-winning battle, like Hannibal's Cannae, that he sought, but that result was not foreordained. In 1862 and 1863, before the two armies became locked in the trenches before Petersburg, Lee fought battles that were decided by chance or by fate or simply by human frailty.

He grasped the enormous advantage in war of holding the initiative, of forcing the enemy to march to his drum, especially so since his was always the smaller army. At every opportunity he aggressively seized the strategic initiative, as he did on taking field command for the first time in June 1862 during the Peninsula campaign.

In fighting McClellan for Richmond in the Seven Days' Battles, which opened in the last week of June, Lee adopted the offensive tactically as well as strategically. While his overall strategy was excellent, his tactics reflected his inexperience: his battle plans were too complicated, his staff work was poor, his orders were too demanding. The closest he came to a Cannae was at Glendale on June 30; Malvern Hill, the next day, was a disaster. Yet Lee had no real alternative to playing the role of aggressor in this week-long battle. To remain on the defensive was to allow McClellan to besiege Richmond, and to lose Richmond was a blow the Confederacy could not have survived, armchair generals to the contrary. In the event, Lee's offensive, flawed as it was, was relentless, and his opponent gave way before it. This was also McClellan's first experience of field command, and he broke under the strain. Lee took note of that lesson.

If Chancellorsville can be considered Lee's tactical masterpiece, his strategic masterpiece was the Second Manassas (Second Bull Run) campaign in August of 1862. In it, demonstrating an unerring sense of time as an element in warfare, he broke John Pope's army, one of the two arrayed against him, before the other one, under McClellan, could join it to overwhelm him. His margin in accomplishing this feat was a matter of only a few hours, but Lee was unruffled. When asked if he was not worried that his advance, under Stonewall Jackson, might be destroyed before he came up with the rest of the army, he replied calmly, "Not at all. I knew he could hold on till we came, and that we should be in position in time." Second Manassas, too, demonstrated how well he had learned the lessons of tactical command during the Seven Days. Now, as Robert Frost put it, "his dispositions for battle were beautiful. His two great divisions under Longstreet and Jackson were like pistols in his two hands, so perfectly could he handle them."

Lee's decision after the victory at Second Manassas to cross his country's northern frontier (as he called the Potomac) and march into Maryland toward Pennsylvania has been much debated. Was it intended as an invasion? A raid? What could he hope to gain by changing the Confederacy's overall posture from defensive to offensive? Lee's rationale was simple and straightforward: Crossing the Potomac was the only way to retain the initiative, and marching north offered the best way toward victory. General McClellan, he had learned, was once again his opponent, and he considered McClellan "an able general but a very timid one." Looking back on the campaign, Lee put the case with nice brevity: "I went into Maryland to give battle," and had all gone as intended, "I would have fought and crushed him."

Of course, all did not go as Lee intended, for chance intervened. A careless courier lost a copy of his campaign plan, and it was found by a Yankee soldier and brought to McClellan. The consequence was the Battle of Sharpsburg (or Antietam), on September 17. Sharpsburg was a battle Lee did not have to fight; so slow was McClellan to act on the lost order that Lee could have slipped back across the Potomac had he wished. Porter Alexander, an artillerist in Lee's army and a particularly astute observer, was blunt in calling it "the greatest military blunder that Gen. Lee ever made." However, Alexander offered the further observation that when General McClellan brought his greatly superior army to the banks of Antietam Creek, "he brought *himself* also." This was the actual reason Lee stood and fought there. He was certain he could beat the timid, cautious McClellan in any pitched battle, and indeed, he did outgeneral him that day and gain a narrow tactical victory, inflicting 20 percent more casualties than he suffered. Even at that, his army was too badly hurt to continue the campaign, and he had to fall back to Virginia. The profit of Sharpsburg was not worth the cost.

To say this is not to say that Lee was being overly aggressive in crossing the Potomac and marching north. With his army intact and rested and operating as he intended on ground of his own choosing, facing a general he was supremely confident he could beat, Robert E. Lee had every reason to believe he would win the showdown battle he sought. In these fall months of 1862 his troops and his lieutenants were in good form and good morale, and he was at the peak of his own powers, and when he insisted that without the mischance of the lost order he would have crushed McClellan, his opinion is worth respect.

The wounding of his army in Maryland forced Lee to surrender the strategic initiative for the first time since taking command, but thanks to the two generals who faced him next, this proved to be no disadvantage. "I fear they may continue to make these changes till they find some one whom I don't understand," Lee said when he learned of McClellan's dismissal after Sharpsburg. He need not have worried. He understood these two perfectly.

December saw McClellan's successor, Ambrose Burnside, hurl his army fruitlessly against the Army of Northern

Virginia at Fredericksburg in the most senseless attack of the war. Longstreet remarked that so long as his ammunition held out and they kept coming, he would kill Yankee soldiers until there were none left in the North. Five months later, in May 1863, it was "Fighting Joe" Hooker's turn to challenge. Lee sarcastically referred to him as "Mr. F. J. Hooker" and once again took cruel advantage of the fact that his opponent was commanding an army in battle for the first time.

At Chancellorsville, Hooker lost his nerve and halted. "For once I lost confidence in Hooker," he admitted, "and that is all there is to it." Seizing the moment, Lee divided his forces in front of an army outnumbering him almost two to one and sent Stonewall Jackson on one of his patented flank marches. Jackson's attack sent the Yankees flying, Lee exerted pressure on all points of the line, and Hooker hastily admitted defeat and took his army back to its starting point. For Lee the great victory was marred by the mortal wounding of Jackson; with Jackson gone, he said, he had lost his right arm.

In opening the Gettysburg campaign a month after Chancellorsville, Lee was once again acting to hold the strategic initiative, and he was once again challenging a general, George G. Meade, who was commanding an army in battle for the first time. It was a familiar pattern, one that Lee had exploited with great success before, and it is not surprising that he would try it again.

In the first two days of the fighting at Gettysburg, Lee came tantalizingly close to winning his Cannae. His blood was up, as Longstreet put it, and he continued the offensive and so committed the deadly mistake of Pickett's Charge. That attack makes the best argument for critics of Lee's overaggressiveness, but the order for it came out of everything Lee was, everything that made him a great general; only this time he failed. "All this has been my fault—it is I that have lost the fight," he told Pickett's surviving soldiers. Still, so imposing was his reputation in that July of 1863 that General Meade was content with the battle's outcome and launched no counterattack and offered no pursuit when Lee retreated to Virginia. "Gettysburg," the historian Shelby Foote sums up, "was the price the South paid for having R. E. Lee."

The two bruised armies sparred inconclusively through the autumn as the war's focus shifted west, where Vicksburg had fallen and the Federals threatened to break through the

Chattanooga gateway to the Deep South. Longstreet's corps was sent west as reinforcement, and Jefferson Davis proposed that Lee go West himself and take command there. He would do so if the president wished, Lee said, but he suggested it be a permanent change; the Western high command would never cordially support a visiting general. Of equal concern, who would command the Army of Northern Virginia in his stead? Jackson was dead and Longstreet was in the West, and Lee could suggest no one else competent for the post. Davis agreed, and Lee remained in the East. In the weakening Confederacy Lee's army was pre-eminent, and Lee was irreplaceable.

Lee's contest against Grant in the spring and summer of 1864, from the Wilderness and Spotsylvania to Cold Harbor and Petersburg, is in many respects as remarkable as anything in his Civil War record. With an army failing steadily and inevitably, against a general who was at last a true match, Lee countered every advance and repelled every charge and inflicted nearly twice the casualties he suffered. At Petersburg the two armies went to ground in a siege that lasted nine months. Here the Army of Northern Virginia was finally brought to bay by Grant, who was the sixth general to attempt it, yet at the same time the effort stalemated the Army of the Potomac, leaving the war in the East on dead center. The Confederacy's two Western generals, Joe Johnston and John B. Hood, could not achieve a comparable stalemate, however, and by the spring of 1865 Lee saw that final defeat was inevitable. "This is the people's war," he said at the time. "When they tire, I stop."

In February he had been appointed general in chief of all the Confederacy's armies, but by then there was little left for him to direct. In line with his earlier call for the entire Southern nation to mobilize for war, he advocated arming the slaves, which act would earn them their freedom. As regards black soldiers in Confederate gray, he said, "I think we could at least do as well with them as the enemy."

Lee felt duty-bound that spring to attempt one last campaign, and he managed to extricate his army from Petersburg and head it westward, hoping to join Joe Johnston in North Carolina and somehow carry on the fight. By the time he approached Appomattox Courthouse he had but eight thousand armed men left and knew he must meet General

Grant and end it.

Gen. Porter Alexander urged Lee not to surrender but instead to let the men scatter to the hills to carry on a guerrilla war against the Yankee invaders. No, said Lee, that would mean ultimate ruin for the South; "a state of society would ensue from which it would take the country years to recover." To destroy what he had fought so hard to preserve would be senseless. "We have now simply to look the fact in the face that the Confederacy has failed." By his surrender, which initiated the surrender of the rest of the Confederacy's forces, Lee performed one of his most lasting services for the Confederate States of America.

When all is said and done, getting right with Robert E. Lee is a task that requires less analysis of his psyche and more analysis of his deeds. He was not by nature eloquent or introspective; even his personal farewell to his army at Appomattox was composed for him by one of his aides. "General Lee has done wonders—and no words wasted," the Charleston diarist Mary Chesnut said of him in 1865. For Henry James there was eloquence enough just in the figure of the man. In the few years left to him after the war, Lee never explained or justified in a memoir, as did so many other generals. Among the major figures of the Civil War, he left the least words and the fewest inner thoughts for historians and biographers to pick over. It was Lee's actions that spoke volumes.

If Douglas Freeman's Lee sometimes has the shadings of a mythic figure, he was surely right to dismiss the idea that there was anything enigmatic about his subject. Lee was simply a professional soldier who found his true calling in war, who, in Bruce Catton's phrase, "understood the processes of war as few men have ever done." Part of that understanding was a Midas's touch for crafting remarkable battlefield feats from limited resources.

Porter Alexander recorded a prophecy about Lee, made early in the war, before he had a record as a battlefield commander, that has been widely quoted. Alexander asked an aide to President Jefferson Davis if he thought Lee had audacity enough to lead a field army. "Lee is audacity personified," the man replied. "His name is audacity, and you need not be afraid of not seeing all of it that you will want to see." Lee's was an instinctive audacity for doing whatever was necessary for winning, and if it resulted in such repulses as Malvern Hill and Pickett's Charge, it was also responsible for the brilliance of Chancellorsville and Second Manassas and a dozen other combats that extended the life of the Confederacy beyond all reasonable expectations. That singular accomplishment is the mark of the man.

—May 1991

THE MIRACLE THAT SAVED THE UNION

by SCARRITT ADAMS

The Union desperately needed an extraordinary warship to counter the ironclad the Confederates were building.

I t was obvious that something very special was needed to confront the ironclad that the Confederacy was furiously building if the Union was to be saved. Yet it took a personal visit of Abraham Lincoln to the somnolent offices of the Navy Department to force the issue, and by then it was so late that the Navy Department had to have a miracle. In short, the contractor would have to build, in a hundred days, a kind of ship that had never been built before, and build it in a desperate race against time.

To sign a contract calling for a miracle in a hundred days was all very well, but there had to be a miracle man to do it. There was probably only one man in the world who could. He was John Ericsson, the great inventor.

Whether Ericsson *would* was another matter. He had become decidedly unenthusiastic about doing business with governments. Napoleon III had turned down his plans for a ship with a movable turret—what Ericsson called a monitor. The British Admiralty had refused him payment for his unique screw propeller on the ground that a rival inventor had already patented one. Ericsson's screw propeller had been demonstrated on a vessel built in England in 1839 and named after his friend Captain Robert F. Stockton of the United States Navy. And it was at Stockton's urging that Ericsson subsequently came to the United States and put one of his propellers on the U.S.S. *Princeton*, the first warship in the world to have one. Unfortunately, during a demonstration firing, the *Princeton*'s big twelve-inch experimental gun exploded, killing Secretary of State Able P. Upshur, Secretary of the Navy Thomas W. Gilmer, and four other persons. Stockton, the skipper of the *Princeton*, turned on his friend Ericsson and made him the scapegoat of the tragedy. In consequence Ericsson vowed never again to deal with Washington, and Stockton continuously opposed the inventor's enterprises. His would be the hidden voice of a widespread Navy coterie in 1861 that was against any such nonsense as what was variously called "Ericsson's Folly," a stupid "cheesebox on a raft," a silly "tin can on a shingle."

That first summer of the Civil War was an especially fretful one for Navy Department officials in Washington. Lincoln had proclaimed a blockade of all Southern ports, but the Navy was seriously hampered by the lack of ships to carry out his order. Worse, after Union forces abandoned the Norfolk Navy Yard, word quickly reached the Capitol that the Confederates, with surprising ingenuity, were building themselves an ironclad ship there. Inasmuch as an armor-piercing shell had yet to be created—there had been no need for one until then—such a vessel was virtually impregnable and could wreak havoc among wooden fighting ships. And the Navy Yard, near the entrance to Chesapeake Bay, was in a strategic position to stymie Union campaigns in Virginia; it controlled the James River approach to Richmond, the Potomac River approach to Washington, and the port of Baltimore as well. An ironclad ship let loose in the bay was obviously a serious threat to the prosecution of the war.

The newfangled ship all covered with iron plates being built by the Confederates was the powerful steam frigate *Merrimack*, burned and scuttled by Union forces when they evacuated Norfolk. The rebels had raised her and were busy refitting her into an ironclad ram that they rechristened the *Virginia*. (The vessel's name has nevertheless come down in history in the Union version.) The Confederates were improvising what looked like a floating barn roof with ports for ten guns. The hull was being cut down to the water line, a long iron-plated superstructure was to be placed on top, and a four-foot cast-iron prow affixed to her bow.

Lincoln had appointed Hiram Paulding, an aged hero of the War of 1812, to "put the navy afloat." Paulding naturally called into consultation the chief of the Bureau of Construction for the Navy, old John Lenthal. Lenthal would have no truck with such nonsense, remarking that building ironclads "was not his trade"; he remained silent thereafter.

At last Gideon Welles, the Secretary of the Navy, sent a message to the special session of Congress meeting on the Fourth of July, 1861, suggesting that a special board be appointed to investigate the feasibility of building one or more ironclad steamers or floating batteries. Congress complied, authorizing the expenditure of $1,500,000 for construction if the board reported favorably.

Then the contractors entered the picture like hawks. The iron interests went to work. Cornelius Bushnell, president of the New Haven, Hartford and Stonington Railroad, one of the foremost of the lobbyists, persuaded the chairman of the Naval Committee to get behind the Ironclad Bill and push it through the House. The Confederate Secretary of the Navy, Stephen R. Mallory, had already issued orders on July 11 "to proceed with all possible despatch" with the *Merrimack*'s rebuilding; it was obvious to all that time was essential.

On August 3 Congress approved the bill and authorized the Secretary of the Navy to appoint a board of "three skilful officers" to look into the matter. Four days later the Navy Department, now moving at unprecedented speed, in a "public appeal to the mechanical ingenuity of our country" issued an advertisement for ironclad steam vessels. The Navy would "receive offers from parties who are able to execute work of this kind." Persons who intended to offer must be quick about it and let the Ironclad Board know in a week—by August 15 precisely. And in less than a month they must have before the board the detailed plans, proposed speed, cost, and building time.

The iron interests and the shipbuilders of New York, Boston, and Philadelphia were in a frenzy of activity. By the deadline sixteen companies had submitted proposals to the Ironclad Board. E. S. Renwick of New York proposed a 6,250-ton giant, 400 feet long, that would speed along at a phenomenal 18 knots and cost $1,500,000. Donald McKay, famed builder of the world's fastest clipper ships, wanted to spend $1,000,000 on his version and take nine months doing it. Cornelius Bushnell submitted plans for still another ship, the

Galena.

John Ericsson was not among the sixteen entrants. One day, however, when Bushnell returned to Willard's Hotel, where he was staying in Washington, he ran into Cornelius DeLamater, a well-known and highly respected machinist. DeLamater was a friend of Ericsson's; indeed, the two had become close associates soon after first meeting in 1839, when Ericsson arrived in the United States. DeLamater's father had bought into, and eventually took over entirely, an ironworks foundry in lower Manhattan, and Ericsson in 1844 had taken up quarters nearby, at 95 Franklin Street.

Bushnell told DeLamater about the plans for the *Galena* that he had submitted to the board; DeLamater suggested that it would be a good idea to check them with Ericsson. Bushnell agreed and took a train to New York.

When Ann, the elderly maid, opened the door at 95 Franklin Street, Bushnell found Ericsson sitting on a revolving piano stool in a combined bedroom-workroom. Bushnell offered to show him the *Galena* plans. Ericsson consented, and the next day, when Bushnell returned, the inventor assured him that they were all right and asked if Bushnell, by the way, would like to see some old plans and a pasteboard model he had of a floating battery, a turreted ironclad with two big guns mounted in a revolving roundhouse. Opening up a dusty box, Ericsson laid open the plans shown to Napoleon III in 1858. Bushnell was impressed, so much so that he took them then and there and rushed off to show them to Gideon Welles, who was visiting in Hartford. The Secretary was equally impressed. He advised Bushnell to take the plans to Washington in a hurry and get them before the Ironclad Board before it concluded its deliberations.

As soon as Bushnell got back to Washington, he looked up two business associates, John A. Griswold, president of the Troy City Bank, and John F. Winslow, a Troy iron-plate manufacturer. Bushnell offered them a quarter interest each in the floating battery if he was awarded the contract. Unable to impress Commodore Joseph Smith of the Naval Board, he got a letter of introduction from Secretary of State William H. Seward to Lincoln, the one man in Washington who could get things done. The three businessmen presented their case to the President, who said: "I don't know much about boats but . . . I will meet you tomorrow at 11 A.M. in Commodore

Smith's office and we will talk it over."

T he members of the Ironclad Board were Commodores Smith and Hiram Paulding, both born in George Washington's time, and Commander Charles H. Davis. They all had a reputation for being extremely cautious and critical. Paulding had already confided to his wife that "ironclads will be more tedious than I thought." Nevertheless he would be inextricably involved in the fortunes of the *Monitor*—as Ericsson later officially named his vessel—not only as a member of the Ironclad Board but later as commandant of the Brooklyn Navy Yard, where it would be his duty to outfit her and send her off to do battle. Smith, who would have more to do with the *Monitor* than anybody else, was chief of the Bureau of Yards and Docks. His reputation for safeguarding the interests of the Navy was such that it was said he always "seemed to sleep with one eye open." Although Smith admired Ericsson, the validity of the plan for a floating battery would have to be very convincingly demonstrated. Davis, the junior member, was dead set against it. With his skill at debate he would be a dangerous opponent. These, then, were the men Bushnell's party would have to persuade.

At the appointed time the President turned up in Smith's office. So did Gustavus Vasa Fox, the dynamic new—and first—Assistant Secretary of the Navy, lobbyist Bushnell, banker Griswold, iron man Winslow, Commodore Paulding, and Commander Davis. Nearly everybody admitted Ericsson's plan was novel. But Davis thought it was silly and ridiculed it. Smith was noncommittal. Lincoln listened for an hour and then in closing the meeting remarked: "All I can say is what the girl said when she put her foot in the stocking: 'I think there's something in it.'" Thus Ericsson's Floating Battery became the seventeenth entry.

The Ironclad Board finished its meetings on September 16. Its formal report turned down fourteen of the seventeen proposals. McKay's proposal was rejected because his ship was too slow. Renwick's eighteen-knot giant cost too much; it would eat up the entire appropriation. But the *Galena* was still in the running, as was an ironclad called *New Ironsides*. And John Ericsson's proposal, entered last, was listed first on the tabulation of the seventeen.

However, when Smith reconvened the board the next

day, Davis prevailed and Ericsson's plan was rejected. It seemed that there would be no *Monitor.*

Lobbyist Bushnell thereupon got to work on the members of the board individually. As a result Paulding and Smith promised they would vote approval if Bushnell could get Davis to go along with them. So Bushnell tackled Davis, a hard nut to crack. Davis was still adamant and told Bushnell that he "might take the little model home and worship it, as it would not be idolatry, because it was made in the image of nothing in heaven above, or the earth below, or in the waters under the earth." There was only one thing left for Bushnell to do. That was to bring Ericsson to Washington to confront Davis in person. Accordingly Bushnell went off to New York, and Commodore Smith helped out by writing to Ericsson that there "seemed to be some deficiencies in the specifications," that "some changes may be suggested," and that "a guarantee would be required."

Convinced by Bushnell that Davis merely wanted a few points about his plan clarified, Ericsson took a train for Washington and on meeting Davis declared: "I have come down at the suggestion of Captain Bushnell, to explain about the plan of the *Monitor.*"

"What," queried Davis, "the little plan Bushnell had here Tuesday? Why, we rejected it *in toto.*"

"Rejected it! What for . . . ?"

"For want of stability. . . ."

"Stability," exclaimed the amazed Ericsson. "No craft that ever floated was more stable than she would be; that is one of her great merits."

Davis, softening, answered: "Prove it . . . and we will recommend it at once."

"I will go to my hotel and prepare the proof . . . and meet your Board at the Secretary's room at 1 o'clock."

In a two-hour presentation Ericsson proved the stability was satisfactory beyond a doubt. After he withdrew, the board deliberated for two more hours, at the end of which they notified Gideon Welles that they were satisfied. Welles called Ericsson to his office late that afternoon and in a five-minute interview told him to get started immediately. The contract could be signed later. Ericsson rushed back to New York to get to work.

Griswold and Winslow now began looking for someone

to build the *Monitor*. They got on a ferry in lower Manhattan and crossed the East River to the heart of the Greenpoint shipbuilding industry. At a plant named the Continental Iron Works they met bearded, thirty-year-old Thomas Fitch Rowland, the proprietor. Griswold and Winslow asked him how much a pound he would charge to make an iron ship for them. Temporizing, Rowland asked what they thought, and they said 4½ cents a pound would be just right. Rowland was experienced in making big things, having once manufactured a quarter-mile iron pipe 7½ feet in diameter for the Croton aqueduct. He was not about to accept a first offer, and it was not until the next day that the deal was agreed upon at 7½ cents a pound.

On October 4 the government contract with Ericsson and his associates was drawn up and signed. It said: "It is further agreed between the said parties that said vessel and equipment in all respects shall be completed and ready for sea in *one hundred days* from the date of this indenture." In addition, a "small-print" clause stated that if the vessel—"an Iron-Clad-Shot-Proof Steam Battery of iron and wood"—was not a success, the party of the first part would have to refund to the government all moneys received.

On the day the contract was signed, Bushnell drove home to Commodore Smith what a good bargain he was getting. "The whole vessel with her equipment," he said, "will cost no more than to maintain one regiment in the field 12 months . . . should [it] prove what we warrant it, will it not be of infinitely more service than 100 regiments?"

Bargain or not, time was still the crucial factor: the *Merrimack*, being constructed in Norfolk, already had her hull, boilers, and engines completed, though the iron sheathing for her sloping deckhouse was not yet ready.

The party of the first part organized to accomplish the impossible. They had to mobilize capital, planners, manufacturers, and shipbuilders into a close-knit, fast-working team. The nerve center would be Ericsson's room on Franklin Street. Griswold, tycoon of Bessemer-process iron, would handle the finances, making all payments. Rowland would build the hull. The revolving turret, the truly unusual feature of the whole project, would be fabricated, appropriately, at the Novelty Iron Works of New York. Machinery, boiler, and turret-turning apparatus would be made in the DeLamater

Iron Works. The iron plates would be rolled out by the Albany Iron Works in Troy. The gunport shields for the turret were to be made by Charles D. Delaney in Buffalo.

Winslow would be the expediter for materials shipped out of Albany. "One hundred days, and they are short ones, are few enough to do all that is to be done," he declared. He wanted the hull-plate specifications immediately because "the making of slabs is the longest part of the operation." On October 12, only eight days after the contract was signed in Washington, Winslow wrote Ericsson: "I am now able to say that every bar of angle iron is now made and ready to go on board of Monday's steamer and be in New York on Tuesday morning. On Tuesday another lot will follow and so on daily until the entire order for hull plates is completed. We shall drive them energetically . . . until you will cry HOLD! in mercy."

Meanwhile Rowland had readied the Continental Iron Works in Greenpoint. Its many buildings sprawled over a large city block from the East River inland. He built a ship house over the building ways large enough to accommodate *Monitor*'s 172-foot-long, 41-foot-wide armored raft and the supporting hull proper.

Rowland made a model of the ship, showing how the armored raft considerably projected over the 124-foot by 34-foot iron hull that supported it. By fitting patterns on the model he determined the exact size of the armor plates needed. He numbered these in sequence so that when the fabricated ones arrived from Troy they could be accurately put together without time-wasting refitting. By October 19 he had submitted his estimate for the woodwork—oak beams, white pine, and oakum, 7,000 spikes, bolts two feet long, millwork, and carpenters' labor, all totalling $11,287 net.

On October 25 Rowland laid the keel. And at long last he also received a formal contract from Ericsson and his associates. By its terms he promised to do the work "in a thorough and workmanlike manner, and to the entire satisfaction of Captain Ericsson, in the shortest possible space of time" and "to launch said battery safely and at his own risk and cost. . . ." Ericsson in turn promised to furnish all the material, pay for the ship house, and pay for constructing the hull at the rate of 7½ cents for each pound of iron used. The furnaces of the Continental Iron Works were fired up.

Ericsson was a demon. He planned and drew and superintended incessantly. Daily he took the ferry over to the shipyard. He climbed all over the building ways, observing everything with a keen and critical eye. In the early morning and late evening he drafted the hundreds of detailed plans at his office. The blueprints flowed directly from him to the various shops, and as soon as the material arrived, each piece was manufactured immediately. If it wasn't right, he was there to adjust it. He made his designs of the utmost possible simplicity in order to speed up the work. "The magnitude of the work I have to do," he said, "exceeds anything I have ever before undertaken."

Commodore Smith was right on top of him. Before the keel was laid, Smith was already worrying about the ventilation, writing on his lined blue notepaper that "sailors do not fancy living under water without breathing in sunshine occasionally." And what's more, he didn't like the plan for the rudder. Ericsson wrote back consolingly: "I beg you to rest tranquil as to the result; success cannot fail to crown the undertaking." But when, the day after the keel was laid, Smith wanted to know how a man five feet eight inches tall could stand in a five-foot-high pilothouse, Ericsson's reply was not altogether satisfactory: "It is an unpleasant task continually to contradict the opinions you express."

At the DeLamater Iron Works, Cornelius DeLamater went about manufacturing the machinery for the turret-turning device and the main propulsion plant, the boilers, and the propeller. "The motive engine," said Ericsson, "is somewhat peculiar, consisting of only one steam cylinder with pistons at opposite ends, a steam tight partition being introduced in the middle. The propeller shaft has only one crank and one crank pin."

Even if it did get made right, and in time, who was going to be smart enough to operate it on board ship? Ericsson was worried about this. He wanted an engineer named Alban C. Stimers, who he thought was the only one in the country for the job. By an odd chance, Stimers had been chief engineer of the *Merrimack* two years before. Ericsson asked for him, and Commodore Smith wrote that Stimers would be there in a week. By then it was November.

The turret was meanwhile shaping up at the Novelty Iron Works, directly across Manhattan from DeLamater's plant. It was a monstrous thing, twenty feet in diameter, nine feet high, and with sides eight inches thick, made of eight layers of plate. It was shotproof. The job required an industrial plant capable of the heaviest kind of work. The ironworks' title, sounding more like a ladies' notion store, hardly suggested anything more substantial than a safety pin. Yet it was a massive iron foundry. Its main building was 206 feet long and 80 feet wide, housing four cupola furnaces and six drying ovens. The world's largest steam cylinder, for the Fall River Line's *Metropolis*, had been built there. (The cylinder was so big that twenty-two people had once sat down to lunch in it.)

Smith wanted to know from Ericsson "more than the specifications state, your plan of putting the turret together." It was hard enough as it was without the commodore's nagging. They were having a tough time making room in the turret for the crew and especially for the recoil of the eleven-inch guns. "I must insist," said Smith, "on the guns having the full length of recoil." Engineer Stimers, now on the scene, said the guns would have to be shortened at least eighteen inches to work in the turret. No, said Smith. The eleven-inch Dahlgren guns "are the guns I intended for it and none others are to be had." The great gunmaker Admiral John Dahlgren reported from the gun factory in Washington that if eighteen inches were cut off the guns, they would lose 50 percent of their effectiveness. So Novelty Iron Works forged ahead, building the tracks in the turret for the two gun carriages. While all this was going on in New York, Delaney, in Buffalo, made the gunport shields for the turret so that they would swing, pendulumlike, to close the ports when the guns were retracted into the turret for loading, thus protecting the crew.

By now it was November 18, and Smith wrote tartly: "I received the copies of the *Scientific American* and regret to see a description of the vessel in print before she shall have been tested." Obviously, the Confederate government would now be alerted to the urgency for launching the rebuilt *Merrimack*.

By Thanksgiving the government made its first payment—a draft on the Navy Agent in New York for $37,500. In the meanwhile banker Griswold had been making weekly cash payments to all the subcontractors for work performed to date.

During December the work moved on steadily, with much less bickering from Washington and a payment of fifty thousand dollars more. The Secretary of the Navy, in his annual report on December 2, said the Ironclad Board had "displayed great practical wisdom" in this new branch of naval architecture. But Smith was not relaxing one bit. He sent a terse warning to Ericsson on December 5 to "push up the work . . . only thirty-nine days left." A week later he feared that the beams under the battery were too small.

At the Continental Iron Works, Rowland's men bolted on the side and deck armor amid rumors that spies had gotten into the shipyard and were passing along a flow of information to Richmond.

C hristmas came and went. On December 30, in his Manhattan shops, Cornelius DeLamater turned on the steam to test the forty-inch cylinder. The slide valves opened and admitted steam, and the great piston moved full stroke and back again. The *Monitor*'s engineering plant was all right. It was loaded in sections onto barges and lightered around the Battery, up the East River to the Continental Iron Works. DeLamater's men followed and began installing it. There was barely room for the boiler, cylinder, and large steam pipes in the eleven feet six inches between bottom and deck.

January of 1862 was the critical month. The contract time would expire; she would have to be launched. Yet the gun problem had not yet been solved. The Brooklyn Navy Yard, where the *Monitor* would have to be fitted out, was having strike trouble. New Year's Day started out with a fierce gale that tore the *North Carolina*, then training the *Monitor*'s crew, away from her pier in the Navy Yard and bashed her stern in.

It was a cold winter. To the touch, iron had the sticky feeling of quick-freezing. The first week of the new year was hardly out before drifting ice filled up the East River, blocked the Brooklyn waterfront, and backed up into Bushwick Creek bordering on the Continental Iron Works. Three days before launching, outside work in shipyards had to be suspended on account of stormy weather.

On January 14 Commodore Smith wrote Ericsson a nasty note on his blue paper, reminding him that "the time for the completion of the shot-proof battery . . . expired on January 12th. . . ." Smith was right, of course; the federal contract had been signed by the government exactly a hundred days before.

But the government, now deeply concerned, did nothing about cancellation, any more than it would hold Ericsson to a part of the contract requiring masts and sails. Washington wanted the *Monitor* badly, under almost any terms. Besides, the government was partly responsible for the delay, since it had not yet been able to provide the guns.

At Novelty a barge was warped under the company's huge forty-ton crane, a landmark towering over its private pier. Sections of the enormous turret were lowered on board, and the barge was towed to the Continental Iron Works. The turret sections were taken into the ship house, placed on the *Monitor*, and assembled. DeLamater's men connected its double train of cogwheels with the small steam engine that would turn it. This completed *Monitor*'s well-known "tin can on a shingle" silhouette.

Practical details were now worked out. The ship, up until this time really nameless, was usually referred to as Ericsson's Battery. Ericsson now proposed to the Navy the name *Monitor*. Twenty-two-year-old Lieutenant S. Dana Greene, the officer who would ride her down the ways on launching, was assigned as executive officer. Rowland prepared for the launching, asked Ericsson to send riggers to assist, and constructed wooden boxes to buoy up the ship's stern lest she plow too deep in the water upon leaving the launching ways.

Smith forwarded the news that the *Merrimack* had been floated out of dry dock on January 25 and urged Ericsson to hold the *Monitor*'s trials as soon as possible.

With some fanfare the *Monitor* moved out of her ship house at 9:45 A.M. on January 30, gathered momentum, and slipped down the inclined ways into the cold waters of the East River, buoyed up by the wooden boxes. The Stars and Stripes flew from the turret and flagstaff. Steam tugs, puffing black smoke and white steam, stood by to help. Ericsson, in company with Lieutenant Greene and Acting Volunteer Master L. N. Stodder, stood on her decks while a top-hatted crowd watched from the ship house and the shores of the river. It was the hundred-first *working* day from the date the contract was signed and the hundredth day from the laying of the keel.

The *Brooklyn Daily Eagle* of January 31 reported: "The launch of the iron-clad battery Ericsson took place yesterday at Rowland's Shipyard, and was highly successful. The vessel is broad and flat-bottomed, with vertical sides and pointed ends, requiring but a very small low depth of water to float in, though heavily loaded with an impregnable armor upon its sides and a bomb-proof deck, on which is placed a shot-proof revolving turret, that will contain two very heavy guns. It is so low in the water as to afford no target for the enemy, and everything and everybody is below the waterline, with the exception of the persons working the guns, who are protected by the shot-proof turret. The vessel will soon be ready for a trial trip, when some idea can be formed as to her usefulness."

Gustavus Fox sent Ericsson a telegram on the landing day to "hurry her to sea as the *Merrimack* is nearly ready at Norfolk."

Things were moving. The *Monitor* needed only guns, crew, and trials and she would be ready. On the day she was launched, the ordnance officer at the Brooklyn Navy Yard told Ericsson he had been authorized to take two eleven-inch guns out of the gunboat *Dacotah* for the *Monitor*, so "if you will send your derricks to the yard the guns can be hoisted out." Ericsson wrote Smith that the *Monitor* was nearing completion, which pleased the old man greatly. "She is much needed now," he replied.

Now it was February. The East River froze over. By the third, Fox had wired Ericsson again that Lincoln wanted to know when the *Monitor* would be ready. Trial time was at hand. On February 5 the two Dahlgren guns were mounted in the turret, "presenting a formidable appearance." On the ninth the main engine was turned over, and the ventilation, on which so much depended, was tested. On the eleventh Paulding wired Washington that she would be ready in a week, but the blacksmith shop in the yard blew up, and Ericsson was having trouble with the turret-turning gear, the piston valves being "too snug."

At last, on February 19, DeLamater's mechanics lighted the fires in the boilers and warmed up the engines. Ericsson boarded the *Monitor*, and she headed out into the river for her first trial trip, in a blinding snowstorm driven by a northeast wind. DeLamater's men soon began having trouble. The little cut-off valves that controlled the admission of steam to the cylinder had unfortunately been put on backward; the vessel could not get up to speed. The valves were adjusted, and that same evening, as the snow changed to a torrential downpour of rain, Thomas Rowland delivered the *Monitor* to Hiram

Paulding at the Brooklyn Navy Yard for fitting out.

Down south in Hampton Roads, Commodore Louis M. Goldsborough, commander of the North Atlantic Blockading Squadron, had a motley array of vessels—old sailing frigates, steamers, and tugs. They were all in danger. The *Merrimack* could sink them at will and, it was feared, proceed north and burn out New York Harbor. Would the *Monitor* never get there?

Washington was in a frenzy. On February 20, the day the *Monitor* was officially finished by her contractors, Gideon Welles sent sailing orders to her skipper, John Lorimer Worden, a veteran naval officer who had only recently been incarcerated as a Confederate prisoner of war: "Proceed with the U.S. Steamer *Monitor* under your command to Hampton Roads, Va. . . ." But in his haste Welles had forgotten that the *Monitor* wasn't even commissioned. She had no crew on board, no provisions, no ammunition. Her battery had not been tested.

The next day a messenger from the American Telegraph Company sped to Ericsson's office on Franklin Street. He bore an envelope addressed to "J. Ericsson, Constructor of Iron Battery." Opening it, Ericsson read: "It is very important that you should say exactly the day the *Monitor* can be at Hampton Roads. Consult with Comdr. Paulding.

G. V. FOX
Ass't Sec'y Navy"

Three days later Griswold, running the *Monitor*'s finances in Troy, wrote hoping that she would be ready in time to stop the *Merrimack*. A northwest gale, so violent that the cupola of the Brooklyn City Hall "occilated like a pendulum," raged in New York Harbor, damaging many vessels. Fortunately the *Monitor* did not suffer. A new underwater cable from Fortress Monroe to Cape Charles was completed, and news of Confederate doings would get north twelve to twenty hours sooner. Rebel Secretary Mallory finally got around to ordering a commanding officer for the *Merrimack*, old disciplinarian Captain Franklin Buchanan, who had been the first superintendent of the Naval Academy at Annapolis and at the time the war broke out had commanded the Washington Navy Yard. But the *Merrimack* still had not been loaded with ammunition for her guns.

On February 25 the *Monitor* was officially commissioned at the Brooklyn Navy Yard. The crew marched over from the *North Carolina* and skidded down the gangway sloping steeply from the pier above to the iron deck of their strange new ship, which floated barely eighteen inches above the river. They could lean over and put their hands in the water. All they saw on her bare decks were the turret, the tiny pilothouse near the bow, and the two small ventilator cowls at the other end. Captain Worden ordered the flag run up. He read his orders and broke his commission pennant. She was at last a ship of the United States Navy. The watch was set and her log started. The new crew loaded on stores, provisions, and ammunition. Ericsson telegraphed Gustavus Fox that the *Monitor* would indeed leave on the morrow.

And so the *Monitor* departed on the morning of February 26 from the Brooklyn Navy Yard for her trip to Rebel waters. It was snowing heavily. She headed bravely down the East River for the Narrows and the open sea. Bushnell, writing from Willard's Hotel in Washington, had "no doubt of her making a good and safe passage to the entire satisfaction of all parties on her arrival at the point of destination." But her steering became difficult, and by the time she was abreast of Wall Street, only a mile downstream, it was out of the question that she could go any farther. Worden reluctantly gave the order to turn around, and the *Monitor* ignominiously returned to the Navy Yard.

Her return caused dismay. Rowland said he could put the *Monitor* in the sectional dock at the foot of Pike Street "with perfect safety, alter her rudder, and have her out in 24 hours." But Ericsson, greatly annoyed, said it was entirely unnecessary to dock the ship, and in fact he made the adjustment without docking her.

At the same time Flag Officer French Forrest, commandant of the Norfolk Navy Yard, was getting desperate for gunpowder for the *Merrimack*. He needed it at once. It would take three full days to fill the *Merrimack*'s cartridge boxes, and it was already February 28.

On March 3 Winslow was writing Ericsson from Troy, supposing the *Monitor* was "ere this en route to Hampton Roads." But she wasn't until the following day, a blustery, cold March 4. A board of experts went on board the *Monitor*. Captain Worden took her out into the open sea off Sandy

Hook for her final checkup. The two eleven-inch Dahlgrens were loaded with fifteen-pound powder charges and solid shot weighting 168 pounds. The pendulumlike gunport shields were swung aside. The gun carriages ran out on their rails until the gun muzzles protruded outside their gunports. They were fired time and again. The new turning mechanism, which had caused Ericsson so much trouble, swung the twenty-foot turret around smoothly. Even the bothersome steering gear worked. The trial was a success, and the board of experts gave the *Monitor* its approval. She returned triumphantly to the yard at five o'clock that evening. Commodore Smith was pleased enough to send a draft for $18,750. But there still was a great deal of work to do. Sailing date was fixed for March 6. Nevertheless Lieutenant Greene, her executive officer, the man who should have known, did not see how they could possibly make it.

Paulding ordered the steamers *Currituck* and *Sachem* to stand by to escort the *Monitor* to Hampton Roads and a tug to take her in tow. It would be a wild trip in the rampaging winter Atlantic. Even Captain Worden thought she might capsize in case of heavy gales.

At about 11 A.M. on Thursday, March 6, the *Monitor* finally left the Brooklyn Navy Yard. She proceeded without difficulty in a light westerly breeze. Opposite Governor's Island the tug took her in tow. Soon the *Monitor* disappeared from view, was through the Narrows and out to sea, heading south.

Friday, March 7, was an angry day at sea. Dreadful things happened on board the *Monitor*. Water poured down through the turret foundations and into the boiler room, unchecked by the makeshift oakum packing that had been added without Ericsson's knowledge. The blowers quit. Men in the engine room nearly suffocated and had to be dragged out. The engine stopped. The captain ordered the tug to tow her inshore close to the coast, where there would be calmer water. Five hours were lost.

At Norfolk, that Friday was a trying day for the Confederacy too. Although the Stars and Bars were run up on the *Merrimack*, her crew was worried. All her officers knew that the ship was not prepared for the heavy work she had to do. Her engines had not been tested. Her water line was her weak part, her Achilles' heel. A well-directed fire here, and she would be done for. Some crew members predicted total failure; few expected to return to Norfolk. Yard workers swarmed all over the ship in a last-minute effort to finish the work.

That evening the *Monitor* got going again. Chief engineer Alban Stimers, despite the discouragement of all hands, insisted that they keep on. Captain Worden kept the deck all night in the tiny pilothouse. The whole crew was already exhausted, choked with fumes and water-soaked. But the *Monitor* steamed steadily on.

It was Sunday morning, March 8. Commodore Goldsborough's blockade squadron rode at anchor in Hampton Roads, engaged in dull routine. He had waited so long for the *Merrimack*, had heard so many cries of wolf, that now on this pleasant day he was lulled into a false sense of security. It was a lovely morning with hardly a ripple on the surface of the bay. Over at Newport News the old fifty-gun frigate *Congress*, commanded by Joseph B. Smith, the commodore's son, waited. Nearby was the *Cumberland*, while over by Old Point Comfort the remainder of the squadron, headed by Van Brunt's steam frigate *Minnesota*, was disposed. Gustavus Fox left Washington and went down to Fortress Monroe, guarding Hampton Roads, to see how the *Monitor* would make out.

Just before 11 A.M. the *Merrimack*'s quick-tempered skipper—hopelessly suffering, said a doctor, from "nervous prostration"—ordered her to sail. She moved out from the pier with workmen jumping ashore as she left. Rebel crowds cheered. Laboring against a strong flood tide, the *Merrimack* steamed ponderously down the Elizabeth River and into Hampton Roads at her top speed of six knots. Dragging her deep, twenty-two-foot hull through the muddy water, with heavy smoke pouring from her stack, she steered poorly. The gunboats *Raleigh* and *Beaufort* escorted her. Shortly after three bells Captain Buchanan called all hands to quarters and told them that "you shall have no reason to complain of not fighting at close quarters. . . ."

The U.S.S. *Cumberland* sent the tug *Zouave* to Pig Point to reconnoiter—to see what all that smoke was coming down the Elizabeth River. After a bit the officers of the *Zouave* saw "what looked to them like the roof of a barn belching forth smoke from a chimney." It was the *Merrimack*. No real worry, though. She was hugging the opposite shore so closely and moving so slowly that obviously she was on no more than a trial run.

At about 4 P.M. the *Monitor* passed Cape Henry and entered the Chesapeake. Her crew heard what sounded like gunfire. It was in fact the *Merrimack* in the act of destroying the *Congress*, whose captain, young Joe Smith, was killed.

A pilot came on board the *Monitor* and told about the havoc the *Merrimack* had created in the Union squadron. The *Minneapolis* was aground, the *Congress* on fire, and the *Cumberland* sunk in fifty-four feet of water. The *Monitor* rushed ahead to the battle area, but it was too late. The victorious *Merrimack* had already retired for the night. So the *Monitor* anchored alongside the *Minnesota* and waited for the dawn.

By 8 P.M. the *Merrimack* was anchored off Sewall's Point. She had lost her prow but was otherwise in fighting trim. Her exhausted crew had to clear away the debris of battle before the cooks could get supper ready at eleven o'clock. After supper the men stayed up to watch the fire they had started over by Newport News. Shortly after midnight the *Congress* blew up. It was not until then that the crew of the *Merrimack*, satisfied, turned in. But they were soon up again, and her anchor was aweigh at 6:20 A.M.

One hundred minutes or so later the *Monitor* and the *Merrimack* met in the momentous first battle between ironclads. The *Merrimack*, accompanied by several steamers, headed directly toward the *Minnesota*, firing at the Union vessel, which had been run aground the previous day. Aboard the *Monitor* Captain Worden gave the order to commence firing, with young Greene pointing and firing the guns himself as they were quickly loaded and reloaded. Five times the two ironclads came so close to each other that they actually touched. The armor of both vessels was proving to be formidable. After two hours of steady combat the *Monitor* broke away briefly to enable her crew to hoist shot into the turret. When the battle was joined again a half hour later, the pilothouse on the *Monitor* was struck and Worden temporarily blinded by the terrific impact. He turned over command to Greene. Stimers was now in charge of the turret guns, and he kept up the firing until suddenly the *Merrimack*, running out of fuel, riding high at the bow, and leaking, broke off contact and headed toward Sewall's Point. Under strict orders to protect the *Minnesota*, Greene did not pursue but instead returned to the *Minnesota*'s side until she was afloat.

The grueling four-and-a-half hour battle had ended in a stand-off, but for all intents it was a Union victory. As Gideon Welles put it: "There is no reason to believe that any of our wooden vessels guarding the Southern Coast would have withstood her [the *Merrimack*'s] attacks any better than the *Cumberland, Congress,* or *Minnesota.* She might have ascended the Potomac, and thrown bombshells into the Capitol of the Union. In short it is difficult to assign limits to her destructive power. But for the timely arrival of the *Monitor* . . . our whole fleet of wooden ships, and probably the whole sea coast, would have been at the mercy of a terrible assailant."

Though a return engagement was expected, none took place, and when in May the Confederates evacuated Norfolk, they decided the *Merrimack* was too unseaworthy for the open ocean and drew too much water to make it up the James River to Richmond, so her own crew destroyed her. The *Monitor,* with young Greene still aboard, was being towed to blockade duty off Beaufort, North Carolina, where she foundered off Cape Hatteras during a storm at sea on December 31, 1862.

John Ericsson continued to build ironclads for the Union navy for the remainder of the war; but the building of the unique *Monitor* had made him a hero—the hero of the "hundred-day miracle."

—December 1975

THE GREAT LOCOMOTIVE CHASE

by STEPHEN W. SEARS

It was headlined "The Most Extraordinary and Astounding Adventure of the War."

O n the pleasant Sunday evening of April 6, 1862, the men of Company H, 33d Ohio Infantry, were relaxing around their campfires near Shelbyville, Tennessee, admiring the Southern springtime and trading the latest army rumors. They were joined by the company commander, Lieutenant A. L. Waddle, who announced that he wanted a volunteer for a secret and highly important expedition behind Confederate lines. Corporal Daniel Allen Dorsey, twenty-three, a former schoolteacher from Fairfield County, Ohio, said that he was willing to take a crack at it, and he was told to report to company headquarters in the morning. As soon as the lieutenant was out of earshot, the catcalls began. "Good-bye, Dorsey!" "Dorsey, you're a goner!" And a final shot from the next tent: "Leave us a lock of your hair, Dorsey!"

That evening and the next day, twenty-two more volunteers were culled from the 33d Ohio and two sister Buckeye regiments, the 2d and the 21st, at Shelbyville. Most of these men, it seems had witnessed just enough action, at Bull Run the previous July or in recent skirmishing in Kentucky, to whet their appetites for more. For them, the Civil War was still an adventure. Three of the men—Wilson Brown, Martin Hawkins, and William Knight—were sought out specifically because of their civilian occupations as railroaders. They were wanted, it was explained, to operate a captured Confederate train.

The three Ohio regiments were part of the Army of the Ohio's 3d Division, Brigadier General Ormsby MacKnight Mitchel commanding. Ormsby Mitchel, fifty-one and flamboyantly handsome, bubbled with imaginative ideas and bold stratagems for bringing down the rebellion. A West Pointer, he had resigned from the army in the 1830s to pursue a varied career that included teaching astronomy and mathematics, practicing law, and building railroads. After Fort Sumter, Mitchel pleaded with Washington, "In God's name, give me something to do!" but thus far he had done nothing very exciting. Now, from his advanced base at Shelbyville, he could look southward and see great opportunities beckoning. At his side, sharing his vision, was a mysterious civilian named James J. Andrews.

Andrews (if that indeed was his real name) remains even today a shadowy figure. The most avid investigator of his life, Charles O'Neill, deduced that he was foreign-born, probably in Finland, but his life is a blank until 1859, when he appeared in Flemingsburg, Kentucky, and took up house painting and clerking in the local hotel. When the war broke out, Kentucky was a deeply divided state, and as the opposing sides competed for its citizens' loyalty, it was riven by intrigue. During the winter of 1861-62 Andrews was very much a part of this intrigue, smuggling medicines into the Confederacy and returning with intelligence reports for the Union command. It is not clear just how much of value was in these reports, but, in any event, Andrews developed bold enough ideas about sabotaging the Confederate railroad network to make him welcome in Ormsby Mitchel's inner circle.

As even the dullest military strategist could see, railroads were the key to the war's logistics: The South not only had less than half the North's railroad mileage, but its system was, for military purposes, eccentrically laid out. Linking the eastern and western theaters of war was but one direct line, and tying into that line was but one link to Atlanta, the second most important munitions center (after Richmond) in the Confederacy. The tie-in point for these vital railroads was Chattanooga, Tennessee, just seventy miles from General Mitchel's headquarters tent. Together, Mitchel and Andrews concocted a scheme aimed at removing the Chattanooga linchpin from the South's war effort.

Confederate prospects in the western theater were not

bright in that spring of 1862. Kentucky was in Union hands, and Yankee forces, such as Mitchel's division, were deep in Tennessee. Other Yankee troops were advancing down the Mississippi, and an army under U. S. Grant was pushing south along the Tennessee River (it would collide with the Rebels at Shiloh even as the Andrews-Mitchel secret mission was being recruited). An immense Federal naval force was at the south of the Mississippi, threatening New Orleans. Losing Chattanooga would be disaster heaped on top of misfortune.

Andrews had focused his spying efforts on the Western & Atlantic Railroad that snaked 138 miles northward from Atlanta through mountainous northern Georgia to Chattanooga. Financed and owned by the state of Georgia, the W & A was one of the best-run roads in the South. A single-track line, with sidings at all principal stations, it was carried across several major streams on covered wooden bridges and through imposing Chetoogeta Mountain in a long tunnel. At Chattanooga it tied into a line from Lynchburg, Virginia, and with the Memphis & Charleston from Memphis.

On Monday evening, April 7, Andrews briefed his twenty-three volunteers. The oldest of them was thirty-two and the youngest eighteen; their average age was twenty-four. One was a civilian, William Campbell, who had wangled himself a place with his friends at the last minute when a 2d Ohio soldier backed out. All of them wore civilian clothes and were armed with pistols. They were impressed by Andrews's appearance and bearing. Corporal Dorsey described him as about thirty-five, "a large, well-proportioned gentleman with a long black silken beard, black hair, [and] Roman features."

They would form small parties, Andrews told them, and make their way southeastward through enemy lines on foot or by whatever means they could find, meeting in Chattanooga the following Thursday afternoon. From there they would take the Western & Atlantic's evening train south to Marietta, Georgia, just above Atlanta. If questioned at any point, they were to say they were Yankee-hating Kentuckians on their way to enlist in the Confederate army. At Marietta on Friday morning they would board the first northbound train and commandeer it—he would explain the plan for doing that just beforehand.

Their objective, said Andrews, was to burn enough bridges behind them to cripple the Western & Atlantic, then ride their stolen train right on through Chattanooga and westward on the Memphis & Charleston to meet General Mitchel's division, which meanwhile would have pushed southward across the Tennessee border to Huntsville, Alabama. With Chattanooga cut off from all reinforcement, Mitchel could move in quickly and capture it. When the town was securely in Federal hands, he might even push on to Knoxville in eastern Tennessee, where it was understood there were thousands of Union-minded citizens eager for the sight of Yankee soldiers. As Corporal William Pittenger remembered it, Andrews summed up their mission by saying, "Boys, we're going into danger, but for results that can be tremendous."

When the party started toward Chattanooga, it ran into immediate trouble with the weather. Rain pelted down steadily, spilling streams over their banks and turning the roads into quagmires that scotched their hopes of hiring farmers' wagons to speed the journey. "The whole face of the country was a vast sheet of water," Private Alf Wilson complained. Traveling in groups of three or four, the Yankees plodded along the sodden roads, slipping into woodsheds and barns to rest or paying for food and shelter at homesteads. Rebel picket posts accepted their cover story and welcomed them to the cause. "With most of us," explained Dorsey, "the idea of keeping mum and talking as little as possible prevailed. We made it a point to appear as insignificant or uneducated as we could." At one general store a native was overheard to remark that the strangers were a "lot of country jakes, who hardly knew enough to come in when it rained."

Seven of the men, tired of walking, crossed the Tennessee River on a ferry west of Chattanooga and brazenly boarded a Confederate troop train for the journey into town. The rest made their slow way along the northern bank of the river to a ferry opposite their goal. The schedule for the mission, however, was in disarray. Helpless to speed up the journey, Andrews had to postpone everything by a day. He assumed that the weather would be an equal hindrance to General Mitchel's march. As he and his men trickled into Chattanooga on Friday, April 11, however, they found the place in an uproar. That morning, they learned, Federal troops had seized Huntsville. Mitchel was on schedule, Andrews a day behind.

How this development would affect the mission Andrews

could only guess. His immediate concern was what it might do to the Western & Atlantic's regular timetable. As his men drifted into the depot to await the southbound evening train, he discovered the count was two short. (Sam Llewellyn and James Smith had run into trouble near the village of Jasper. To allay further suspicious questioning of their cover story, they had promptly enlisted in a nearby Rebel light artillery unit, hoping to desert at the first opportunity and make their way back to Union territory.)

Andrews and his raiders boarded the evening train without event and, as Alf Wilson later described it, "were soon moving off into Dixie at a good rate of speed." "This," he added, "was a much easier and expeditious way of getting on than the tedious marching of the previous four days." They noted with interest the numerous bridges that carried the Western & Atlantic across meandering Chickamauga Creek. It was midnight when they left the train at Marietta and wangled beds in the town's two hotels. Porters were instructed to wake them before dawn.

Early the next morning, Saturday, April 12, Andrews held a final briefing in his hotel room. The men were instructed to board the northbound morning mail train and be prepared for action during the twenty-minute breakfast stop at Big Shanty, Georgia, eight miles up the line. When the crew and passengers left the train to eat, Andrews explained, he and engineers William Knight and Wilson Brown and fireman Alf Wilson would commandeer the engine. The others were to move swiftly into one of the head cars after it was uncoupled from the cars behind. "If anyone interferes," he ordered, "shoot him, but don't fire unless you have to."

At first light, right on schedule, the morning mail train from Atlanta arrived at the Marietta station. Its locomotive was the powerful woodburner *General*, built for the Atlantic & Western in 1855 by the Rogers, Ketchum and Grosvenor Works in Paterson, New Jersey. Behind the tender were three empty boxcars, slated to bring commissary stores out of Chattanooga on the return trip, then a string of passenger cars. The Yankees took seats in one of these coaches, according to Dorsey, "in a sleepy, drowsy manner . . . indifferent to all surroundings." Again the count was two short. (Martin Hawkins and John Porter had reached the depot only in time to see the train puffing off down the track. They had been at another hotel, and the porter had failed to wake them in time. "I can't describe my feelings at that moment . . . ," Porter would recall. "There we were in the heart of the Confederacy, knowing that if we were suspected of anything wrong we could expect death.")

When the train pulled into Big Shanty at 6:45 A.M., the passengers hurried to Lacy's Hotel to find places at the breakfast table. With them went conductor William Allen Fuller, engineer Jeff Cain, and the foreman of the W & A's machine shops, Anthony Murphy, who was along on an inspection trip. The moment they were out of sight, Andrews, engineers Knight and Brown, and fireman Wilson quietly stepped down on the off-side of the train, pulled the coupling pin behind the three boxcars, and checked that the switches were in their favor. As the Yankee crewmen ambled up to the *General* and climbed aboard, Andrews casually waved the rest of the raiders into the third boxcar. Fifty feet away, sentries at a large Confederate training camp watched the strange performance in puzzlement. At Andrews's signal, Knight abruptly threw open the throttle, the big driving wheels spun for a moment, and then the *General* bounded away.

In Lacy's dining room, foreman Murphy glanced up from his breakfast to see the abbreviated train speeding off. "Someone is moving your engine!" he shouted to conductor Fuller. The crew tumbled out onto the platform, raising the alarm, and the Rebel sentries loosed a few futile shots at the stolen train disappearing around a curve. Murphy's best guess was that the thieves were deserters from the nearby training camp, taking this unorthodox method of putting distance between themselves and Confederate authorities.

"Fuller, Cain, and myself concluded in a few minutes that our duty was to proceed after them," Murphy later testified. The Great Locomotive Chase was joined.

The pursuers' immediate problem was finding something to pursue it with. Big Shanty lacked a telegraph station, so there was no way to send a warning up the line, but that did not deter conductor Fuller. Tough and ambitious, twenty-five-year-old William Fuller had risen rapidly through the W & A ranks, and he took the theft of his train as a personal insult. Trailed by Cain and Murphy, he started off along the track at a fast run. Assuming the thieves had limited railroading experience, he expected to find his stolen train abandoned a few miles up the line.

The *General*, however, was rolling steadily northward at its regular pace. Andrews knew that on the single-track line he would have to hold to the timetable in order to pass the morning's three scheduled southbound trains at station sidings. Acquiring a crowbar from a track-repair crew they encountered, the raiders paused to take up rails to hinder any pursuit, paused again to cut the wire beyond the first telegraph station they reached, and headed on toward Kingston, thirty miles north of Big Shanty. At Kingston, according to the timetable, they would encounter the first of the southbound trains from Chattanooga.

Fuller, meanwhile, was setting some kind of track record. "I ran two and a half miles, and when I say run, I don't mean trot, gallop or pace. I mean run," he later recalled. When he reached the repair crew and heard its story, he began to doubt the deserter theory. The thieves, whoever they were, seemed to have no trouble operating the stolen train. Fuller took the repair crew's pole car—a small handcar pushed along by poles, much as a keelboat was propelled upstream by poling—and went back to collect the panting Murphy and Cain. Setting off northward once more, the three Georgians discovered the break in the telegraph line. That confirmed it: they were not simply chasing a few Southern farm boys trying to evade soldiering but a bank of Yankees bent on something considerably more serious.

Redoubling their efforts, the pursuers twice rounded curves only to be hurled off the track where the raiders had lifted rails. They dragged the pole car across the gaps and labored on. Fuller, who was now fighting mad, set out for Etowah station, where a branch track from the Cooper Iron Works angled into the main line. Cooper's, he knew, kept a small switching engine named the *Yonah*. "On we pressed and pushed," Fuller recounted. "When our strength was nearly gone, we hove in sight of Etowah, and to our great delight the engine was there." The little *Yonah* was nothing much as locomotives went, but it was a vast improvement over the pole car. Within minutes Fuller, Cain, and Murphy had steam up and were pounding along at full throttle for Kingston, fourteen miles away. It was now raining steadily.

Some forty-five minutes before the Georgians piled aboard the *Yonah*, the Yankee raiders had reached Kingston and backed onto the station siding to await the southbound freight due momentarily. The unexpected arrival of the abbreviated, three-car train, manned by strangers, raised a small commotion, but the resourceful Andrews was ready with an improvised story. He was a Confederate officer on a mission of the highest military priority, he confided to the station agent. General P. G. T. Beauregard, commander of the field army at Corinth, Mississippi, was desperately short of ammunition after the fighting at Shiloh, and this was a special train impressed to carry powder to the embattled Rebels. The moment the southbound freight passed, he would be on his way.

When the freight arrived, however, it bore on its last car a red flag, indicating that an unscheduled train was following. Andrews demanded an explanation. The conductor said that the high command in Chattanooga was evacuating stores and rolling stock because of the threatening Yankee force at Huntsville—Mitchel's division. Expressing a cold fury he no doubt deeply felt, Andrews order the freight to move on down the main track so that the extra train, when it arrived, would not block his powder train. "I must be off the first possible minute," he snapped.

After an agonizing delay, the extra arrived at Kingston— and it, too, had a red flag on the rearmost car. There was too much rolling stock in Chattanooga for one locomotive to handle, the conductor reported, and a second section had to be made up. By now the sixteen raiders closed up in the "powder train" were decidedly nervous. "A thousand conjectures will spring up at such times . . . ," Corporal Pittenger later wrote. "To be shut up in the dark, while for all we knew the enemy might be concentrating an overwhelming force against us, was exceedingly trying . . . ." Engineer Knight strolled over to the boxcar containing the men, leaned his back against the door, and said in a low voice, "Boys, we've got to wait a while more for one more train that's behind time, and the local folks around are getting edgy. If you're called, be ready to jump out and fight."

At last came the welcome whistle of the extra's second section. Like its two predecessors, it was ordered by Andrews to pull on through the station to unblock his northbound train. A very long sixty-five minutes after reaching Kingston, Andrews himself threw the siding switch, and the stolen train rolled out onto the main line again. Just four minutes later,

William Fuller arrived on the scene aboard the *Yonah.*

The gallant little switch engine had made the fourteen-mile run from Etowah in fifteen minutes, only to face the same jam-up that had frustrated the Andrews raiders. Fuller immediately realized that trying to clear the line of the three southbound freights was hopeless. Again he took to shanks' mare to reach the head of the tangle, two miles away. A branch line from Rome, Georgia, tied into the main line just north of the station, and fortuitously the daily Rome train was waiting on it. With the telegraph still dead—the Yankees had stopped to cut the wire soon after they cleared Kingston—Fuller commandeered the Rome train and once more set out in pursuit.

The raiders were meanwhile pushing hard for Adairsville, ten miles north of Kingston, where two more scheduled southbound trains were to be passed. So far as they knew, there was no alarm out for them. Their cover story was so convincing that at one stop to take on wood and water the Georgian on duty later confessed, "I'd as soon have suspected Mr. Jefferson Davis himself as a man who talked with the assurance Andrews did." As a precaution, however, Andrews ordered a halt four miles short of Adairsville to take up a rail and load up with crossties to serve as tinder for their bridge burning. At this time the Yankees suddenly spotted the smoke of a pursuing train. With a violent effort they tore the rail loose and resumed their run for Adairsville.

Balked by the torn-up track, Fuller had to abandon the Rome engine and for the third time that morning dash northward on foot. His fury was now tinged with desperation. According to the timetable, he knew, once beyond Adairsville the Yankees would have a clear track all the way to Chattanooga.

As Fuller hurried along in the pelting rain, with only foreman Murphy able to keep pace with him, the raiders pulled into the Adairsville station—and found only a local freight waiting on the siding. Due to the confusion in Chattanooga, the conductor told Andrews, the trailing southbound passenger train was running half an hour late. "I'll have to go out at once," Andrews insisted. "If the Yankees attack Beauregard, he hasn't powder enough for a three-hour fight." The conductor cautioned him to run slowly and send a flagman ahead at every curve. "I'll attend to that," Andrews assured him. The moment the *General* was out of sight around the first curve, however, he ordered Knight to open the throttle wide. They had to reach the next station, Calhoun, before the Chattanooga train did or they would be hopelessly blocked. The *General*, fireman Alf Wilson related, "rocked and reeled like a drunken man, while we tumbled from side to side like grains of popcorn in a hot frying pan."

They won the race to Calhoun by the slimmest of margins. The southbound passenger train was just pulling out of the station when its engineer heard their screaming whistle and hurriedly reversed far enough to clear the siding switch. Once more Andrews told his story of rushing to General Beauregard's aid, and once more it got him out on the main line.

Ahead of Andrews was a clear track, but behind him his tenacious pursuers were closing the gap. Just below Adairsville the strong-legged Fuller and Murphy had encountered the southbound local freight, pulled by the *Texas*, a locomotive of the same class at the *General*. They piled aboard, shunted all the freight cars off on the Adairsville siding, and raced off northward, pushing the *Texas* flat out in reverse. For the first time that day, after running almost seven miles, poling a handcar, and riding a switch engine and the small branch-line Rome engine, the two Georgians were in command of a locomotive fully capable of testing the *General* and its captors. At Calhoun, they too bypassed the southbound passenger train, stopping only long enough to spread the alarm among the local militia.

Near Resaca, five miles north of Calhoun, was a long trestle over the Oostanaula River, one of the raiders' prime targets. "Some of the first exhilaration we'd felt after capturing the train at Big Shanty was again ours," Corporal Pittenger recalled, "as we whistled swiftly on for a mile or more, and then stopped to cut the wire, and to take up a rail—as we hoped—for the last time." They bent to their work, prizing up the spikes with their crowbar and trying to wrench the rail loose with a fence rail. "At that instant, loud and clear from the south, came the whistle of the engine in pursuit," Pittenger wrote. "By the sound, it was near and closing in fast. A thousand thunderclaps couldn't have startled us more."

If the tale of the Great Locomotive Chase has a turning point, it was reached here along this deserted stretch of the Western & Atlantic just north of Calhoun, approximately halfway between Big Shanty and Chattanooga. Thus far James Andrews had been nothing short of brilliant. He had brought his nineteen men through every anticipated danger and improvised his way through dangers entirely unexpected. He had no reason to doubt that the track ahead was clear. Of the quality and tenacity of the pursuit he knew nothing. (The Yankees believed it was simply the last train they had passed; "If we'd been told the full story, we would have thought it too wild and improbable to believe," Pittenger remarked.) The rail they were trying to lift was well loosened, needing but a few more minutes' effort, and they would be free of pursuit and able to go about their bridge burning in comparative safety. Yet Andrews chose not to stand and fight long enough to finish the job. Perhaps it was simply the man's make-up. That, at any rate, was Pittenger's view. In temperament, he wrote, Andrews "delighted in strategy" rather than "the plain course of a straight out-and-out fight with the pursuing train." The *General* started off again, leaving the rail loose but still in place. Carefully guiding the *Texas* over the danger spot, Fuller and Murphy resumed the chase.

Andrews's delight in strategy was soon evident. Taking advantage of his brief lead, he ordered the last boxcar uncoupled, reversed the *General*, and sent the car hurtling back down the track. But as with every other surprise he had encountered that eventful day, Fuller was undaunted. He too reversed course, neatly picked up the runaway boxcar in full flight, and then headed north again, pushing it ahead of him. The raiders dropped a second car in the middle of the covered bridge over the Oostanaula, with the same result. Fuller simply shunted the two cars off at Resaca and continued northward.

Above Resaca the Western & Atlantic wound tortuously through rough country, forcing the Confederates aboard the pursuing *Texas* to proceed carefully, alert for obstructions and ambushes. Obstructions there were. Behind nearly every curve the Yankees had tossed crossties onto the track from the supply in their remaining boxcar. Fuller perched on the tender, signaling back to Murphy and the *Texas*'s engineer, Peter Bracken, when the track ahead was blocked. They then heaved over the forward lever, and the *Texas*, driving wheels spinning, would slide to a stop—sometimes with nothing to spare. "Looking back at it now," Murphy later recalled, "our whole course seems reckless in the extreme. But we were young then, and youth takes chances that are appalling to old age." At one point near Tilton on a straight stretch of track the Yankees managed to lengthen their lead enough to stop for badly needed wood and water.

With their engine replenished, they made one more attempt to permanently block pursuit. By now the technique was down pat. One team cut the telegraph line, another piled up obstructions on the track, engineers Knight and Brown checked and oiled the locomotive, and the rest of the party labored to lift a rail. But Andrews, despite the pleading of several of his men, refused to permit an ambush assault on the Rebel train, and time ran out. The moment the *Texas* came into view, Andrews cried "All aboard!" and the raiders bolted off, leaving the track intact.

The two locomotives thundered on—at times reaching speeds of a mile a minute—through Dalton, through the long tunnel under Chetoogeta Mountain, across the first of the long bridges over Chickamauga Creek, past Ringgold station. Andrews had ordered the men to set fire to the remaining boxcar in the hope of dropping it off inside one of the covered bridges—to at least partially accomplish the mission—but the day-long rain had soaked everything combustible. "Our fire burned aggravatingly slow," Corporal Dorsey complained.

A mile or so short of Graysville, near the Georgia-Tennessee border, the *General* began to flounder. Boiler water was low and the firewood was gone. "The game was almost up . . ." said Dorsey. "The grand old iron steed was dying in his tracks." The *General* had carried them nearly one hundred miles from Big Shanty, but it could carry them no farther. "Andrews now told us all that it was 'every man for himself,' that we must scatter and do the best we could to escape to the Federal lines," Alf Wilson testified.

Before dashing into the woods, engineer Knight threw the *General* into reverse, but steam pressure was too low and the pursuing *Texas* easily picked up the slow-moving engine. Fuller sent a messenger back to the militia garrison at Ringgold to order a roundup of the fugitives. "My duty ended here," he reported matter-of-factly. After six hours of high adventure, he had his stolen train back.

The Andrews party would later blame their failure on the one-day delay in executing the mission. They maintained that had the raid taken place on schedule, before Chattanooga was alarmed by General Mitchel's capture of Huntsville, the Western & Atlantic would have been clear of the extra trains that held them up so long at Kingston. Nor would any bridge-burning efforts have been hampered by Saturday's day-long rain. The theory is not improbable, considering how narrow was their margin of defeat despite all the unforeseen complications. By the same token, however, there is little reason to believe that conductor Fuller's pursuit would have been any less vigorous twenty-four hours earlier. Be that as it may, the Yankees' gallant failure was not redeemed by any action on General Mitchel's part.

After taking Huntsville on Friday, Mitchel put a brigade aboard a captured train and, on Saturday, while the Great Locomotive Chase was convulsing northern Georgia, steamed eastward to Stevenson, Alabama, thirty miles from Chattanooga. There he halted, apparently to await the arrival of his raiding party. But the fact that while waiting he burned a rail bridge in front of him suggests that he had already abandoned any hope of seizing Chattanooga by a bold *coup de main*. Perhaps like the rest of the Federal high command in that spring of 1862, he was suddenly overwhelmed by caution. Or perhaps, like Andrews, he "delighted in strategy" rather than a slugging match. In any event, Chattanooga remained safely in Confederate hands.

For the raiders, what an Atlanta newspaper headlined as "The Most Extraordinary and Astounding Adventure of the War" was far from ended when they abandoned the *General* and took to the woods. They soon discovered they were abroad in an alien land.

The news of the Yankee raiders spread rapidly across northern Georgia. In a matter of hours Confederate cavalry patrols were guarding every crossroad and examining every farmer's lane. The farmers themselves formed posses and with shotguns and butcher knives and tracking dogs tramped across the fields and woodlands, corralling any stranger they encountered.

Without maps or compasses, most of Andrews's men wandered aimlessly, and one after another they were stopped and questioned—and seized. The story that had worked for them in Tennessee—that they were Kentuckians seeking to join the Rebel army—did not work this far south. Posing as a Confederate officer, Andrews got within a dozen miles of

Bridgeport, Alabama, with two of his men before they tried their bluff once too often and were captured.

Privates Alf Wilson and Mark Wood developed the best cover story of all, claiming that *they* were pursuing the Yankees. They made it to the Tennessee River east of Chattanooga, stole a canoe, and floated all the way down the river past Chattanooga to Stevenson, Alabama, where they expected to find Federal troops. The Federals had left, however; even so, the two had almost talked their way past a Rebel patrol when a civilian rushed up and pointed them out as Yankees. He had been a passenger on the train they commandeered.

Martin Hawkins and John Porter, who had been left behind in Marietta, were taken trying to enlist in the 9th Georgia. Only James Smith and Sam Llewellyn, who early in the mission had joined a Confederate unit to escape detection, successfully deserted and made their way back to Union lines.

Since the twenty-two Yankees had been captured in civilian clothes well inside Southern territory, there was strong pressure on the Confederate authorities to hang them as spies. The raiders' one hope, they realized, was to maintain that they acted under orders and were subject to the rules of war for military prisoners. They were quick to point out the threat of retaliation by the Federal command. "When taunted about the fate that awaited us," Corporal Dorsey wrote, "we had a stereotyped reply: "Hang and be d--d. Our fellows will hang twenty of you for every one you hang of this party.""

Andrews had little faith in this line of defense for himself. He was known to the Confederate high command for his earlier smuggling of medicines into the South, and it was now obvious that he was a double agent. He had no illusions about his fate. According to Pittenger, he remarked to his fellow prisoners, "Boys, I have often thought I'd like to see what's on the other side of Jordan." Late in April, Andrews was tried as a spy by a military court in Chattanooga, and on May 31—after a review by Secretary of War Leroy P. Walker and President Jefferson Davis—the verdict was announced. James Andrews was found guilty as charged and sentenced to death by hanging.

The next night Andrews and Private John Wollam used a jackknife one of the raiders had managed to conceal to pry loose the bricks in the wall of their Chattanooga jail and escape. Two days later, however, Andrews was retaken (Wollam evaded capture for a month) and on June 7 the leader of the raiders was taken to a gallows a block from Peachtree Street in Atlanta and hanged. "He died bravely," conductor Fuller reported.

In the meantime, a dozen of the Yankees were transferred to Knoxville and seven of them, chosen at random, were tried by a military court—not for the attempt on the Western & Atlantic, which could be considered a legitimate military target, but for spying on Confederate military camps. All seven were found guilty, brought to Atlanta, and sentenced to death. They were Privates Samuel Robertson, Perry G. Shadrach, Samuel Slavens, and George D. Wilson, Sergeant-Major Marion A. Ross, Sergeant John Scott, and William Campbell, the civilian who had joined the expedition at the last minute.

Standing on the gallows on June 18, Wilson spoke the last words for all of them: "The seven of us have been condemned here as spies. We aren't that, as even those who convicted us knew. . . . A lot of you are going to live to be sorry for what you're now doing. More than that, you're going to see the Stars and Stripes waving again over the ground this scaffold stands on."

After the mass execution, the Confederate authorities had second thoughts about this solution to the problem of the "Yankee bridge burners," as the Southern press described them. For four months the fourteen survivors sweated out their captivity. In mid-October they heard a rumor from their jailer that they too would be tried, and on October 16 they staged a mass breakout from their Atlanta prison.

After adventures that rivaled the locomotive chase itself, eight of the raiders made good their escape. Heading off in all directions to confuse pursuit, they eventually reached Federal forces in such widely scattered places as central Tennessee; Corinth, Mississippi; Lebanon, Kentucky; and Apalachicola, Florida. The experience of William Knight, the engineer who had piloted the stolen *General*, was typical: "We had spent forty-seven days and nights, passing over some of the roughest country that ever laid out of doors."

In March 1863 the six raiders still in Confederate hands were exchanged. All the survivors were awarded the Congressional Medal of Honor, the first recipients of that decoration. Corporal William Pittenger was invalided out of the army later in 1863, but the rest of the raiders remained in uniform until the war's end. On the other side, William Fuller and Anthony Murphy continued to serve the Confederacy until there were no trains left to run. General Ormsby Mitchel's military career went nowhere after his aborted attempt on Chattanooga, and in October 1862, at a new post on the North Carolina coast, he died of yellow fever.

Whether the Andrews raiders, had they succeeded, could have shortened the Civil War will never be known. But beyond question the Great Locomotive Chase fully merited that Atlanta newspaperman's description: it was indeed an extraordinary, astounding adventure.

—December 1977

BELLE BOYD

by RICHARD F. SNOW

The adventures of the heroine spy.

S he began her career as a spy and ended it as an actress, and there are no two professions more thickly larded with myth and lies. At least one historian, despairing of seeing anything real behind the mists, concluded that she had never lived at all. But Belle Boyd did exist and was, in the words of Douglas Southall Freeman, "one of the most active and most reliable of the many secret woman agents of the Confederacy."

She was born in 1844 to a prosperous Virginia store owner and raised like any other young woman of her background: a course of studies in French, music, and the classics at Mount Washington Female College, followed by her introduction into Washington society. When the war broke out, she returned home ablaze with secessionist sentiments and set about raising money for the cause. Her military career began on Independence Day, 1861, when, as she told it, drunken Federal soldiers who had occupied Martinsburg the day before began looting houses, bent on stealing cherished keepsakes and insulting the occupants. At the Boyds' they produced "a large Federal flag, which they were now preparing to hoist over our roof in token of our submission to their authority." Belle's mother, who heretofore had watched the hooligans' depredations with saintly resignation, now stepped forward and said, "Every member of my household will die before that flag shall be raised over us." One of the soldiers replied in "offensive" language, and Belle shot him dead.

The Federal command did nothing about it; in fact,

seemed to admire her pluck. Certainly her looks had something to do with this. The pictures show us a long, rather dour face with too much nose, but her contemporaries universally found her attractive. "Perhaps Miss Boyd wasn't beautiful," one wrote, "or as beautiful, physically, as some other women, yet there was something beautiful about her . . . something a man never forgot." Another praised her "no-care-madcap-devil-of-a-temperament that pleases." It would save her again and again.

After killing the soldier, Belle began smuggling information to the Confederate forces nearby. Enthusiastic and inexperienced, she put down the messages in her own handwriting, was soon caught, and let off with a reprimand.

This daunted her not at all, and she took to roaming the Shenandoah Valley, gathering intelligence for Jackson. Again arrested, she was taken to Baltimore, and once more released. She returned to Virginia and settled for a while with her aunt just south of Winchester in Front Royal, the scene of her most famous exploit.

On May 23, 1862, Stonewall Jackson, punching north through the valley on the offensive that would bring him all the way to the Potomac, prepared to move against Front Royal. The Union forces, falling back from the town, planned to burn the bridges behind them. Belle found out about it.

She describes what she did then in her postwar autobiography, a book much maligned for its inaccuracy. The historian Curtis Carroll Davis, however, who probably knows more about Belle's career than anyone alive, annotated the volume with great care, and found it to contain far less fantasy than many such memoirs. In any event, Belle "did not stop to reflect . . . [but] started at a run down the street, which was thronged with Federal officers and men. I soon cleared the town and gained the open fields . . . hoping to escape observation until such time as I could make my way to the Confederate line. . . . I had on a dark-blue dress, with a little fancy white apron over it, and this contrast of colors, being visible at a great distance, made me far more conspicuous than was just then agreeable." Union pickets opened fire, and "the rifle-balls flew thick and fast about me, and more than one struck the ground so near my feet as to throw the dust in my eyes." With artillery bursting around her, she finally gained the Rebel lines, and delivered her message. Jackson at once attacked the bridges, took them intact, and then wrote Belle a note which she kept all her life, but which has not survived: "I thank you, for myself and for the army, for the immense service that you have rendered your country to-day."

Belle was captured when Federal troops reoccupied the town. She was famous now, and Secretary of War Stanton himself drafted the order that had her jailed in Washington. There, a New York *Tribune* reporter saw her wearing "a gold palmetto tree beneath her beautiful chin, a Rebel soldier's belt around her waist, and a velvet band across her forehead, with the seven stars of the Confederacy shedding their pale light therefrom." The *Herald*'s man was less dazzled; he dismissed her as "an accomplished prostitute."

Released in an exchange of prisoners, she was again arrested, again let go, and in 1864, took ship from Wilmington with Confederate dispatches bound for England. Her blockade runner was taken and boarded by a Union warship. Belle destroyed her documents. Her last mission was over. She was a few weeks shy of twenty years old.

Her charm apparently survived the rigors of campaigning; Samuel Hardings, the Union officer who took command of her captured ship, promptly asked her to marry him. "His every movement," she said, "was so much that of a refined gentleman that my 'Southern proclivities,' strong as they were, yielded ... to the impulses of my heart." He died shortly after the war, however, leaving her penniless in England with an infant daughter. She published her autobiography, made far less money from it than she had hoped, and, in 1866, turned to the stage, opening in Manchester in a romantic comedy by Bulwer Lytton. She was an immense success, and continued to be when she returned to America.

She married again—this time to an English military man—but it was not a happy match. "My health was failing," she said years later in a brief, pathetic statement, "and I went with my husband to California. Just previous to the birth of my little son my mind gave way and my child was born in the asylum for the insane at Stockton, Cal. My boy was buried there."

Her eventual recovery, and the birth of two more daughters, did not reconcile her to her husband. She divorced him in 1884 and, less than six weeks later, married Nat High, an actor seventeen years her junior. She returned to the stage, giving dramatic recitations, but found herself forced to play second-class houses. The war had been over for twenty years, and people were beginning to forget.

On Sunday, June 10, 1900, she wrote her daughters from Evansville, Wisconsin, where she planned to give a recitation for the local Grand Army of the Republic: "I feel like a criminal not sending you money. But I have only been able to play one night, and sent you all I had . . . over expenses, 2.00"

The next morning a heart attack killed her. The women's auxiliary of the G.A.R. raised the money for her funeral, and four Union veterans lowered her coffin into Northern soil.

—February 1980

CRISIS AT THE ANTIETAM

by BRUCE CATTON

Upon the clash of arms near a little Maryland creek hung the slave's freedom and the survival of the Union.

Awhitewashed Dunker church without a steeple, a forty-acre field of corn that swayed, head-high and green, in the September sun, an eroded country lane that rambled along a hillside behind a weathered snake-rail fence, and an arched stone bridge that crossed a lazy, copper-brown little creek—these unimpressive features of a quiet Maryland landscape made the setting in which one of the greatest moments of crisis in American history came to a solution on the bloody day of September 17, 1862.

The crisis involved nothing less than the continued existence as one nation of the United States, an existence which was in a fair way to come to an end in the middle of that wartime September and which got past its hour of greatest danger because of the tremendous shock of battle. In all the American Civil War, no single day was bloodier or more costly than that one day of battle on the hills and fields overlooking Antietam Creek in western Maryland; nor did any single combat in that war go so far toward putting this American crisis on the road toward solution.

Things had not been going well for the Union cause in the summer of 1862. The great drive to capture Richmond, in which the picturesque young General George B. McClellan led the Army of the Potomac down to the very suburbs of the Confederate capital, had failed in the smoke and clamor of the famous Seven Days' Battles—seven days in which Robert E.

Lee, outnumbered and seemingly doomed to defeat, had led McClellan into confusion, had roundly whipped his army, and had driven general and troops to an uneasy refuge at Harrison's Landing, a steaming mud flat far down the James River, many miles from the goal which had been so nearly within reach.

President Abraham Lincoln's government had scrambled frantically to retrieve the situation, without luck. A new Federal army, styled the Army of Virginia, had been organized and put under command of General John Pope and sent down overland to get the Confederates under control; but Lee and his famous lieutenant, Stonewall Jackson, had run rings around General Pope—and on the famous field of Bull Run, less than thirty miles from Washington—had shattered his army in a defeat so ignominious that Pope himself was shelved and sent to Minnesota to fight Indians for the rest of the war, while the remnants of his army crept back to Washington to be united with McClellan's Army of the Potomac, brought back from the James River to help defend the national capital.

So as September began, the cause of the Union looked very dark. In the West things were no better, with Confederates led by Braxton Bragg marching north into Kentucky. On the home front there was much gloom; the high hopes of spring (when people believed the war would be won in another month or so) had been replaced by bewilderment and discouragement, and the most influential members of Lincoln's Cabinet suspected that General McClellan might actually be a pro-Southern sympathizer who did not especially want to win the war at all. The vital spark in the Northern war effort seemed to have died and there did not appear to be any good way to bring it back to life.

Worst of all, General Lee's triumphant Army of Northern Virginia—ragged, weary, worn to a shadow by the heavy fighting it had been through, but powerfully imbued with the notion that there was no Yankee army anywhere that could not be licked—had crossed the Potomac River and was marching up on an invasion of the Northern heartland, aiming apparently at nothing less than the conquest of Pennsylvania and the capture of Washington.

Along with this—as if it were not enough to make a man-sized crisis—there was the open threat of decisive European intervention on the side of the Confederacy. The British government was openly sympathetic with the South, and the papier-mache emperor of France, Napoleon III, was clearly ready to grant recognition and material aid if the British would just take the lead. This the government in London seemed prepared to do. The prime minister and foreign secretary were preparing to suggest to the cabinet that England take the lead in inducing a concert of powers to step in and bring this American war to an end—which, under the circumstances, could mean nothing less than independence for the Confederacy. They were waiting only to see what came of Lee's invasion of the North. If it went as it seemed likely to go, Britain would act.

Lincoln had been trying desperately to remedy matters, but at the moment there was little he could do. To revive the Northern war effort, it seemed to him that he must somehow bring into full play the vigor and determination of the abolitionists. Thus far, official policy was that the war was being fought for the sole purpose of restoring the Union and that the issue of slavery had nothing to do with it. To Lincoln it was clear that he must now broaden the base; if this could now be made a war against slavery, as well as a war for reunion, it would become a thing in which no British government would dare to intervene.

To bring this about, Lincoln had on his desk a draft of what would eventually be the Emancipation Proclamation. But he could not issue it yet. Secretary of State Seward had warned him: We have been beaten and our armies are in retreat—get this out now and it will look like a cry of despair, an appeal to the black race for help, rather than a statement of our purpose to help the black race. . . . The proclamation could not be issued until the North had won a victory.

So Lincoln did what he could. To the poorly reorganized Army of the Potomac, which was moving up into Maryland to try to catch and defeat Lee, he restored General McClellan, despite the grumbling of important Cabinet members and party leaders. This done, he could only wait for the test of battle. If Lee could be beaten, European intervention could be averted and final victory could perhaps be counted on; if he could not be beaten, then there would presently be two independent nations rather than one between Canada and the Rio Grande. Seldom in American history has so much been at stake on one battle.

During the first two weeks of September the rival armies sparred for an opening. Lee moved west of South Mountain, a long spur of the Blue Ridge that runs fifty miles northeast from the Potomac, cutting through western Maryland up into Pennsylvania. Screened by his cavalry, which held the South Mountain passes with infantry support, Lee evolved a daring plan. There was a Federal post at Harpers Ferry held by 12,000 troops, and it seemed to Lee that his invasion would go more smoothly if this post could first be gobbled up. While McClellan, who was still east of South Mountain, was trying to find out precisely where the Confederate Army might be, Lee divided his forces and sent half of his army, under Stonewall Jackson, doubling back to capture Harpers Ferry.

It worked just as Lee had anticipated. Jackson surrounded the post before the Federals knew what was going on, got artillery into position to bombard it, and forced its surrender. There was, however, one incident.

A copy of Lee's orders setting forth the whole plan was somehow lost, to be picked up by two Federal soldiers as they bivouacked on a field near the town of Frederick, Maryland. It was sent to McClellan, who immediately realized that Lee had divided his army and that the Army of the Potomac was actually nearer to its separate pieces than those separate pieces were to each other.

McClellan was a capable general, but he usually moved very slowly, and Lee had banked heavily on this fact, gambling that he could capture Harpers Ferry and reunite his army before McClellan could interfere. Ordinarily, this gamble would probably have worked. But finding the lost order spurred the usually sluggish McClellan into action. He put his army on the road, broke through the South Mountain passes, and set out to destroy the scattered portions of the Army of Northern Virginia.

He did not move quite fast enough to save the Harpers Ferry garrison, and Jackson scooped up his 12,000 prisoners, along with a good deal of matériel which the Confederates needed very badly. But McClellan's sudden move did put a serious hitch in Lee's invasion plans. Before he could do anything about entering Pennsylvania, Lee had at all costs to reassemble his army and fight off this thrust of McClellan's. Hard-riding couriers went galloping down the roads of western Maryland with orders, and the weary Confederates—from Hagerstown, from Boonsboro, from Crampton's Gap, and from Harper's Ferry itself—were ordered to move at once to Sharpsburg, a little town just north of the Potomac. If McClellan wanted to fight, they would fight there. If they won, then they could go on with the invasion. If they lost—well, Lee had enormous confidence in them; he did not think they were going to lose.

These Confederates were very weary men, a point that needs to be emphasized because it had much to do with the circumstances under which the battle would be fought. Since the middle of June they had marched many dusty miles and had fought many furious battles, and they were on the edge of exhaustion. When Lee led them across the Potomac, thousands upon thousands of them had simply given out, unable to move any farther; from straggling alone, Lee suffered a temporary loss during the first two weeks in September of between 10,000 and 20,000 men. The army that would reunite at Sharpsburg would be very far under strength. If all of its units reached the scene—a matter about which there was some doubt—Lee would have no more than 45,000 men of all arms; and McClellan was on the scene with more than 95,000. Not until the final desperate campaign of Appomattox would Lee enter a major battle with his strength so badly depleted.

But if the Confederate army was thin it was full of high spirits. It had not yet lost a battle, and its members—from the humblest private up to the commanding general—believed they would win this one. What were Yankees for, if not to be beaten? The Confederate soldier might be ragged and shoeless, doomed to exist on insufficient rations and poorly served by his supply department, but he had the habit of victory, and with a gun in his hands he was as dogged a fighting man as the world has ever seen.

Lee put his men in position on the high ground just north of Sharpsburg on September 16, while McClellan's host assembled on the hills opposite, on the far side of Antietam Creek. Why McClellan did not open an immediate attack is beyond fathoming. Understrength as his army was, Lee had hardly more than half of it on the scene; the greater part of the segment that had taken Harpers Ferry was still on the road, and most of it would not arrive until the next day. McClellan's numerical advantage was overwhelming. His real strength, to be sure, was not as great as it looked on paper; he had nearly 97,000 men on his rolls, but nearly 20 percent of these were in noncombat assignments and would not go into action. Nevertheless, he had every advantage, and a full-dress attack on September 16 would almost certainly have driven Lee's men into the Potomac.

But McClellan, as has been said, was a leisurely character. Also, for some unaccountable reason, he always believed that he was outnumbered. So now he was cautious, spending long hours appraising the situation, waiting for his troops to get into position, making plans and revising them, leaving nothing to chance . . . with the fate of the nation resting on what he was doing and with Lee's absentees plodding along under a broiling sun, coming up to the hills to get into the fight. In the end the whole day of September 16 passed with nothing more serious taking place than clashes between outposts.

Lee's position was strong, but it had no depth. The Potomac River comes down from the north at Sharpsburg and then swings sharply to the east, with Sharpsburg lying inside the bend. Coming down parallel to the big river, and only a few miles east of it, is Antietam Creek, with rolling high ground folded in between creek and river. It was on this thumb of land that Lee's army was waiting for battle. The position was good—the Yankees would have to come uphill to fight—but it was shallow; if the line broke anywhere the entire army might be destroyed.

Lee had two principal subordinates—the famous Jackson and the almost equally famous General James Longstreet, a very tough fighter who was at his best on a defensive assignment. Jackson held the left—the high ground around a little Dunker church, a mile or so north of Sharpsburg—with infantry massed in a big cornfield north of the church and in a grove flanking the cornfield to the east: a cornfield owned by a man named Miller, known forever after simply as *the* cornfield. Center of the line, angling south and a little east from the Dunker church, was held by a division led by General D. H. Hill, under Longstreet's general supervision; it occupied a sunken lane which went zigzagging along near the crest of a rolling hill—a natural trench, as good as a fort. South of this position, on a hilltop just east of Sharpsburg, Longstreet had more men and artillery, with his extreme right posted to the south and east on some low hills overlooking the looping course of the Antietam.

Having spent the day of September 16 arranging his own masses opposite this position, McClellan ordered an attack at dawn on September 17, and in the earliest light of day the fighting began.

The first move was entrusted to McClellan's First Army Corps, led by General Joseph Hooker—"Fighting Joe," they called him—a florid, handsome man much admired by his troops. A thin drizzle dimmed the early light as Hooker got his corps into line and began to move south, along the road that ran from Sharpsburg north toward Hagerstown. His objective was the Dunker church position.

Hooker had three divisions in line—16,000 men, on paper; actually, about 9,000 in action. Preceded by skirmish lines, these approached the cornfield, found it full of armed Southerners, and wavered to a halt. On a ridge immediately behind the Federal infantry, Hooker ordered up guns, and 36 of them swung into action there, banked up hub to hub. They opened fire on the cornfield, plastering it unmercifully; men who watched said that cornstalks flew in the air, and knapsacks, muskets, and bit of human bodies. Then the bombardment died down and the Federal infantry moved in.

Through the cornfield and the wood just east of it, Hooker's divisions made their advance, clearing their way despite a murderous fire and coming out at last on open ground facing the Dunker church—where they were hit by a vicious counterattack, John B. Hood's division of Mississippi and Texas troops, which drove them back to their starting point. Reinforcements came up: the Federal Twelfth Corps, under General Joseph K. F. Mansfield, which regained the wood lot and the cornfield, driving out Hood's men and the remnants of the original Confederate line. Mansfield was killed, Hooker was wounded, and the two corps had fought themselves out so completely that they could advance no farther. Hooker later wrote that by this time, over most of the cornfield, the corn had been cut down by rifle and cannon fire as completely as if reapers had gone through with sickles; and Hood admitted that on no other field in all the war was he so constantly worried by the fear that his horse would step on some wounded man.

Again it was time for reinforcements, and McClellan now sent in his Second Corps, let by a white-haired old regular named Edwin Sumner. Sumner had three divisions, each one numbering five or six thousand combat men, and he led one of these in across the burnt-out cornfield and into a woodland that flanked the Dunker church on the north and west, aiming to break in the extreme left of the Confederate line. His advance was unopposed, or nearly so, at first, and he reached a position where a wheel to the left would drive away the last of Jackson's men—and then he ran into an ambush.

Portions of Lee's army were still coming in, finishing the cruel hike from Harpers Ferry, and some of these reached him that morning in the nick of time. Lee sent them to Jackson's aid, and they hit Sumner's leading division in the flank, crumpling it with one savage blow and driving the whole division north in wild retreat with heavy loss. For a moment it looked as if the whole right of McClellan's army might be involved in the rout, but Hooker's huge line of guns on the ridge to the north was a rallying point, and the triumphant Confederates were driven back to the Dunker church position. Across the cornfield—which by now, in its littered forty acres, contained at least 10,000 casualties from both armies—the rival forces glared at each other; and although they continued to exchange rifle and artillery fire for the rest of the day, the real fighting in that part of the field was over . . . stalemate.

Now Sumner brought his other two divisions up to attack the Confederates in the sunken road. Attack after attack followed in bewildering sequence, with trim Union divisions moving up to the deadly little lane, breaking under Confederate fire, retreating, and reforming for another attack. The Confederate position here was very strong, but the Union advantage in numbers was great, and toward noon one of Sumner's division commanders, General Israel B. Richardson, gained a hilltop where his infantry could enfilade the sunken roadway. The Confederates wavered and finally broke, and the triumphant Northerners swarmed in and took full possession of the position. The lane was so fearfully heaped with dead and wounded men that soldiers on both sides referred to it, forever after, simply as Bloody Lane.

Lee was now on the edge of final defeat. The center of his position was lost, and there were no reinforcements in sight. General D. H. Hill had taken a musket and, with a handful of stragglers he had rallied, was fighting like a foot soldier, while Longstreet was helping the gunners in a mangled battery. One determined push, here and now, would have broken Lee's line beyond recall, and the Army of Northern Virginia might have been destroyed. But McClellan was worried. The men who had taken Bloody Lane were exhausted, General Richardson was mortally wounded, it seemed to McClellan that the entire right of his line was frazzled and unable to fight any more, and the troops that might have been sent in to exploit this success he held in reserve lest Lee mount a counterattack. (A counterattack, just then, was the one thing Lee could not possibly manage; he could only hold on, hoping against hope that his men could stay where they were. But this truth never dawned on McClellan.)

So the fighting died out along the center, just as it had died out farther north, and now the action shifted to the southern end of the line—the chain of low hills overlooking Antietam Creek. Here McClellan's Ninth Corps, under General Ambrose E. Burnside, moved into action.

It moved ineptly, for Burnside somehow fed his four divisions into action one at a time, instead of massing them for a concerted attack, and although he had a numerical advantage of four or five to one he was never able to make it fully effective. He succeeded, finally, in storming the little stone bridge that led across the stream and dusted the Confederates off the hills that overlooked it. He got one division across the creek by a ford, a mile downstream; and after a long delay, in which ammunition was brought forward and lines were rearranged, he sent his men moving on to take the town of Sharpsburg, get between Lee and the Potomac, and make complete victory possible.

There was not a great deal Lee could do to prevent this, apparently. His understrength army had been fearfully mangled. He had lost at least 10,000 men, and many of the survivors had been blown loose from their commands and could not be reassembled before dusk. The ones who remained were fighting as hard as men have ever fought, but the odds by now were overwhelming. Poorly as Burnside had put his divisions into action, they were about to win.

Then—at the last minute of the last hour—up came Confederate reinforcements: A. P. Hill's division from Harpers Ferry, exhausted after a seventeen-mile hike in which General Hill personally, with sword in hand, had pricked laggards out from fence corners and out from under shady trees. This Hill was not a cautious man. A McClellan would have reflected that if he drove his men too hard most of them would fall out, and he would have arrived, with everything in tiptop shape, at nine o'clock next morning, eighteen hours too late but with everybody present and accounted for. Hill did it the other way; he drove his men unmercifully, and he lost at least half of his division along the way, but the ones who survived arrived on the scene at the exact moment when they were needed, and just now, with Burnside's blue soldiers preparing to walk in on Sharpsburg and kill the Southern Confederacy forever, A. P. Hill's beat-out soldiers, dust in their mouths and on their clothing, came stamping up the hill from the Potomac and smote Burnside in the flank.

It was the push that settled things. The Yankees who were under the gun fell back. Burnside, fully as cautious as McClellan, conceived that he was in trouble and acted that way; his advance elements were ordered to withdraw, his numerical advantage evaporated because he no longer thought it existed, and in a short time he was sending frantic messages to McClellan announcing that he believed he could hold his position if he were heavily reinforced.

And so, as a smoky dusk came down, the great battle of the Antietam came to an end, with a Union army, which did not know it had won, digging in for a last-ditch stand and with a Confederate army, which had been pounded to the last inch of human endurance, grounding its arms and making the best bivouac it could on a field that already stank with the hideous odor of unburied corpses. The battle was over: human beings had done the worst they could do to each other and nothing in particular had been settled, and perhaps tomorrow the thing would start all over again.

Perhaps: the word needs to be underscored. The most amazing thing about this battle is that Lee held his army in position all through the day of September 18, daring an opponent who had twice his numbers and five times his reserves to come and fight him if he had the nerve. McClellan did not have the nerve. He held his forces together throughout the eighteenth, wondering if he might not be attacked and hoping that he could hold his army in hand if that happened; and on the night of September 18, Lee pulled his army out of its lines and went back across the Potomac to rest and recruit and see if he could build the army up to something like the strength it used to have. (As it turned out, he could, and as a result the war went on for two and one-half years longer.)

So that was the battle of the Antietam; a bloody standoff, with 25,000 men in the two armies shot down in twelve dreadful hours, and with neither side winning anything in particular. And yet, even though he had played his hand with ruinous caution and had missed all the opportunities that were open to him, McClellan had won the decisive victory of the war—one of the great, decisive victories in American history.

He had won it, mostly, because he had not lost it. He had won it because, even though the fight itself was no better than a draw, Lee had had to retreat afterward; because of this battle, his dream of an invasion of the North had come to nothing. And since this dream faded out and was lost in the mist and shadows of time, the companion dream—the great, overriding threat to the continued existence of the American nation— also became dark and died.

Lee's invasion failed. So England decided not to recognize the Confederacy, and the possibility that Europe would settle the American Civil War went out the window. With England out, France also was out; from September 17 on, the South would win if it could gain a clear-cut decision on the battlefield and not otherwise. After the Antietam the Confederacy never again came within 24 hours of final victory; after this fight the Stars and Bars were on the downward slope, with great darkness lying at the end of the slide.

Even more: Lincoln now had the victory which he had to have. It was a shadowed victory, no victory at all technically, not much of a victory even judged by the long-term pull; but still a victory, a turning back of the Confederate invasion, a triumph over an army which up until that crucial September day had had just about everything going its way.

So Lincoln issued the Emancipation Proclamation and the course of American history thereafter was different.

The Emancipation Proclamation in many ways was one of the weakest state papers ever issued in the United States. It decreed the end of slavery in precisely those areas where the writ of the Federal government did not run—namely, in those states that, as yet unconquered, were still in rebellion; it left slavery untouched in the "loyal" states like Maryland and Kentucky; in many ways it was nothing more than a pious statement of intent.

Yet it had immense power. It finally determined that the Civil War was not merely a war for reunion but also a war to end human slavery; turned it from a family scrap into an incalculable struggle for human freedom, and thus made it a fight in which no civilized outsider could possibly intervene. It harnessed to the Union cause the basic dreams and aspirations of the race, and nailed to the American flagpole the charter of human rights. Everything in American history—and within reason, in world history—would be different after this. The bloody showdown in the cornfield and along the sunken lane and over the little stone bridge that spanned the narrow Antietam had enabled the nation to take a decisive step forward along the road to destiny.

The Antietam was a badly fought battle: badly fought, that is, in the sense that it was miserably directed. To be sure, it was fought magnificently by the enlisted men who had to pay the bill for their generals' decisions. The casualty list of 25,000 killed and wounded for the two armies, in a struggle that lasted only from dawn to dusk, gives it rank with the most dreadful battles ever waged by man. But the great point about it is that it brought the country to and through a moment of enormous decision. Out of it came reunion and freedom, neither one fully attained even a century later, but each one riveted into the American consciousness in a way time cannot undo.

What America is and hopes to be dates from the fight along Antietam Creek. The fight cost an enormous number of lives, and inflicted pain and disability on many thousands more; but in the infinite economy of the advance of the human race it may have been worth what it cost.

—August 1958

THE SLAVES FREED

by STEPHEN B. OATES

The long and tortuous path to the boldest of presidential acts.

When the cold, fastidious Mississippian rose to speak, a hush fell over the crowded Senate chamber. It was January 21, 1861, and Jefferson Davis and four other senators from the Deep South were here that day to announce their resignations. Over the winter, five Southern states had seceded from the Union, contending that Abraham Lincoln's election as President doomed the white man's South, that Lincoln and his fellow Republicans were abolitionist fanatics out to eradicate slavery and plunge Dixie into racial chaos. Though the Republicans had pledged to leave the peculiar institution alone where it already existed, Deep Southerners refused to believe them and left the Union to save their slave-based society from Republican aggression.

For his part, Jefferson Davis regretted that Mississippi had been obliged to secede, and he had spent a sleepless night distressed about the breakup of the Union and fearful of the future. To be sure, he loved the idea of a Southern confederacy; and he had warned Republicans that if the South could not depart in peace, a war would begin, the likes of which man had never seen before. But today, as he gave his valedictory in the Senate, Davis was sad and forlorn, his voice quavering. He bore his Republican adversaries no hostility, he said, and wished them and their people well. He apologized if in the heat of debate he had offended anybody—and he forgave those who had insulted him. "Mr. President and Senators," he said with great difficulty, "having made the announcement which the occasion seemed to me to require, it only remains for me to bid you a final adieu."

Several senators were visibly moved, and there were audible sobs in the galleries. As Davis made his exit, with Southern ladies waving handkerchiefs and crying out in favor of secession, Republicans stared grimly after him, realizing perhaps for the first time that the South was in earnest, the Union was disintegrating.

As Lincoln's inauguration approached and more Southern congressmen resigned to join the Confederacy, Republicans gained control of both houses and voted to expel the secessionists as traitors. Senator Lyman Trumbull of Illinois pronounced them all mad, and Charles Sumner of Massachusetts exhorted the free states to stand firm in the crisis. Michigan's Zachariah Chandler vowed to whip the South back into the Union and preserve the integrity of the government. And Ben Wade of Ohio predicted that secession would bring about the destruction of slavery, the very thing Southerners dreaded most. "The first blast of civil war," he had thundered at them, "is the death warrant of your institution."

After the events at Fort Sumter, Wade, Chandler, and Sumner called repeatedly at the White House and spoke with Lincoln about slavery and the rebellion. Sumner was a tall, elegant bachelor, with rich brown hair, a massive forehead, blue eyes, and a rather sad smile. He had traveled widely in England, where his friends included some of the most eminent political and literary figures. A humorless, erudite Bostonian, educated at Harvard, Sumner even looked English, with his tailored coats, checkered trousers, and English gaiters. He was so conscious of manners "that he never allowed himself, even in the privacy of his own chamber, to fall into a position which he would not take in his chair in the Senate. 'Habit,' he said, 'is everything.'" Sumner spoke out with great courage against racial injustice and was one of the few Republicans who advocated complete Negro equality. Back in 1856 Representative Preston Brooks of South Carolina had beaten him almost to death in the Senate Chamber for his "Crime Against Kansas" speech, and Sumner still carried physical and psychological scars from that attack. The senator now served as Lincoln's chief foreign policy adviser, often accompanied him on his carriage rides, and became the President's warm personal friend.

Zachariah Chandler was a Detroit businessman who had amassed a fortune in real estate and dry goods. Profane, hard-drinking, and eternally grim, Chandler had been one of the founders of the national Republican party and had served on the Republican National Committee in 1856 and 1860. Elected to the Senate in 1857, he had plunged into the acrimonious debates over slavery in the West, exhorting his colleagues not to surrender another inch of territory to slaveholders. When Southerners threatened to murder Republicans, brandishing pistols and bowie knives in the Senate itself, Chandler took up calisthenics and improved his marksmanship in case he had to fight. Once civil war commenced, he demanded that the government suppress the "armed traitors" of the South with all-out warfare.

Now serving his second term in the Senate, Benjamin Franklin Wade was short and thick chested, with iron-gray hair, sunken black eyes, and a square and beardless face. He was blunt and irascible, known as "Bluff Ben" for his readiness to duel with slaveholders, and he told more ribald jokes than any other man in the Senate, but he also had a charitable side: once when he spotted a destitute neighbor robbing his corn-crib, Wade moved out of sight in order not to humiliate the man. Once the war began, he was determined that Congress should have an equal voice with Lincoln in shaping Union war politics. According to diplomat Rudolf Schleiden, Wade was "perhaps the most energetic personality in the entire Congress." "That queer, rough, but intelligent-looking man," said one Washington observer, "is old Senator Wade of Ohio, who doesn't care a pinch of snuff whether people like what he says or not." Wade hated slavery as Sumner and Chandler did. But like most whites of his generation, he was prejudiced against blacks: he complained about their "odor," growled about all the "Nigger" cooks in Washington, and insisted that he had eaten food "cooked by Niggers until I can smell and taste the Nigger . . . all over." Like many Republicans, he thought the best solution to America's race problem was to ship all Negroes back to Africa.

As far as the Republican party was concerned, the three senators belonged to a loose faction inaccurately categorized as "radicals," a misnomer that has persisted through the years. These "more advanced Republicans," as the Detroit *Press and Tribune* referred to them, were really progressive, nineteenth-century liberals who felt a powerful kinship with English liberals like John Bright and Richard Cobden. What advanced Republicans wanted was to reform the American system—to bring their nation into line with the Declaration's premise—by ridding it of slavery and the South's ruling planter class. But while the advanced Republicans supported other social reforms, spoke out forthrightly against the crime and anachronism of slavery, and refused to compromise with the "Slave Power," they desired no radical break from basic American ideals and liberal institutions. Moreover, they were often at odds with one another on such issues as currency, the tariff, and precisely what rights black people should exercise in American white society.

Before secession, the advanced Republicans had endorsed the party's hands-off policy about slavery in the South: they all agreed that Congress had no constitutional authority to menace slavery as a state institution; all agreed, too, that the federal government could only abolish slavery in the national capital and outlaw it in the national territories, thus containing the institution in the South where they hoped it would ultimately perish. But civil war had removed their constitutional scruples about slavery in the Southern states, thereby bringing about the first significant difference between them and the more "moderate" and "conservative" members of the party. While the latter insisted that the Union must be restored with slavery intact, the advanced Republicans argued that the national government could now remove the peculiar institution by the war powers, and they wanted the President to do it in his capacity as Commander-in-Chief. This was what Sumner, Wade, and Chandler came to talk about with Lincoln. They respected the President, had applauded his nomination, campaigned indefatigably in his behalf, and cheered his firm stand at Fort Sumter. Now they urged him to destroy slavery as a war measure, pointing out that this would maim and cripple the Confederacy and hasten an end to the rebellion. Sumner flatly asserted that slavery and the rebellion were "mated" and would stand or fall together.

Lincoln seemed sympathetic. He detested human bondage as much as they did, and he wanted to stay on good terms with advanced Republicans on Capitol Hill, for he needed their support in prosecuting the war. Moreover, he respected the senators and referred to men like Sumner as the conscience of the party.

Yet to the senators' dismay, he would not free the slaves, could not free them. For one thing, he had no intention of alienating moderate and conservative Republicans—the majority of the party—by issuing an emancipation decree. For another, emancipation would almost surely send the loyal slave states—Delaware, Maryland, Kentucky, and Missouri—spiraling into the Confederacy, something that would be calamitous to the Union. Then, too, Lincoln was waging a bipartisan war with Northern Democrats and Republicans alike enlisting in his armies. An abolition policy, Lincoln feared, would splinter that coalition, perhaps even cause a new civil war behind Union lines.

Though deeply disappointed, the three senators at first acquiesced in Lincoln's policy because they wanted to maintain Republican unity in combating the rebellion. Sumner told himself that at bottom Lincoln was "a deeply convinced and faithful anti-slavery man" and that the sheer pressure of war would force him to strike at Negro bondage eventually.

On July 4, 1861, the Thirty-seventh Congress convened with a Rebel army entrenched less than thirty miles away. Republicans controlled both houses, and the advanced Republicans quickly gained positions of leadership out of proportion to their numbers. Many had been in Congress for years, and their uncompromising stand against slavery expansion and concessions to secessionists had won them accolades from all manner of Republicans. Like Chandler, several advanced Republicans had helped establish the national party; all were prominent in their state parties. Their prestige, skill, and energy—Chandler, for example, routinely put in eighteen-hour workdays—had helped bring them to positions of power on Capital Hill.

In the Senate, advanced Republicans chaired nearly all the crucial committees. Sumner ran the committee on foreign relations, Chandler the committee on commerce, and Wade the committee on territories. In addition, Lyman Trumbell of Illinois, a dry, logical speaker with sandy hair and gold-rimmed spectacles, headed the judiciary committee. Henry Wilson, Sumner's Massachusetts colleague, a stout, beardless, red-faced businessman who had once been a shoemaker's apprentice, held Jefferson Davis's old job as chairman of the committee on military affairs. William Pitt Fessenden of

Maine, impeccably dressed in his black jackets and black silk ties, famous for his forensic duels with Stephen A. Douglas before the war, chaired the finance committee and cooperated closely with Salmon Chase, Lincoln's Secretary of the Treasury. Fesseden had been born out of wedlock—a terrible stigma in that time—and the awful, unspoken shame of his illegitimacy had made him proud and quick to take offense, intolerant of human failings in others as well as himself. He and Sumner had once been friends, had called one another "my dear Sumner" and "my dear Fessenden," and often entered the Senate arm in arm. But Fessenden had taken umbrage at what he thought were Sumner's haughty airs, and their friendship had changed to bristling animosity. Fessenden remained "old friends" with Wade and Chandler, though, and also hobnobbed with Jacob Collamer of Vermont, a Republican conservative.

Advanced Republicans were equally prominent in the House. There was James Ashley of Ohio, an emotional, dramatic man with a curly brown mane, who chaired the committee on territories. There was George Washington Julian from Indiana, protégé of Joshua "Old War Horse" Giddings and a contentious, frowning individual who proved himself a formidable antislavery legislator. There was portly, unkempt Owen Lovejoy of Illinois, brother of Elijah, the abolitionist martyr; an eloquent antislavery orator, he headed the committee on agriculture. Like Sumner, Lovejoy was a close friend of Lincoln's—"the *best* friend I had in Congress," the President once remarked—and strove to sustain administration policies while simultaneously pushing the main cause of emancipation.

Finally there was sixty-nine-year-old Thaddeus Stevens of Pennsylvania, who controlled the nation's purse strings as chairman of the powerful committee on ways and means. Afflicted with a clubfoot, Stevens was a grim, sardonic bachelor with a cutting wit ("I now yield to Mr. B.," he once said, "who will make a few feeble remarks") and a fondness for gambling that took him almost nightly to Washington's casinos. To the delight of his colleagues, he indulged in witticisms so off color that they had to be deleted from the *Congressional Globe*. A wealthy ironmaster with a Jekyll-and-Hyde personality, he had contributed generously to charities and causes, crusaded for public schools in Pennsylvania, and defended fugitive slaves there. Crippled, as Fawn Brodie has noted, Stevens spoke of bondage "in terms of shackled limbs and a longing for freedom to dance." He lived with his mulatto housekeeper, Lydia Smith, and there is strong evidence that they were lovers. Antimiscegenation laws made marriage impossible, and their liaison not only generated malicious gossip but probably kept Stevens from becoming what he most wanted to be—a United States senator. He liked to quote the Bible that "He hath made of one blood all nations of men," yet he never championed complete equality for blacks—"not equality in all things," he once asserted, "simply before the laws, nothing else." Serving a fourth term as congressman, this bitter, intimidating, high-minded man was to rule the Civil War House and become "the master-spirit," said Alexander McClure, "of every aggressive movement in Congress to overthrow the rebellion and slavery."

As the session progressed that summer, congressional Republicans demonstrated remarkable harmony. They all wanted to preserve the Union and help the President fight the war through to a swift and successful conclusion. In agreement with Lincoln's slave policy, congressional Republicans also voted for the so-called Crittenden-Johnson resolutions, which declared that the sole purpose of the war was to restore the Union. For the sake of party unity, most advanced Republicans reluctantly supported the resolutions, too. But they agreed with Congressman Albert Riddle of Ohio that slavery ought to be destroyed. "You all believe that it is to go out, when it does, through convulsion, fire and blood," Riddle stormed on the House floor. "That convulsion is upon us. The man is a delirious ass who does not see it and realize this. For me, I mean to make a conquest of it; to beat it to extinction under the iron hoofs of our war horses."

For the advanced Republicans, the first chance to strike at slavery came late in July, after the Union rout at Bull Run. Observing that rebel forces used slaves to carry weapons and perform other military tasks, the advanced Republicans vigorously championed a confiscation bill, which authorized the seizure of any slave employed in the Confederate war effort, and they mustered almost unanimous Republican support in pushing the measure through Congress. Border-state Democrats like John J. Crittenden of Kentucky complained that the bill was unconstitutional, but most Republicans agreed with

Henry Wilson that "if traitors use bondsmen to destroy this country, my doctrine is that the Government shall at once convert those bondsmen into men that cannot be used to destroy our country." In war, Republicans contended, the government had every right to confiscate enemy property—including slave property—as legitimate contraband. Though the bill was hardly a general emancipation act, advanced Republicans hailed its passage as an important first step. They were glad indeed when Lincoln signed the bill into law and commanded his armies to enforce it. At last the President appeared to be coming around to their views.

But they had misunderstood him. When General John Charles Frémont, commander of the Western Department, ordered that the slaves of all Rebels in Missouri be "declared freemen," Lincoln pronounced this a dangerous and unauthorized political act that would alienate the loyal border and commanded Frémont to modify his order so that it accorded strictly with the congressional confiscation act. Though border Unionists applauded Lincoln, advanced Republicans were dismayed that he had overruled Frémont's emancipation decree. Sumner declared that Lincoln "is now a dictator." Wade charged that Lincoln's opinions on slavery "could only come of one, born of 'poor white trash' and educated in a slave State." And Fessenden denounced the President for his "weak and unjustifiable concession to the Union men of the border States."

Still, the Frémont episode did not cause an irreparable split between Lincoln and the advanced Republicans, as some writers have claimed. In fact, when Lincoln subsequently removed the general from command, Trumbull, Chandler, and Lovejoy sustained the President, conceding that the celebrated Pathfinder and first standard-bearer of their party was a maladroit administrator. But in the fall and winter of 1861, advanced Republicans did mount an all-out campaign to make the obliteration of slavery a Union war objective. One after another they came to the White House—Wade, Chandler, and Trumbull, Sumner, Julian, and Lovejoy—and implored and badgered the President to issue an emancipation proclamation on military grounds. With the war dragging on, they insisted that slavery must be attacked in order to weaken the Confederate ability to fight.

Moreover, they argued, slavery had caused the conflict

and was now the cornerstone of the Confederacy. It was absurd to fight a war without removing the thing that had brought it about. Should Lincoln restore the Union with slavery preserved, Southerners would just start another war whenever they thought the institution threatened, so that the present struggle would have been in vain. If Lincoln really wanted to salvage the Union, he must hurl his armies at the heart of the rebellion. He must tear slavery out root and branch and smash the South's arrogant planters—those mischievous men the advanced Republicans believed had masterminded secession and fomented war. The annihilation of slavery, Julian asserted, was "not a debatable and distant alternative, but a pressing and absolute necessity." So what if most of the country opposed emancipation lest it result in an exodus of Southern blacks into the North? "It was the duty of the President," he said, "to lead, not follow public opinion."

Sumner, as Lincoln's foreign policy adviser, also linked emancipation to opinion overseas. There was a strong possibility that Britain would recognize the Confederacy as an independent nation—potentially disastrous for the Union since the Confederacy could then form alliances and seek mediation, perhaps even armed intervention. But, Sumner argued, if Lincoln made the destruction of slavery a Union war aim, Britain would balk at recognition and intervention because of her own antislavery tradition. And whatever powerful Britain did, the rest of Europe was sure to follow.

Also, as Sumner kept saying, emancipation would break the chains of several million oppressed human beings and right America at last with her own ideals. Lincoln and the Republican party could no longer wait to remove slavery. The President must do it by the war powers. The rebellion, monstrous and terrible though it was, had given him the opportunity.

But Lincoln still did not agree. "I think Sumner and the rest of you would upset our applecart altogether if you had your way," he told some advanced Republicans one day. "We didn't go into the war to put down slavery, but to put the flag back; and to act differently at this moment would, I have no doubt, not only weaken our cause, but smack of bad faith. . . . This thunderbolt will keep." And in his message to Congress in December of 1861, the President declared that he did not want the war degenerating into "a violent and remorseless revolutionary struggle." He was striving, he said, "to keep the integrity of the Union prominent as the primary object of the contest."

Advanced Republicans were deeply aggrieved. Fessenden thought the President had lost all hold on Congress, and Wade complained that not even a galvanic battery could inspire Lincoln to "courage, decision and enterprise."

"He means well," wrote Trumbull, "and in ordinary times would have made one of the best of Presidents, but he lacks confidence in himself and the *will* necessary in this great emergency."

By year's end, though, Lincoln's mind had begun to change. He spoke with Sumner about emancipation and assured the senator that "the only difference between you and me on this subject is a difference of a month or six weeks in time." And he now felt, he said, that the war "was a great movement by God to end Slavery and that the man would be a fool who should stand in the way. But out of deference to the loyal border states, Lincoln still shied away from a sweeping executive decree and searched about for an alternative. On March 6, 1862, he proposed a plan to Congress he thought would make federal emancipation unnecessary—a gradual, compensated abolition program to begin along the loyal border and then be extended into the rebel states as they were conquered. According to Lincoln's plan, the border states would gradually remove slavery over the next thirty years, and the national government would compensate slaveholders for their loss. The whole program was to be voluntary; the states would adopt their own emancipation laws without federal coercion. At the same time (as he had earlier told Congress), Lincoln favored a voluntary colonization program, to be sponsored by the federal government, that would resettle liberated blacks outside the country.

On Capitol Hill Stevens derided Lincoln's scheme as "diluted milk-and-water-gruel." But other advanced Republicans, noting that Lincoln's was the first emancipation proposal ever offered by an American President, acclaimed it as an excellent step. On April 10 the Republican-controlled Congress endorsed Lincoln's emancipation plan. But the border-state representatives, for whom it was intended, rejected the scheme emphatically. "I utterly spit at it and despise it," said one Kentucky congressman. "Emancipation in the cotton States is simply an absurdity. . . . There is not enough power in the world to compel it to be done."

As Lincoln promoted his gradual, compensated scheme, advanced Republicans on Capitol Hill launched a furious antislavery attack of their own. They sponsored a tough new confiscation bill, championed legislation that weakened the fugitive-slave law and assailed human bondage in the national capital as well as the territories. What was more, they won over many Republican moderates to forge a new congressional majority so far as slavery was concerned. As the war ground into its second year, moderate Republicans came to agree with their advanced colleagues that it was senseless to pretend the Union could be restored without removing the cause of the rebellion.

So, over strong Democratic opposition, the Republican Congress approved a bill that forbade the return of fugitive slaves to the Rebels, and on March 13, 1862, Lincoln signed it into law. Congress also adopted legislation which abolished slavery in Washington, D.C., compensated owners for their loss, and set aside funds for the voluntary colonization of blacks in Haiti and Liberia, and Lincoln signed this as well. Democrats howled. One castigated the bill as an entering wedge for wholesale abolition, another predicted that liberated Negroes would crowd white ladies out of congressional galleries. Washingtonians accused the "abolitionists" in Congress of converting the capital into "a hell on earth for the white man." Republicans brushed aside all such criticism. "If there be a place upon the face of the earth," asserted a Minnesota Republican, "where human slavery should be prohibited, and where every man should be protected in the rights which God and Nature have given him, that place is the capital of this great Republic."

In June the Republican Congress lashed at slavery again: it passed a bill that outlawed human bondage in all federal territories, thus overriding the Dred Scott decision, and Lincoln signed the measure into law. Congress and the President also joined together in recognizing the black republics of Haiti and Liberia, a move that would facilitate colonization efforts in those lands. Meanwhile, a fierce debate raged over the second confiscation bill, which authorized the seizure and liberation of all slaves held by those in rebellion. Advanced Republicans not only pushed the bill with uninhibited zeal but also advocated that emancipated blacks be enlisted in the army. But even some Republicans thought full-scale confiscation too drastic, and "conservatives" like Jacob Collamer of Vermont, Orville Browning of Illinois, and Edgar Cowan of Pennsylvania sided with the Democrats in denouncing the bill as uncivilized and unconstitutional. "Pass these acts," cried one opponent, "confiscate under the bills the property of these men, emancipate their negroes, place arms in the hands of these human gorillas to murder their masters and violate their wives and daughters, and you will have a war such as was never witnessed in the worst days of the French Revolution, and horrors never exceeded in San Domingo."

On July 4, in the midst of the debate, Sumner hurried back to the White House and admonished Lincoln to attack slavery himself. Sumner was extremely disappointed in the President, for he did not seem a month or six weeks behind the senator at all. In fact, Lincoln recently had overruled another general, David Hunter, who liberated the slaves inside his lines, and again the advanced Republicans had groaned in despair. Now, on July 4, Sumner urged "the reconsecration of the day by a decree of emancipation." The senator pointed out that the Union was suffering from troop shortages on every front and that the slaves were an untapped reservoir of manpower. "You need more men," Sumner argued, "not only at the North, but at the South, in the rear of the Rebels; you need the slaves." But Lincoln insisted that an emancipation edict was still "too big a lick." And, in a White House interview, he warned border-state legislators that his gradual, state-guided plan was the only alternative to federal emancipation and that they must commend it to their people. Once again they refused.

On July 17, five days after Lincoln spoke with the border men, Congress finally passed the second confiscation bill. If the rebellion did not end in sixty days, the measure warned, the executive branch would seize the property of all those who supported, aided, or participated in the rebellion. Federal courts were to determine guilt. Those convicted would forfeit their estates and their slaves to the federal government, and their slaves would be set free. Section nine liberated other categories of slaves without court action: slaves of Rebels who escaped to Union lines, who were captured by federal forces or were abandoned by their owners, "shall be deemed captives of war, and shall be forever free." On the other hand, the bill exempted loyal Unionists in the rebel South, allowing them to retain their slaves and other property. Another section empowered Lincoln to enlist Negroes in the military. Still another, aimed at easing Northern racial fears and keeping Republican unity, provided for the voluntary resettlement of confiscated blacks in "some tropical country." A few days later Congress appropriated $500,000 for colonization.

Controversial though it was, the second confiscation act still fell short of genuine emancipation. Most slaves were to be freed only after protracted case-by-case litigation in the courts. And of course, the slaves of loyal masters were not affected. Yet the bill was about as far as Congress could go in attacking slavery, for most Republicans still acknowledged that Congress had no constitutional authority to eradicate bondage as a state institution. Only the President with his war powers—or a constitutional amendment—could do that. Nevertheless, the measure seemed a clear invitation for the President to exercise his constitutional powers and annihilate slavery in the rebellious states. And Stevens, Sumner, and Wilson repeatedly told him that most congressional Republicans now favored this. On the other hand, conservatives like Orville Browning beseeched Lincoln to veto the confiscation bill and restore the old Union as it was. "I said to him that he had reached the culminating point in his administration," Browning recorded in his diary, "and his course upon this bill was to determine whether he was to control the abolitionists and radicals, or whether they were to control him."

For several days, Lincoln gave few hints as to what he would do, and Congress awaited his response in a state of high tension. Finally, on July 17, he informed Capitol Hill that he agreed entirely with the spirit of the confiscation bill, remarking that "the traitor against the general government" deserved to have his slaves and other property forfeited as just punishment for rebellion. While he thought some of the wording unfortunately vague, he nevertheless raised no objection to the sections on slave liberation. He did, however, disagree with other portions on technical grounds, especially those which permanently divested a Rebel of the title to his land, and Lincoln hinted that he would veto the bill as a consequence. To avoid that, congressional Republicans attached an explanatory resolution removing most of Lincoln's complaints. Satisfied, the President signed the bill and commanded the army to start enforcing it after sixty days.

Even so, several advanced Republicans were angered by Lincoln's threatened veto and peeved by what they perceived as his legalistic quibbling when the Union was struggling for its life against a mutinous autocracy founded on slavery. Julian, for his part, thought Lincoln's behavior "inexpressibly provoking," and when Congress adjourned, he called at the White House to find out once and for all where the President stood on emancipation and all-out war against the Rebels. Julian said he was going home to Indiana and wanted to assure his constituents that the President would "co-operate with Congress in vigorously carrying out the measures we had inaugurated for the purpose of crushing the rebellion, and that now the quickest and hardest blows were to be dealt." Complaining that advanced Republicans had unfairly criticized him, Lincoln said he had no objection at all to what Julian wished to tell his constituents. In Indiana that summer, Julian announced that Lincoln had now decided on a radical change in his policy toward slavery.

In August Sumner learned that Lincoln had at last decided to issue an emancipation proclamation. Convinced that the peculiar institution could be destroyed only through executive action, Lincoln actually had drawn up a draft of the proclamation and read it to his Cabinet. But couldn't Sumner have predicted it? Lincoln had let Secretary of State William H. Seward dissuade him from issuing the edict until after a Union military victory. At the White House, Sumner demanded that the decree "be put forth—the sooner the better—without any reference to our military condition." But the President refused, and Sumner stalked out, dismayed again at what he once called Lincoln's "immense *vis inertiae*." The senator feared that only the confiscation act would ever free any slaves.

But in September Lincoln came through. After the Confederate reversal at Antietam, he issued his preliminary emancipation proclamation, a clear warning that if the rebellion did not cease in one hundred days, the executive branch would use the military to free *all* slaves in the rebel states—those belonging to secessionists and loyalists alike. Thus the President would go beyond the second confiscation act—he would handle emancipation himself, avoid tangled litigation over slavery in the courts, and vanquish it as an institution in the South. He believed he could do this by the war powers, and he deemed it "a fit and necessary military measure" to preserve the Union.

The advanced Republicans, of course, were delighted. "Hurrah for Old Abe and the proclamation," Wade exulted. Stevens extolled Lincoln for his patriotism and said his proclamation "contained precisely the principles which I had advocated." "Thank God that I live to enjoy this day!" Summer exclaimed in Boston. "Freedom is practically secured to all who find shelter within our lines, and the glorious flag of the Union, wherever it floats, becomes the flag of Freedom." A few days later, Sumner announced that "the Emancipation Proclamation . . . is now the corner-stone of our national policy."

As it turned out, though, the preliminary proclamation helped lead to a Republican disaster in the fall by-elections of 1862. Northern Democrats already were angered by Lincoln's harsh war measures, especially his use of martial law and military arrests. Now, Negro emancipation was more than they could bear, and they stumped the Northern states beating the drums of Negrophobia and warning of massive influxes of Southern blacks into the North once emancipation came. Sullen, war-weary, and racially antagonistic, Northern voters dealt the Republicans a smashing blow as the North's five most populous states—all of which had gone for Lincoln in 1860—now returned Democratic majorities to Capitol Hill. Republicans narrowly retained control of Congress, but they were steeped in gloom as it convened that December.

Though most Republicans stood resolutely behind emancipation, Browning and other conservatives now begged Lincoln to abandon his "reckless" abolition policy lest he shatter his party and wreck what remained of his country. At the same time, Sumner and Wade admonished Lincoln to stand firm, and he promised that he would. On January 1, 1863, the President officially signed the final proclamation in the White House. In it Lincoln temporarily exempted all of Tennessee and certain occupied places in Louisiana and Virginia (later, in reconstructing those states, he would withdraw the exemptions and make emancipation mandatory). He also excluded the loyal slave states because they were not in rebellion and he lacked the legal authority to uproot slavery there. With these exceptions, the final proclamation declared that all slaves in the rebellious states "from henceforth shall be free." The document also asserted that black men—Southern and Northern alike—might now be enlisted in Union military forces.

All in all, the advanced Republicans were pleased. Perhaps the President should not have exempted Tennessee and southern Louisiana, Horace Greeley said, "but let us not cavil." Lincoln had now "played his grand part" in the abolition of slavery, Julian declared, and "brought relief to multitudes of anxious people." "On that day," Sumner wrote of January 1, 1863, "an angel appeared upon the earth."

In truth, Lincoln's proclamation was the most revolutionary measure ever to come from an American President up to that time, and the advanced Republicans took a lot of credit for goading him at last to act. Slavery would now die by degrees with every Union advance, every Northern victory.

Now that Lincoln had adopted emancipation, advanced Republicans watched him with a critical eye, making sure that he enforced his edict and exhorting him to place only those firmly opposed to slavery in command of Union armies. In February rumor had it that if Lincoln wavered even once in his promise of freedom to the slaves, Wade would move for a vote of "no confidence" and try to cut off appropriations. But Lincoln did not waiver. Even though a storm of anti-Negro, anti-Lincoln protest broke over the land, the President refused to retract a single word of his decree. "He is stubborn as a mule when he gets his back up," Chandler said, "& *it is up* now on the Proclamation." "His mind acts slowly," Lovejoy observed, "but when he moves, it is *forward*."

In the last two years of the war, Lincoln and the advanced Republicans had their differences, but they were scarcely locked in the kind of blood feud depicted in Civil War histories and biographies of an earlier day. Several advanced Republicans did oppose Lincoln's renomination in 1864 because the war was going badly and they thought him an inept administrator. In addition, Sumner, Stevens, and Wade clashed bitterly with Lincoln over whether Congress or the President should oversee reconstruction. Sumner, Julian, Chandler, and a handful of other legislators also insisted that Southern black men be enfranchised. But Lincoln, sympathetic to Negro voting rights, hesitated to force them on the states he reconstructed. Nevertheless, in April 1865, he publicly endorsed limited Negro suffrage and conceded that the black man deserved the right to vote.

In truth, despite their differences, Lincoln and the advanced Republicans worked together closely. And they stood together on several crucial issues: they all wanted to abolish slavery entirely in the South and to muzzle the rebellious white majority there so that it could not overwhelm Southern Unionists and return the old Southern ruling class to power. They also came to see that colonization was probably an unworkable solution to the problem of racial adjustment. All Lincoln's colonization schemes had foundered, and anyway most blacks adamantly refused to participate in the Republicans' voluntary program. In place of colonization, the Lincoln administration devised a refugee system for blacks in the South, a program that put them to work in military and civilian pursuits there and prepared them for life in a free society. And in 1864 the Republican Congress canceled all funds it had set aside for colonization efforts.

Most important of all, advanced Republicans cooperated closely with Lincoln in pushing a constitutional amendment through Congress that would guarantee the permanent freedom of all slaves, those in the loyal border as well as in the rebel South. Since he had issued the proclamation, Lincoln and his congressional associates had worried that it might be nullified in the courts or thrown out by a later Congress or a subsequent administration. As a consequence, they wanted a constitutional amendment that would safeguard the proclamation and prevent emancipation from ever being overturned. Accordingly, in December 1863, Iowa senator James F. Wilson introduced an emancipation amendment in the Senate, and the following February Trumbull reported it from the judiciary committee, reminding his colleagues that nobody could deny that all the death and destruction of the war stemmed from slavery and that it was their duty to support this amendment. In April the Senate adopted it by a vote of 38 to 6, but it failed to muster the required two-thirds majority in the House.

After Lincoln's re-election in 1864, advanced Republicans joined forces with the President to get the amendment passed. In his message that December, Lincoln conceded that this was the same House that earlier had failed to approve the amendment. But since then a national election had taken place which Lincoln insisted was a mandate for permanent emancipation. If the present House refused to pass the amendment, the next one "almost certainly" would. So "at all events," the President said, "may we not agree that the sooner the better?"

As December passed, Republicans who sponsored the amendment plotted with Lincoln to pressure conservative Republicans and recalcitrant Democrats for their support. On January 6, 1865, a heated debate began over the amendment, with James Ashley quoting Lincoln himself that "*if slavery is not wrong, nothing is wrong.*" A week later, Thaddeus Stevens, still tall and imposing at seventy-two, limped down the aisle of the House and closed the debate with a spare and eloquent address, declaring that he had never hesitated, even when threatened with violence, "to stand here and denounce this infamous institution." With the outcome much in doubt, Lincoln and congressional Republicans participated in secret negotiations never made public—negotiations that allegedly involved patronage, a New Jersey railroad monopoly, and the release of Rebels kin to congressional Democrats—to bring wavering opponents into line. "The greatest measure of the nineteenth century," Stevens claimed, "was passed by corruption, aided and abetted by the purest man in America." When the amendment did pass, by just three votes, a storm of cheers broke over House Republicans, who danced, embraced one another, waved their hats and canes. "It seemed to me I had been born into a new life," Julian recalled, "and that the world was overflowing with beauty and joy." Lincoln, too, pronounced the amendment a "great moral victory" and "a King's cure" for the evils of slavery. When ratified by the states, the amendment would end human bondage in America.

See, Julian rejoiced, "the world *does* move." He could have added that he and his advanced Republican colleagues, in collaboration with their President, had made it move, had done all they could in the smoke and steel of civil war to right their troubled land with its own noblest ideals.

—December 1980

LEE'S GREATEST VICTORY

by ROBERT K. KRICK

During three days in May 1863, the Confederate leader took astonishing risks to win one of the most skillfully conducted battles in history. But the cost turned out to be too steep.

The ability of Robert E. Lee and Thomas J. ("Stonewall") Jackson never showed itself more vividly than during three days of battle in May 1863 around a rustic crossroads called Chancellorsville. At the battle's denouement, which might be considered the highest tide of the Confederacy, the two Virginians capped a reversal of fortunes as dramatic as any recorded in more than three centuries of American military affairs.

During the last day of April the Federal commander Joseph Hooker had stolen a march on Lee as completely as anyone did during the entire war. In an amazing strategic initiative Hooker took his army far around Lee's left, across two rivers, and into an admirable position around Chancellorsville. His fellow general George G. Meade, a saturnine man and no admirer of Joseph Hooker when in the sunniest of moods, exclaimed jubilantly on April 30: "Hurrah for old Joe! We're on Lee's flank and he doesn't know it."

The army with which Joe Hooker stole his march on Lee was a tough, veteran aggregation that had suffered from ill use at the hands of a series of inadequate leaders. Most recently Ambrose E. Burnside had butchered more than twelve thousand of his brave men in a hopeless attack near Fredericksburg the preceding December. Earlier the Army of the Potomac had endured mishandling from a boastful bully named John Pope, whose tenure in command was numbered in days, not in months, and the brilliant but timid George B. McClellan had led the same regiments to the brink of victory—but never quite over the threshold—on famous fields in Virginia and Maryland.

General Hooker's rise to high rank during the war grew from a blend of training at West Point and experience in Mexico, with more than a tincture of political maneuvering. Bravery under fire in the 1862 campaigns won the general a name for valor and the nickname Fighting Joe. (According to some accounts the catchy name was coined by accident when two newspaper headlines—THE FIGHTING and JOE HOOKER—overlapped in some fashion.) Hooker had shamelessly schemed against Burnside, motivated in part by a wholesome distaste for Burnside's ineptitude but also by a powerful degree of personal ambition.

Abraham Lincoln concluded in January 1863 that Burnside must go and reluctantly identified Hooker as the officer to inherit the mantle. In a patient and appropriately famous letter the President bluntly informed Hooker that he was appointing him despite the "great wrong to the country" inherent in his behavior toward Burnside. "I have heard, in such way as to believe it," Lincoln continued, "of your recently saying that both the Army and the Government needed a Dictator. Of course it was not for this, but in spite of it, that I have given you the command. Only those generals who gain success, can set up dictators. What I now ask of you is military success, and I will risk the dictatorship."

During the three months between Hooker's appointment and the onset of the campaigning season, Lincoln must have been very much gratified by the accomplishments of his new commander. A contemporary wrote that Hooker when young was a "very expert" baseball player, who could "take a ball from almost in front of the bat, so eager, active and dexterous were his movements." When applied to military administration, that same controlled zeal made the Army of the Potomac a much improved military implement. Joe Hooker ironed ineptitude and indolence out of the medical services, flogged quartermaster and commissary functions into a fine pitch of efficiency, revitalized the cavalry arm, and inaugurated an intelligence-gathering system far ahead of its time in that staff-poor era. The soldiers noticed the changes and took heart from them.

The men also relished their new commander's reputation as a profane, hard-drinking sort of fellow. "Our leader is Joe Hooker, he takes his whiskey strong," they sang in admiration of one of the general's two most widely mooted social traits. The other rumored trait resulted in a persistent tradition that remains in circulation to this day. General Hooker's campaign to tighten up the Army of the Potomac extended to controlling the prostitution that flourished on its fringes. Supposedly the general's name somehow became an appellation for the quarry of the overworked provost detachments enforcing his order. Joe Hooker's own reputation as a womanizer fed the story conveniently. Firm evidence that the etymology of the word *hooker* antedates 1863 by more than a decade has done little to check the legend.

Hooker's ranking subordinates by and large did not share the enthusiasm of the men in the ranks. The officer corps of the Old Army was a generally conservative body, both politically and morally. One immediate subordinate, the intensely pious O. O. Howard, doubtless felt particularly uneasy about Hooker, and Hooker reciprocated. Soon after the war he told an interviewer that Howard was "a good deal more" qualified to "command a prayer meeting" than an army corps. "He was always a woman among troops," said Hooker. "If he was not born in petticoats, he ought to have been, and ought to wear them. He was always taken up with Sunday Schools and the temperance cause."

Other corps commanders of note included George G. Meade and Daniel E. Sickles. General Meade, the snappish patrician who was destined to replace Hooker, seems in retrospect the most capable man who wore Union general's stars in the war's Eastern theater. Dan Sickles, by contrast, was a bawdy, rambunctious adventurer. Three years before Chancellorsville he escaped conviction for the public murder of his wife's lover on the then novel ground of temporary insanity. After the war he served as intermittent paramour to the queen of Spain.

Federal operations at Chancellorsville suffered dramatically from two absences. Much of Hooker's cavalry spent the crucial days on a largely irrelevant raid, leaving the main army bereft of its essential screening-and-reconnaissance function. Worse, the army's enormously capable chief of artillery, Henry J. Hunt, was off in a rear area, where Hooker had consigned him after the two had quarreled.

The men of the Army of Northern Virginia benefited from any number of subjective advantages over their familiar foemen of the Army of the Potomac, but no Southerner could help worrying over the apparent disparity of force. Although no one knew enemy strengths with precision—and, in fact, often neither side could firmly establish its own strength—Federals north of the Rappahannock clearly had a vast preponderance in numbers. The actual figures approximated 130,000 against 60,000.

The Northern army brought seven corps to the field of Chancellorsville. The Confederates countered with two, and one of the two was at less than one-half of its strength. The missing divisions had gone southeastward to the vicinity of Suffolk, Virginia, in quest of the foodstuffs that already dwindled at an alarming rate. The question now was whether the agrarian South could feed its armies on its own soil.

The two supporting arms that came up short for Hooker at Chancellorsville never looked better on Lee's side of the line than they did in that spring of 1863. The colorful Southern cavalry general James E. B. Stuart, universally called Jeb after his initials, stood at the height of his personal and professional powers, tirelessly alert and active and energetic. As for the Southern artillery, it continued to labor under tremendous disadvantages in weaponry and ammunition but during the past winter had revolutionized its tactics by converting to a battalion system. Since the first whiff of gunpowder, cannon had suffered from the tendency of infantry officers to misuse the big guns simply as larger infantry weapons. In 1861 batteries assigned to brigades fought under infantry direction, often from positions at either end of the line. High ground, low ground, heavy enemy pressure, or no enemy pressure, it was all the same: Put the guns with the infantry. But now Confederate artillery would move and fight in clusters, usually of at least four four-gun batteries, and the higher-ranking artillerymen commanding these larger clusters would enjoy some degree of autonomy. Some of the South's brightest and best young men rode at the head of the reorganized guns.

Federal horsemen attempted to open the campaign that led to the Battle of Chancellorsville at the end of the second week in April. Gen. George Stoneman, commanding Hooker's cavalry, was to take the greater part of the available mounted force and cross the Rappahannock far upstream northwest of Fredericksburg, Virginia. The horse soldiers, Hooker hoped, would ricochet with deadly effect through Confederate rear areas, freeing Federal prisoners, tearing up railroads, breaking an aqueduct on the James River, and forcing a frightened Lee to fall back from Fredericksburg. In the event, heavy rains sluiced the bottoms out of Virginia's clay roads, and the raiding force did not cross the Rappahannock until April 29, after a substantial portion of Hooker's infantry had done so. Still, it is hard to avoid blaming the delay as much on Stoneman as on uncooperative weather.

Once launched, the cavalry raid caromed almost aimlessly about central Virginia, causing some localized discomfort but achieving not a thing of real military worth. Stuart detached just enough regiments to contain the raid within certain wide limits, harassing its rear and flanks and gathering in stragglers. One of the interesting reflections modern students draw from the Chancellorsville campaign is that the Federal cavalry raid, prudently checked by just the right number of Confederates, presaged in mirror image the cavalry situation a few weeks later at Gettysburg. There Stuart wasted his substance in a meaningless raid while his army fought blindly, and the Federals reacted prudently. It was as though the Federals had gone to school at Chancellorsville on the apt use of the mounted arm, with Stuart as teacher.

In the last two days of April, Hooker brought to a successful conclusion the huge turning maneuver that placed the center of his flanking element at the country crossroads of Chancellorsville. That polysyllabic name, whose ending suggests a busy settlement, actually belonged to a single building. The Chancellor kin who built the heart of the structure late in the eighteenth century expanded it into a wayside inn opened in 1815. By 1860 two additions had swelled the building into a really sizable structure, but dwindling traffic on the roads that met in the yard had reduced its function to that of a one-family residence. The Chancellors called their home Chancellorsville in the same fashion that other Southern homes were called Mount Vernon or Belle Hill. No one else lived within a half-mile of the crossroads, and only a few within several miles.

An environmental feature that contributed to Chancellorsville's meager dimensions also levied a heavy impact on military operations nearby. The land lay largely desolate under the dense, scrubby growth of a region known as the Wilderness of Spotsylvania. About seventy square miles of the Wilderness sprawled along the south bank of the Rapidan and Rappahannock rivers, stretching about three miles farther south than Chancellorsville and about two miles farther east. A numerically superior army ensnarled in those thickets, and confined to easy maneuver only on the few poor roads, would lose much of its advantage.

Joe Hooker pushed the head of his mighty army eastward to the edge of the Wilderness early on Friday, May 1, 1863. About three miles from the Chancellorsville crossroads the Federals came face-to-face with a commanding wrinkle of the earth's surface, atop which stood a little wooden Baptist church bearing the name of Zoan. The Zoan Church ridge represented about as succulent a military prize as Joe Hooker could have found just then in his zone of operations. It was high ground (none higher to the east, short of Europe); it straddled a key road; and most important, it rose on open ground just east of the entangling tendrils of the Wilderness.

Confederates on top of the prize ridge had been feverishly digging earthworks overnight on the orders of the division commander Richard H. Anderson. Despite the trenches, Hooker could have dislodged Anderson's relative handful of men and occupied Zoan Church without much exertion. Perhaps he would have, had not Stonewall Jackson ridden into the uncertain tableau and dominated the unfolding action with his force of personality. Stonewall ordered Anderson's men to pack their entrenching equipment and attack. Anderson left no account of his reaction, but he must have wondered how he and Jackson and a few assorted regiments could accomplish much.

As Jackson began pressing against the Northerners lapping around the western base of the ridge, he used two critically important parallel roads. The old Orange Turnpike came out of Fredericksburg past Zoan, through Spotsylvania County, and then on to Orange County and Orange Courthouse. About a decade before the Civil War local entrepreneurs had undertaken to supplant that century-old thoroughfare with a toll road paved on one of its lanes with planks. Elsewhere in the vicinity men of vision were putting their money into railroads; but trains and their trappings required vast capital outlay, and the plank-road people reasoned that everyone owned wheeled wagons already.

The brand-new Orange Plank Road proved to be a wretched idea economically, but in May 1863 it drew troops of both sides like a magnet because it formed a second usable corridor through the Wilderness. Hooker had moved east on both the Turnpike and the Plank Road, which near Zoan Church ran generally parallel to and a mile or so south of the older right-of-way. As the morning wore on, Confederates pushed west against both heads of Hooker's army on the two roads.

Jackson, soon joined by Lee in person, superintended an almost chaotic blend of Confederate regiments and brigades in the advance. Southern units arriving from various points funneled off into the Turnpike or the Plank Road at Jackson's whim and in response to unfolding exigencies, without much regard for command and control at levels below the corps commander in person. Their elan and their leader's determination were steadily reclaiming the ground of the earlier Federal advance when yet another transportation corridor swung the action entirely into the Confederate column.

Just before the war more prescient investors had founded and funded a railroad to run from Fredericksburg out to Orange and into fertile Piedmont Virginia. By the time the conflict halted work, the route had been surveyed and the line graded. The level stretch of cuts and fills and grades lay uncluttered by even the first stringers or rails, but it constituted a convenient third passage through the Wilderness. The unfinished railroad ran westward, parallel to the two wagon roads and about a mile south of the Plank Road. Gen. A. R. ("Rans") Wright's brigade, three regiments and a battalion of infantry from Georgia, sliced ahead along that convenient conduit and forced a reorientation of the Federal line by ninety degrees. Contending lines that had stretched for miles from north to south readjusted to Wright's lunge. Hooker's right swung up away from Wright and left the Federals at the end of the first day of battle (and the first day of May) arrayed in a huge, irregular, shallow V. The apex of the broad V lay at or near Chancellorsville while one arm ran northeast toward the river and the other sprawled west toward Wilderness Church.

Before Jackson and Wright buffeted his right, Hooker himself had squandered a wonderful opportunity on his left. The V Corps of the Army of the Potomac, ably led by Meade, began May 1 by moving steadily eastward along the River

Road. This fourth east-west route curled far north of the Turnpike and the Plank Road and led eventually past Banks Ford on the river into Fredericksburg. Meade moved vigorously ahead until his skirmishers reached the vicinity of Mott's Run, within hailing distance of Banks Ford. Federals holding the southern mouth of that ford would serve a number of highly desirable ends. By that hour, however, Joe Hooker had recoiled from the presence of the legendary Stonewall Jackson with such abruptness that he sought no opportunities, only shelter. Hooker had collapsed within himself, and now he began inexorably pulling his mighty and well-tempered army down with him.

General Hooker dished out bravado loudly and often during the Chancellorsville campaign, but his boasts seem in retrospect to have been feeble attempts to brace up his own wavering spirits. On the evening before his advance of May 1, Hooker drummed out a staccato general order assuring his men "that the operations of the last three days have determined that our enemy must either ingloriously fly or come out from behind his defenses and give us battle on our own ground, where certain destruction awaits him." There can be little doubt that Hooker really meant that. Lee surely would react to Hooker's clever and successful movement to Chancellorsville, and to the Federal cavalry roaming in his rear, by sidling south away from the unhappy combination facing him. Good ground on the North Anna River would allow the Confederates a chance to regroup and start over. Even after a century and a quarter it is difficult to come to grips with Lee's daring choice. At the·time Hooker clearly was flabbergasted.

With a difficult May 1 behind him, Hooker blustered anew. "It's all right . . . I've got Lee just where I want him," the Federal commander insisted to an incredulous subordinate. At headquarters Hooker declared, "The rebel army is now the legitimate property of the Army of the Potomac." To another audience he said, "The enemy is in my power, and God Almighty cannot deprive me of them." And he finally summarized his professed contentment in a written circular to his corps commanders. "The major general commanding trusts," he wrote incautiously, "that a suspension in the attack to-day will embolden the enemy to attack him." The first three boasts proved to be empty, but Hooker's written wish came true with a vengeance.

Across the lines that evening of May 1 the Confederate commanders weighed the situation somewhat more judiciously. Just about a mile from Hooker's headquarters at Chancellorsville, Lee and Jackson crouched together over a small fire on seats improvised from abandoned U.S. cracker boxes. R. E. Lee, who had ridden up toward the river on his right in a personal reconnaissance during the afternoon, told Jackson that poor roads, steeply cut stream beds, and Federals dense on the ground combined to deny the Confederates any opportunity there.

The two men sent their respective engineer officers on a moonlit scout directly toward the enemy center at Chancellorsville. T. M. R. Talcott of Lee's staff later wrote vividly of that tense experience. His companion, J. Keith Boswell of Jackson's staff, had no chance to record his impressions; Boswell fell dead from a volley that struck him as he rode at Stonewall's side a few hours later. The two capable young men came back convinced that the Federal center offered no opening whatsoever for an assault.

Other young men scouting through the darkness of the Wilderness sent back reports through the night that gradually suggested a way to get at Hooker. It would be horribly risky under the circumstances, but perhaps Lee and Jackson might be able to snake a column westward all the way across the enemy's front, around his right, and clear up behind him. Stonewall's favorite preacher, Beverly Tucker Lacy, knew some of the ground in the western reaches of the Wilderness because his brother lived there. Charles Beverly Wellford, a veteran of the army and now running the family iron furnace just down the road, knew more of the ground. Catharine Furnace (named for the matriarch of the Wellford clan) burned charcoal in enormous volume and owned thousands of acres nearby from which to harvest charcoal wood. Jackson's mapmaker Jedediah Hotchkiss, a converted New York Yankee now as zealously Southern as any native, wandered the woods roads with Wellford and Lacy and came back with some sketches. Jeb Stuart sent cavalry in the same direction under General Lee's boisterous twenty-seven-year-old nephew Fitzhugh Lee.

Very early on May 2 Lee reached his decision. Jackson would take two-thirds of the already heavily outnumbered Army of Northern Virginia and disappear on a daylong march over the horizon. With startling nonchalance the two commanders agreed that Lee would stand firm and act belligerent with no more than seventeen thousand men at his back while Jackson ventured far out on a limb with twice that many troops. An attack by Hooker of even moderate earnestness would simply destroy the Confederate army.

A rough pencil sketch of the roads showed that the desperate gamble might have a chance. Lee and Jackson and others pored over the map. At one point the army commander carefully arranged a handful of broomstraws on the edge of a box and then, by way of example to Jackson, swept them helter-skelter onto the ground. Jackson had a last quiet word with his chief, then rode away. R. E. Lee and Stonewall Jackson never met again.

Lee at once set out upon the delicate mission of beguiling his opposite number. The tactical dogma of the day held that one or at most two companies of the ten that made up a regiment should go forward on skirmish or outpost duty. Those advance guards could give early warning of approaching enemy, fire a quick volley, and then scurry back to the main line. Driving in hostile skirmishers was familiar business; so was finding their comrades behind them in a ratio of about nine to one. On May 2 Lee sent swarms of skirmishers toward the enemy, sometimes using all his men out in front, leaving no main line but creating the impression of great strength. Confederate units launched vigorous feints that Federals repulsed stoutly and with some smugness. Meanwhile, Jackson pushed on through the woods toward Hooker's rear, carrying a quiver full of thunderbolts.

Jackson's fabled flank march actually unfolded with far less stealth than any Confederate wanted. Barely one mile beyond the intersection where Lee and Jackson parted, the flanking column ran into its first taste of trouble. On high ground just before the road dropped into a bottom around Catharine Furnace, a gap in the woods allowed Federals a mile and a quarter away to see the Southerners moving steadily past the open space. Of course Northern artillery opened fire at the closely packed target; of course the Confederates double-timed past the hot spot. General Lee knew of this early difficulty, but then there began a long, tense silence that dragged on for endless hours.

The long-range shells spiraling across more than a mile annoyed their intended victims and no doubt hurt a few of them, but they constituted no real military impediment. A more serious threat gradually developed at the second milepost when Dan Sickles pushed his troops southward to the vicinity of Catharine Furnace to find out what all those moving Southerners were up to. Men of the 23d Georgia spread in an arc above the furnace as a flank guard fought against an increasing tide of Federals. The Georgians finally fell back to the cut of the same unfinished railroad that had played a role the day before in shaping the battle lines. By this time Jackson's entire infantry column had marched past. The Georgia regiment fell apart finally, and all but a handful of men became prisoners. Emory Fiske Best, the regiment's twenty-three-year-old colonel, was among those who escaped. A court-martial cashiered him just before Christmas, but his 23d Georgia had done well for a long time.

The bluecoats of Sickles's corps who captured the Georgians were pleased by their success, but in fact their prime quarry had eluded danger. The last two infantry brigades in Jackson's column turned back and easily repulsed any further advance by Sickles beyond the railroad. High open ground around the Wellford house, bisected by the narrow woods road climbing out of dense thickets, provided the Southern rear guard with a ready-made stronghold. The extensive trains of ambulances and ordnance wagons scheduled to follow Jackson's infantry avoided the furnace pressure point by detouring around it to the south and west on another set of primitive traces. Jackson was free to pursue his great adventure.

The narrowness of the wagon tracks Jackson followed toward his goal proved to be both a blessing and a curse. The Southern column needed secrecy, and the Wilderness that closed in all around provided it. But the column also needed to move fast, and that the primitive roads did not encourage. Even so, Jackson's two-week-old circular about marching habits kept the march moving: two miles in fifty minutes, then ten minutes' rest, then do it again, and again, and again.

A little more than four miles from his starting point Stonewall Jackson reached the Brock Road. This was the main north-south route in the vicinity, and it led north around the enemy right. Jackson turned south. Someone attributed to Stonewall the military aphorism "Always mystify, mislead, and surprise the enemy." Moving the wrong way with almost thirty thousand men might accomplish that end, if anyone was watching. The wrong-way march lasted only long enough to cross two gentle ridgelines. Then Jackson turned off into the trees again on another set of woods tracks and angled northward parallel to the Brock Road.

Soldiers marching at the head of Jackson's corps rejoiced when, about two miles beyond the detour, they came to a small stream flowing across the road. Standing water dotted gullies throughout the Wilderness, but the stream supplied them with their first source of drinkable water along the route. It gurgled across the road at just about precisely the halfway point along the march. When Jackson's van reached the stream, the tail of his attenuated corps had not left the starting blocks six miles to the rear.

Officers prodded dusty and tired men through the enticing water and on their way. When Jackson reached the Brock Road again, he poured his troops onto it, and they surged northward. At the intersection of the Plank Road he planned to turn right and cover the two miles to Wilderness Church, there to demolish Hooker's dangling flank. Gen. Fitzhugh Lee met Jackson at the intersection and led him east on the Plank Road to show him why that idea no longer made good sense. From a high plateau in the yard of a farmer named Burton, young Lee pointed out to Jackson the Federal line running west beyond Wilderness Church. To attack down the Plank Road would be to hit the enemy in front, canceling most of the advantages won by so much sweat and at such great risk.

Stonewall Jackson was about the most famous man on earth that spring; Fitz Lee knew he had served him well and prepared to bask in the glow of a deserved kudos. Instead, the dour Stonewall gazed intently across the intervening ground at his quarry without a glance at his disappointed benefactor. Turning without a word, Jackson hurried back to the head of his column on the Brock Road and pointed it up the road still farther north. Two extra miles of marching would complete the wider circuit now necessary. Good generals adapt to tactical verities, and Jackson was very good indeed at what he did. He paused long enough to scribble a four-sentence dispatch to Lee, then headed eagerly on with his men.

The Federals on whom Jackson planned to unleash his tidal wave belonged to the XI Corps under O. O. Howard. General Howard was new to his post, but the men in the ranks knew Jackson all too well. Stonewall had brought them to grief more than once in the past year while they served under Gen. Nathaniel Banks and Gen. Franz Sigel. That unhappy past, combined with the German origins of many of the men, left them the unpopular and misunderstood outcasts of the Army of the Potomac. After the battle many of them came to believe, or at least to claim, that they had known full well that Confederates by the tens of thousands lurked in the woods. But in the late afternoon of May 2, without access to hindsight, the infantrymen of the XI Corps whiled away their last moments of grace playing cards and writing letters and cooking food that they would never eat. Several miles away Joe Hooker sat on the veranda of the pleasant Chancellorsville Inn and composed brash communiqués.

General Jackson could not wait for his entire column to snake through the narrow woods and uncoil across Howard's exposed flank. Despite all the risks he had successfully run and the superb opportunity that lay before him, Jackson knew that the inexorable slide of the sun toward the horizon had now become his greatest foe. The stern, devout Jackson was about as close to an Old Testament warrior as the Civil War produced, but he could not make the sun stand still. After pushing two-thirds of his men into three long, parallel lines, Jackson could wait no longer.

The two main Confederate lines, separated by only about one hundred yards, stretched for nearly a mile on either side of the Turnpike. They stood squarely at right angles to the unwitting Federal line strung out along the road and facing south. When the Southern avalanche struck, the bravest Northerner turning to confront this surprise attack from the rear would be outflanked by a mile to his right and a mile to his left. In naval parlance, Jackson had "crossed the T" on his quarry by forming the cap of the T and looking down its shank.

Sometime after 5:00 P.M. Stonewall Jackson reached under his coat and pulled his watch out of an inside pocket. Conflicting accounts place the moment at 5:15 or as late as 6:00. Jackson looked up from the watch at the handsome, capable Robert E. Rodes, a Virginian commanding the division waiting in the front line. "Are you ready, General Rodes?"

"Yes, sir."

"You can go forward then."

That quiet colloquy launched the II Corps and moved thousands of men through the brightest moment of the fabled Army of Northern Virginia. A nod from Rodes to a young officer named Blackford, who had grown up in nearby Fredericksburg but commanded Alabamians on this day, triggered the attack. Bugles told skirmishers to advance. About twenty thousand infantrymen followed close behind through dense brush that tugged at their tattered uniforms. As the Rebels gained momentum, they broke into a hoarse, savage roar that escalated into the spine-chilling high-pitched shriek of the Rebel yell.

The dense two-mile line of Southern soldiers drove forest animals in front of its advance like beaters flushing game on an African safari, and many Northern troops got their first intimation that something was afoot in the woods behind them when animals scurried and fluttered past, hurrying eastward. Some Federals laughed and cheered the bizarre natural phenomenon. Then the paralyzing tremolo of the Rebel yell came floating after the wildlife.

Howard's unfortunate division and brigade commanders generally did their best in an impossible situation. No soldiers could have stood in the circumstances thrust upon the XI Corps—even had the Confederates been unarmed, and the Federals equipped with twentieth-century weapons not yet dreamed of. Troops simply do not stand when surprised from behind by hordes of screaming enemies. Leaders with those foreign names that made the rest of the army look askance encouraged brief rallies that inevitably spilled back in rout. Schurz, Krzyzanowski, Schimmelfennig, von Gilsa, von Einsiedel, and dozens more scrambled in vain to stem the wide and deep tide sweeping against and over them.

Capt. Hubert Dilger won a great name for himself by firing a piece of artillery with steadfast courage in the face of Jackson's legions. This freshly immigrated German, known as Leatherbreeches because of some doeskin pants he wore, retired so stubbornly that Army legend held that he fell back only by reason of the recoil of his gun at each discharge.

Federals fleeing from the intolerable spot whence Jackson had erupted found little support as they ran eastward. Dan Sickles had taken most of his III Corps down toward the furnace to cope with Jackson's rear guard. The panicky fugitives ran back not onto a stalwart line of friends but into a comfortless vacuum.

Only the failure of one inept Confederate officer saved the Federal army from unmitigated disaster. Alfred H. Colquitt was a Georgia politician of starkly limited military attainments. Chance put this weak reed on the right end of Jackson's four-brigade frontline cutting edge. The spare fifth brigade of the front division fell in just behind Colquitt, ready to deploy into the first good seam popped open by the attack. Colquitt and his peers operated under strict orders to move straight and steadily ahead, ignoring matters on either side; they would exploit Jackson's strenuously won advantage while other troops tidied up around the edges and behind them.

Despite his unmistakable instructions, Colquitt came to a dead stop shortly after the attack began. One of the general's staff excitedly reported enemy off to the right. The highly capable young Stephen Dodson Ramseur of North Carolina, commanding the brigade just to the rear and stymied by Colquitt's halt, found to his immense disgust that "not a solitary Yankee was to be seen" in that direction. Colquitt had single-handedly obliterated the usefulness of two-fifths of Jackson's front line. Almost immediately after the battle Lee sent Colquitt into exile far away from the Army of Northern Virginia; by contrast, Georgians thought enough of Colquitt to elect him governor twice and then send him to the U.S. Senate.

Even without the 40 percent of his front line lost through incompetence, Jackson had enough men in place to sweep the field. His troops devoured more than two miles of the Federal line in about two hours. But near the end of their triumphant plunge toward Chancellorsville the Southerners were themselves taken by surprise as the result of a bizarre accident. The 8th Pennsylvania Cavalry had spent that afternoon at the commanding artillery position known as Hazel Grove, about one mile south of the Turnpike at a point two miles east of where Jackson struck. An acoustical shadow kept those troopers and others around them from hearing, or at least clearly comprehending, the disaster that had befallen their friends far away to their right and rear. When the Pennsylvanians responded to a routine but outdated order to head north to the main road, then east to Hooker's headquarters at Chancellorsville, they stumbled into the midst of Jackson's columns.

Surprised Southerners quickly dispersed the equally surprised Pennsylvania boys, who fought bravely but vainly in a sea of gray. Gen. Alfred Pleasonton, who had command of the Federal cavalry, later wove the charge of the 8th into a vast panorama of self-serving lies that he concocted as his official report of the battle. Eventually Pleasonton won his well-earned reputation as the Civil War's Munchausen, but at the time the survivors could only fume impotently.

As darkness fell, the men of the Federal XI Corps completed a frantic run for shelter that in many instances took them all the way back to the river and across the pontoon bridges. One officer called these German fugitives the Flying Dutchmen; another, hoarse from his vain efforts to shout up a rally, said that "the damned Dutchmen ran away with my voice." To finish with these poor XI Corps fellows, it must be reported that they ran afoul of similarly grotesque bad luck a few weeks later at Gettysburg and suffered an almost identical thrashing. Before year's end, though, many of the same men participated in the dramatic spontaneous charge that captured Missionary Ridge in Tennessee.

Dan Sickles's boys of the Federal III Corps blundered through their own personal nightmare after darkness fell. Thousands of them crashed about in the baffling Wilderness, far south of the position they had left when ordered to explore the area around Catharine Furnace and southwest of friendly lines still intact. When the III Corps troops groped back toward Chancellorsville in the darkness, they bumped into blazing muskets and thundering cannon, all fired by the Federal XII Corps. The number of men killed by friends in this hellish, confused pitch-black tangle cannot be ascertained with any certainty. Some Northern witnesses marveled that anyone survived, and Gen. Henry Warner Slocum, commanding the XII Corps, wrote that "the damage suffered by our troops from our own fire . . . must have been severe."

When this combat between bluecoats erupted, Confederates in the vicinity ducked for cover and expected the worst, only gradually coming to the soothing understanding that the storm excluded them. Meanwhile, a handful of Confederates as confused as were Slocum and Sickles inflicted a mortal wound on their own hero—and perhaps on the national prospects of their young country.

Stonewall Jackson's considerable military virtues did not

include an intuitive grasp of terrain. Perhaps because of that, the general customarily worked hard and long in seeking understanding of ground where he would fight. In the smoke-smeared moonlight that evening of May 2, Jackson rode out before the amorphous tangle of troops that constituted his front line. The general and an entourage of staffers and couriers poked about in the Wilderness, looking for a route that would provide access to some point behind Chancellorsville, blocking the Federal retreat. When the little cavalcade headed back toward Confederate lines, it came athwart two North Carolina brigades. The noise of the horses prompted one of the brigades to fire a wild volley obliquely across the road from its southern edge. An officer with the general shouted a desperate plea to cease firing. "You are firing into your own men!" he yelled.

The major of the 18th North Carolina, just north of the road, bellowed: "It's a lie! Pour it into them, boys!"

This volley struck dead Jackson's faithful engineer officer, J. Keith Boswell, and inflicted mortal hurts on at least three others in the party. Three of its bullets hit Stonewall Jackson. Two shattered his left arm; the third pierced his right hand. Horrified subordinates gathered around the stricken leader, bound his wounds, and laboriously carried him from the field. At one point three young staff members lay around Jackson's litter in a hurricane of artillery fire, shielding him with their bodies as canisters struck sparks from the road all around them. Twice men carrying a corner of the litter went down. The second time Jackson fell squarely on his mangled shoulder, renewing the arterial bleeding that already had cost him much of his vitality. Eventually the worried and sorrowful party delivered their general to a field hospital near Wilderness Tavern. There his medical director amputated Jackson's savaged arm just below the shoulder early on May 3. The bullet extracted from the general's right palm was round, one of the projectiles fired by the obsolete smoothbore muskets still carried by a surprising number of ordnance-poor Confederate units.

By the time Jackson awakened from his anesthetic, artillery fire from the nearby battlefield was shaking the earth beneath him. During the night after Jackson's wounding, command of his corps passed to Jeb Stuart, who was dragooned into this unaccustomed temporary role because the only available infantry general of adequate rank had been wounded soon after Jackson went down. Col. Edward Porter Alexander, a fine young artillerist from Georgia, reported to Stuart that a high, open knoll called Hazel Grove offered a wonderful artillery vantage point and persuaded the general to capture it. At about 1:00 A.M. Stuart sent J. J. Archer's brigade of Tennessee and Alabama regiments to the vicinity, and at the first hint of dawn the Southern troops stormed out of the woods into the clearing. They reached the hilltop just in time to capture four guns and one hundred men of a Federal rear guard; Joe Hooker had decided during the night to abandon Hazel Grove, the key to the battlefield.

The newly installed battalion system of artillery, which ensured ready availability of ample guns in large, mobile masses, allowed Alexander to rush about fifty pieces of the right size and type to Hazel Grove. There they took under fire the Federal artillery some twelve hundred yards away at Fairview (still another Chancellor family farmhouse) and at the Chancellorsville crossroads itself. Although the gunners of the Army of Northern Virginia had achieved well-earned fame, they were accustomed to suffering under the fire of better-made and more modern Federal weapons that hurled far more reliable ammunition. The advantage of ground offered by Hazel Grove, however, combined with successful implementation of the battalion concept, resulted in a situation in which, said the army's leading historian, Douglas Southall Freeman, "the finest artillerists of the Army of Northern Virginia were having their greatest day."

One particularly noteworthy round fired from Hazel Grove spiraled over Fairview and headed unerringly for the Chancellorsville Inn. As the shell descended toward its target, General Hooker was leaning against one of the large white porch columns, looking out from the second-story veranda. The shell did not explode (an all-too-typical result from the Southern perspective; one officer on this day insisted that he kept track and only about every fifteenth round went off). The hurtling iron hit Hooker's pillar, though, and the impact knocked it and pieces of the porch in every direction. Lt. Col. Logan Henry Nathan Salyer of the 50th Virginia lay across the top of a piano in the inn's first-floor parlor, where Federal captors had taken him after he went down with a saber wound in the head. Salyer roused himself enough to ask scurrying staff officers what had happened, and they responded with an early and inaccurate report that Hooker had been killed. Salyer rejoiced quietly, but in fact Hooker was only stunned and paralyzed. He ostensibly conveyed to Gen. Darius N. Couch the command of the army, but as the day continued, it became apparent that he retained so many strings on Couch that the latter really wielded no substantial authority.

General Couch and his colleagues recognized that their army still enjoyed clear advantages in numbers and position. Could they commit the large body of unused men to action, they might still grind Lee's weak force to bits, Jackson's dazzling success of the previous day notwithstanding. But Hooker held his army passive and allowed Lee the luxury of choosing the time and place at which decisive actions developed.

Nevertheless, R. E. Lee experienced considerable difficulty on the morning of May 3. Almost all of the Federal infantry lines that Lee had to break that morning stood in the dense Wilderness. Southern brigades plunged into the brush and fought blindly against equally bemused Northern units, generally accomplishing little and ballooning the already dreadful casualty lists. Other brigades wandered through the storm without either doing much good or suffering much loss. "It would be useless to follow in detail the desperate fighting which now ensued. . . ." That admission by Edward Porter Alexander, a ranking Confederate officer who revisited the field after the war before writing a classic history, suggests the nature of the woods fighting on May 3.

Among the casualties of this hours-long brawl was Gen. Hiram G. Berry of Maine, shot down with a mortal wound as he crossed the road near Chancellorsville. But perhaps the most important Federal casualty, viewed from the long perspective of posterity, was Col. Nelson Appleton Miles of the 61st New York. Miles went down with a bullet in the abdomen, recovered, and went on to become commander in chief of the U.S. Army near the turn of the century. At about the time Miles gained his highest command, private citizens both North and South purchased huge chunks of the battlefield of Chancellorsville in hopes that the War Department would accept them as a donation to form a national military park on the order of those newly designated at Gettysburg and elsewhere. The Army chose not to accept the largess of those public-spirited preservationists. Gettysburg was one thing, but the scenes in which the U.S. Army had been humiliated in 1863 (and where a rebellious Southerner punctured General Miles) certainly did not deserve protection. The portion of the battlefield preserved today, amid a sea of modern development, contains only a small fragment of what our forebears sought to protect almost a century ago.

Early during the woods fighting two Confederate generals became casualties of different sorts. Gen. John R. Jones of Virginia was one of Stonewall Jackson's special projects that turned out poorly. Jones had been accused of cowardice so blatant that it resulted in a formal court-martial, a shocking event in the general officer corps of an army fabled for its bravery. The court cautiously exonerated Jones two weeks before Chancellorsville. On May 3, however, the demands of combat among the bullets snapping through the trees proved to be too much for Jones. He left the field and resigned.

Another of Jackson's projects, E. F. Paxton, went into the morning's fight with the unshakable premonition that he would be killed at once. Paxton had known Jackson as a fellow communicant at Stonewall's beloved Presbyterian church before the war. When Paxton lost an election to be major of the 27th Virginia, Jackson calmly found means to promote him several ranks to brigadier general, out of reach of the whims of the electorate. Much of the army disdained this proceeding as another instance of Jackson's much mooted wretched judgment in selecting subordinates. Paxton had had little opportunity to confirm or disprove this conventional wisdom when he led his famous Stonewall Brigade into action on May 3. He knew he would not survive the battle and prepared for death by studying his wife's photograph and reading his Bible by the scant predawn light. Moments after the action opened Paxton fell dead, surviving only long enough to reach for the pocket where he kept his treasured pictures.

Over all of the infantry chaos that morning there throbbed the steady rhythm of Confederate artillery at Hazel Grove, building to a crescendo that won the battle for Lee. The two divisions that had remained with Lee for the past day and a half pressed toward Chancellorsville from the south and east. Jackson's men under Stuart closed in from the west. Before the morning was far gone, the two Confederate wings reunited at last, ending that aspect of Lee's incredible gamble and providing the general with the chance to reassert direct control over his whole army. Gradually the consolidated Southern force swept Hooker's brave but poorly led legions back to the Chancellorsville intersection. A brief, confused stand there bought Hooker a few minutes. Then Confederates swarmed over the crossroads and around the burning inn in a frenzied victory celebration.

Into this animated scene rode R. E. Lee on his familiar gray horse. "His presence," wrote an officer who was there, "was the signal for one of those outbursts of enthusiasm which none can appreciate who have not witnessed them. The fierce soldiers with their faces blackened with the smoke of battle, the wounded crawling with feeble limbs from the fury of the devouring flames, all seemed possessed with a common impulse. One long, unbroken cheer, in which the feeble cry of those who lay helpless on the earth blended with the strong voices of those who still fought, rose high above the roar of battle, and hailed the presence of the victorious chief. He sat in the full realization of all that soldiers dream of—triumph; and as I looked upon him in the complete fruition of the success which his genius, courage, and confidence in his army had won, I thought that it must have been from such a scene that men in ancient days rose to the dignity of gods."

The impromptu celebration fizzled out when dreadful news arrived from Fredericksburg. Lee's eleven-thousand-man rear guard there, under Gen. Jubal A. Early, had been facing twice as many Federals under Gen. John Sedgwick. When a Mississippi colonel named Thomas M. Griffin incautiously (and against regulations) accepted a flag of truce during the morning of May 3, Northern officers saw just how thin was the line opposing them. Adjusting their formations and tactics accordingly, the Federals pounded across the plain below Marye's Heights and burst over the stone wall and Sunken Road that had caused their army so much grief the previous December. This penetration of the rear guard opened a path to Lee's rear for Sedgwick's force. A government photographer accompanying the advancing Federals took some shots of the captured ground, among them one of freshly dead Mississippians in the Sunken Road that gave stark testimony of the price of their colonel's impolitic behavior. The film captured one of the most graphic views of battle dead taken during the entire war.

Sedgwick's apparently wide-open opportunity to slice

westward and do Lee some harm came to an abrupt obstacle about four miles west of Marye's Heights, at Salem Church. Gen. Cadmus Marcellus Wilcox and his brigade of five tough, veteran Alabama regiments began May 3 guarding Banks Ford on the Rappahannock River, two miles due north of Salem Church. Wilcox moved alertly toward Fredericksburg and the action developing there during the morning. When Early's line at Marye's Heights fell apart, Wilcox hurried across country and threw skirmishers in Sedgwick's path. The Alabama men retarded their enemy's advance from positions on each gentle crest and at fence rows perpendicular to the road. Finally at Salem Church they made a stout stand.

Lee received the bad news from eastward with the same calm poise he always displayed, but his heart must have sunk within him. He turned Gen. Lafayette McLaws onto the Turnpike back toward Salem Church and later followed in person. Wilcox and his men stood at bay near the little brick building when McLaws arrived with reinforcements. The simple Southern Baptist sanctuary, built in 1844 by the farming brethren who worshiped in it, now served as a make-do fortification. Blue-coated infantry charged up to and around the building while Alabamians fired out the windows. Hundreds of men fell in the yard, in the church itself, and in the small log church school sixty yards to the east.

But McLaws and his men made the Salem Church ridge too strong to breach, and fighting flickered out late on May 3. The next day Confederates from the church and from Early's bypassed rear guard bottled Sedgwick up with his back to the Rappahannock. Soon after midnight of May 4-5, this Union detachment retreated back over the river under desultory shell fire and light infantry pressure.

Salem Church survives today, covered both inside and out with battle scars. All but a tiny fragment of the Salem Church ridge, however, disappeared during the past few years as gas stations and shopping centers destroyed the battlefield. Huge earth-moving machines chewed up and carried away the ground of the ridge itself, leaving the building a forlorn remnant of the historic past isolated on its little vestigial crest.

After Sedgwick headed for cover at the end of May 4, Lee could return his attention to Hooker's main army. The Federals had built a strong and deep line of earthworks shaped like an enormous capital V. The flanks were anchored on the river, and the apex stretched south to a point only one mile north of Chancellorsville. Within that sturdy fastness Joe Hooker continued to cooperate with Lee's objectives by holding his force quietly under the eyes of Southern detachments that he outnumbered by about four to one. When Lee was able to return to the Chancellorsville front on May 5, the men he brought back with him from around Salem Church improved the odds to some degree but not nearly enough to approach parity. Federal losses totaled about eighteen thousand during the campaign, but Lee had incurred some twelve thousand casualties as well and was still greatly overmatched. Even so, the Confederate commander was looking for some means to launch a renewed offensive against Hooker when, on the morning of May 6, his scouts reported that all the Federals had retreated north of the river during the night.

That same day, Joe Hooker announced in an order to the entire army: "The events of the last week may swell with pride the heart of every officer and soldier of this army. We have added new luster to its former renown . . . and filled [the enemy's] country with fear and consternation." By contrast, Lee's congratulatory order to his troops, dated May 7, gave thanks to God "for the signal deliverance He has wrought" and encouraged divine services in the army to acknowledge that debt.

Historians continue to discuss many aspects of the campaign without any hint of unanimity. Was Joe Hooker drunk most of the weekend? After the war the general conclusion was that he had stopped drinking on accession to army command, leaving him unsettled after a lifetime of consistent bibulousness; new evidence suggests that he did indeed indulge his habit during the Chancellorsville weekend. Did R. E. Lee conclude from the evidence of his incredible victory that there was virtually nothing his battle-tested infantry could not do, leading to overconfidence at Gettysburg? The army had performed at an astoundingly high level during the first three days of May, and Lee soon did ask nearly impossible feats from it; on the other hand, the leaders of a tenuous revolutionary experiment could hardly afford to play conservatively against staggering negative odds.

Chancellorsville gave Lee the leverage to move the war out of torn and bleeding Virginia. His raid into Pennsylvania held the potential for great success, but it came to grief at

Gettysburg, two months to the day after Chancellorsville.

The combination of bold strategy and even bolder tactics employed by the Confederate leaders at Chancellorsville turned an apparently impossible situation into a remarkable triumph. But the most important scenes in that tragic drama ultimately unfolded not around the old inn or at Hazel Grove but in an outbuilding of a country house twenty-five miles to the southeast at Guinea Station. Stonewall Jackson seemed to be recovering favorably from the loss of his arm when an ambulance carried him to the Chandler place at Guinea on the hot fourth of May. His progress continued good for two more days at this new resting place farther from the dangers and distractions of the front. Then, early on the morning of May 7, Jackson awakened with a sharp pain in his side that his medical staff readily and worriedly diagnosed as pneumonia. The disease made rapid inroads on the general's weakened system, and doctors began to hint that he might not recover.

The grim news spread through the ranks. The loss of mighty Stonewall would transform the glorious name of Chancellorsville into the blackest of blots. Mrs. Jackson reached her husband's bedside on May 7, and three days later it was she who had to rouse Thomas Jackson from his delirium to warn him that he was dying. "I will be an infinite gainer to be translated," the fading man responded, and later: "My wish is fulfilled. I have always desired to die on Sunday."

In the early afternoon of a lovely spring Sunday, May 10, Stonewall Jackson called out for Gen. A. P. Hill and for Maj. Welles J. Hawks of his staff as his mind wandered to battles won and streams crossed at the head of his troops. At three o'clock a spell of calm intervened, broken only by the sobs of family and friends in the room and by the general's desperate gasping for breath. As the clock neared the quarter hour, Jackson spoke quietly from the bed: "Let us cross over the river, and rest under the shade of the trees." Then, as he so often had done during the year just past, Stonewall Jackson led the way.

—March 1990

THE END OF
THE *ALABAMA*

by NORMAN C. DELANEY

Captain Semmes was spoiling for a fight—and Captain Winslow of the Kearsarge *was waiting for him, just off Cherbourg.*

Early in 1864 the Confederate States Steamer *Alabama* left the Indian Ocean and headed for European waters. Her captain, Raphael Semmes—tired, ill, and bad-tempered after almost three years commanding Confederate raiders—noted in his journal on May 21: "Our bottom is in such a state that everything passes us. We are like a crippled hunter limping home from a long chase." During almost two years at sea the *Alabama* had never been long enough in any port for a thorough overhaul of her hull, rigging, and engines. Since her fires had never been allowed to go out, flues and pipes had not been properly cleaned. As First Officer John McIntosh Kell observed, the ship was "loose at every joint, her seams were open, and the copper on her bottom was in rolls."

On April 23 Semmes had made a target of a captured vessel. Shot and shell were used "with reasonable success," according to Semmes. Others thought differently. Of twenty-four rounds fired, only seven were seen to have any effect. Some observers attributed this to bad shooting, but there were other possibilities, of which Kell gradually became aware. Upon investigation, he found that many of the shell fuses were faulty. It would later be found that a large quantity of powder had become damp because of the magazine's proximity to the condensing apparatus. Even the supply of powder put up in cartridges and stored in copper tanks, which Semmes assumed was still in good condition, had—he would later admit—

deteriorated "perhaps to the extent of one-third of its strength." The size of the problem would not be known until weeks later. But there was no question that the *Alabama* needed to be put up in dry dock for repairs that would take at least a month.

At midday on June 11, 1864, the *Alabama* dropped anchor at Cherbourg, France. During her twenty-two months at sea, she had overhauled 294 vessels, fifty-five having been burned and ten others released on bond. It was a record that would not be equalled by any other Confederate raider. The presence of the *Alabama* at Cherbourg was an embarrassment to the French authorities there. Since the docks were naval property, only Emperor Napoleon III—away on a vacation— could give the necessary permission for her to be docked. However, Semmes was allowed to land his prisoners and take on coal.

On June 14 the U.S.S. *Kearsarge*, commanded by John A. Winslow, appeared off the breakwater. Semmes had learned the day before of her coming and faced three alternatives: he could continue waiting for permission to dry-dock, he could leave Cherbourg at once without taking on coal, or he could fight. If he made the first choice, he would lose most of his crew, and the Federals would be waiting in greater strength for him to leave. And Semmes—who was actually spoiling for a fight—had no intention of making a getaway. When the *Kearsarge* steamed into view, Lieutenant Kell, glass in hand, stood on the quarter-deck trying to make out her hull, rigging, and battery. He saw a "smooth black hull" but— since her principal guns were pivoted—could learn little of her battery. However, Semmes believed that he had adequate knowledge of the *Kearsarge*, since he had seen her at close range two years earlier at Gibraltar. He was convinced that the *Alabama* was a match for her.

Soon after the arrival of the *Kearsarge*, Semmes summoned Kell to his cabin. Kell, twenty years later, gave a newspaper reporter his recollection of Semmes's words: "I have sent for you to discuss the advisability of fighting the *Kearsarge*. As you know, the arrival of the *Alabama* at this port has been telegraphed to all parts of Europe. Within a few days, Cherbourg will be effectually blockaded by Yankee cruisers. It is uncertain whether or not we shall be permitted to repair the *Alabama* here, and in the meantime, the delay is to our advantage. I think we may whip the *Kearsarge*, the two vessels being of wood and carrying about the same number of men and guns. Besides, Mr. Kell, although the Confederate States government has ordered me to avoid engagements with the enemy's cruisers, I am tired of running from that flaunting rag!''

Kell was not convinced that the decision to fight was a wise one, but—as he later confided to his wife—he "could not remonstrate with Captain Semmes." Instead, he reminded him of their defective powder and of the fact that, at target practice in April, only one in three fuses had been good. Semmes shrugged off Kell's concern, saying, "I will take the chances of one in three." Kell said, "I'll fit the ship for action, sir."

Soon after the *Kearsarge* had arrived, Semmes had sent a statement to Winslow (through the American consul at Cherbourg) of his intention to fight. He received no reply from Winslow, who had earlier been advised by Secretary of the Navy Gideon Welles: "To accept or send a challenge would be to recognize the pirates on terms of equality, elevating them and degrading our own." But Winslow had no intention of allowing the *Alabama* to escape. It was arranged with the American consul that men be stationed each night on the bluff overlooking the harbor. They were to fire signal rockets in the event that Semmes tried to leave port under cover of darkness.

By June 18 Semmes felt that his ship and crew were ready. He refused to be influenced by the "unanimous feeling" of the French port authorities, who advised that he should avoid combat with a "superior force." Kell had been assiduous in preparing the *Alabama*'s battery, magazine, and shell rooms. But when Captain George Terry Sinclair, Confederate naval agent in Europe, arrived at Cherbourg from Paris only hours before the battle, he found the officers looking, "rough, jaded, and worn out." He observed of Semmes: "He seemed to have weighed the matter well in his own mind, and determination was marked in every line of his faded and worn countenance." Before disembarking, Sinclair advised Semmes to keep his ship at a respectful distance from Winslow's powerful eleven-inch pivot guns.

The evening before the fight Kell wrote letters to his wife Blanche and his mother, knowing that they might be his last. He had good reason for gloom, for two of his three young children had died of diphtheria ten months before, and some of his wife's frantic letters from Vineville, Georgia—pleading for his return—had finally reached him.

Sunday, June 19, 1864. The day was bright and cloudless, with only a slight haze. On the *Alabama* the fires had been started shortly after 6 A.M. As Semmes inspected his men, dressed in clean white frocks and blue trousers, he commented on their smart look. He also remarked to Lieutenant Arthur Sinclair: "If the bright, beautiful day is shining for our benefit, we should be happy at the omen." The officers, in their best uniforms, were tense with excitement as they paced the decks. Decks and brass work were immaculate from recent holystoning and polishing, and overhead flew the Confederate ensign. Musing over his prospects, Semmes surprised his fifth lieutenant by asking: "How do you think it will turn out today, Mr. Sinclair?" Sinclair, unaccustomed to being consulted by his captain, replied (as he recalled it later): "I cannot answer the question, sir, but can assure you the crew will do their full duty and follow you to the death." Semmes answered, "Yes, thats true," and began pacing the quarter-deck.

Kell continued to be the busiest officer aboard as he supervised the final preparations for battle. The decks were sanded and tubs of water placed along the spar deck as a precaution against fire. Then the men were sent to their stations.

At about 9:45 A.M. the *Alabama* got under way. She passed in front of the French ironclad frigate *Couronne*, which had started her own fires hours earlier. The *Couronne* would escort the Confederate raider to the three-mile limit to make certain that there was no violation of French territory. As the *Alabama* passed the liner *Napoleon*, the crew of the French vessel manned the rigging and gave three rousing cheers; then their band broke out with "Dixie." Thousands of spectators— Confederate and Union sympathizers alike—were arrayed upon the hillsides, on the breakwater, atop buildings, and aboard vessels. Among those best situated to watch the fight were wealthy Englishman John Lancaster and his family, vacationing aboard their private yacht *Deerhound*. That morning at breakfast the family had held a vote to determine whether to attend church services or watch the fight from their yacht. The children all elected to see the action. In addition to the *Couronne* and the *Deerhound*, a few pilot and fishing boats trailed along. Aboard one pilot boat was the artist Edouard Manet, equipped with pencils, colors, and sketchbook. Manet would produce one of the most accurate representations of the *Alabama-Kearsarge* engagement. A Cherbourg photographer had brought his equipment onto the old church tower over-looking the harbor, and he would take at least one recogniz-able photograph of the fight (but one that, unfortunately, has since been lost).

After the *Alabama* steamed around the breakwater and sighted the *Kearsarge*, three miles away, Semmes headed his ship directly toward the enemy. The starboard battery was prepared for action. Semmes ordered Kell to have all hands piped aft, where the men heard an address by their captain well calculated to arouse them: "Officers and Seamen of the *Alabama!*—You have, at length, another opportunity of meeting the enemy—the first that has been presented to you since you sank the *Hatteras!* In the meantime you have been all over the world, and it is not too much to say, that you have destroyed, and driven for protection under neutral flags, one half of the enemy's commerce, which, at the beginning of the war, covered every sea. This is an achievement of which you may well be proud;, and a grateful country will not be unmindful of it. The name of your ship has become a house-hold word wherever civilization extends. Shall that name be tarnished by defeat? The thing is impossible! Remember that you are in the English Channel, the theatre of so much of the naval glory of our race, and that the eyes of Europe are at this moment, upon you. The flag that floats over you is that of a young Republic, who bids defiance to her enemies, whenever, and wherever found! Show the world that you know how to uphold it! Go to your quarters." The sailors cheered enthusi-astically, shouting "Never! Never!" at mention of defeat.

Aboard the *Kearsarge*, shortly after 10 A.M. the signal bell had just summoned the men for divine service. Captain Winslow, wearing a rather rusty-looking uniform, was open-ing his Bible when the lookout gave the cry, "Here she comes! The *Alabama!*" Winslow closed the Bible and told a cabin boy to bring his side arms. He ordered the drummer to sound quarters. James Wheeler, acting master, ran to the hatchway of the wardroom mess and shouted to the startled officers below, "She's coming! She's coming and heading straight for us!"

Within two minutes all the men were at their stations. It is likely that they recalled Winslow's remark of three days earlier: "My lads, I will give you one hour to take the *Alabama*, and I think you can do it!" Running on a full head of steam, the *Kearsarge* was turned northeastward to open sea. Winslow wanted the battle to be fought well outside the three-mile limit both to avoid any incident with the French authorities and to prevent Semmes from escaping. Aware that he would have a greater advantage at close range, he ordered his guns loaded with five-second shell and sighted for five hundred yards.

After reaching the three-mile limit, the *Couronne* turned and left the *Alabama*, which was still headed toward the *Kearsarge*. Meanwhile, the *Kearsarge* had moved seven miles out to sea before turning around. Then, as the two vessels steamed directly at each other, the decks of the *Kearsage* were sanded. Winslow's plan was to run down the *Alabama* or, "if circumstances did not warrant it, to close in with her."

Semmes, standing on the horse block, the highest point on deck, had his glasses trained on the *Kearsarge*. His two pivot guns were rotated to starboard, as he intended to engage the enemy on that side. Semmes realized that the two 11-inch Dahlgrens on the *Kearsarge* gave the Federals an advantage at close range, while his own hundred-pound Blakely pivot gun was most effective at long range. He had it set for two thousand yards and loaded with solid shot. Lieutenant Richard F. Armstrong—commanding the gun—was instructed to have his gunner aim low, at the hull of the *Kearsarge*. Better to fire too low than too high, Semmes told his men, as the ricochet of their shot over the smooth water would remedy any defect in their vertical aim.

It was now about 11 A.M., forty-five minutes since they had rounded the breakwater. A mile and a quarter's distance from the *Kearsarge*, the *Alabama* sheered, discharging her Blakely. The shot went high. The *Kearsarge*, on full steam, came with such speed that the *Alabama* was able to discharge only two more shots, which were also too high and damaged only the rigging.

Suddenly Winslow sheered off, presenting his starboard battery. The men responded instantly to his order: "All the divisions! Aim low for the waterline! Fire! Load and fire as rapidly as possible!" The thirty-pound rifle gun on the topgallant forecastle, manned by the marine detachment, was the first fired. A shell struck the *Alabama* near her forward port, throwing out splinters and wounding a man at a gun. Another sailor later recalled: "He leaped away with a leg smashed, and another man at the next gun fell dead. The shell caught our slide rack, and I think the man was killed by one of our own shot, which was thrown against him by the shell of the *Kearsarge*." The *Alabama* next received a full broadside. Winslow had intended to run under the *Alabama*'s stern, but Semmes's keeping his broadside exposed prevented this. At five hundred yards both ships were forced into a circular track under full steam, moving in opposite directions and each fighting her starboard side. The positions of the ships reminded one Yankee sailor of "two flies crawling around on the rim of a saucer." They would make seven complete circles before the end of the action, gradually lessening the distance between them by about a hundred yards.

The action was not continuous on both sides. An assistant engineer on the deck of the *Kearsarge* was able to see shot and shell from the *Alabama* "skip like stones ... thrown to ricochet until they burst to windward with a hollow roar, sending aloft a shower of glittering spray." The *Alabama* fired at least two shots for every one of the *Kearsarge*. Although Kell believed that his men "handled their guns beautifully," he would also give due credit to his adversary: "She came into action magnificently." He was standing near the eight-inch pivot gun commanded by Lieutenant Joseph Wilson when an eleven-inch shell exploded through the gun port and—as Kell later recalled—wiped out "like a sponge from a blackboard one-half of the gun's crew." A second shell killed one man and injured others. Then a third shell from the *Kearsarge* struck the gun carriage and spun around on deck without exploding. Seaman Michael Mars, compressor man, quickly picked it up and threw it over the side. Lieutenant Wilson, in a state of shock at being struck by blood and limbs, was in no condition to continue his command. Mars signalled to Kell, requesting permission to clear the deck. Kell bowed his head in assent, and the remains were shovelled into the sea. After the deck had been resanded, the places of Wilson and the dead and wounded were filled on Kell's order by Midshipman Edward Anderson and eight men from a nearby thirty-two-pound gun. They worked coolly and methodically.

About twenty minutes after the action began, the spanker

gaff that flew the *Alabama*'s colors was shot away, and the flag fell to just above the deck. Another flag was immediately raised at the mizzenmast head. At about the same time, a shell from the *Alabama* struck the hull of the *Kearsarge*. The men on the *Alabama* cheered, believing they had "knocked her engines to pieces," before they realized there was little damage.

Positioned on the horse block to best direct the maneuvering of the *Alabama*, Semmes left his gunners with "no particular orders" during the action. However, it was later claimed by his sailors that he offered a reward to the men who could silence the two 11-inch Dahlgrens that were causing such havoc aboard his ship. Semmes is reported to have said of his opponents during the fight: "Confound them, they've been fighting twenty minutes, and they're cool as posts."

Kell distinguished himself throughout the battle, and the captain later praised his "coolness and judgment." Lieutenant Sinclair in his *Two Years on the Alabama*, written many years later, recalled "The Luff's" behavior: "From point to point of the spar-deck in his rapid movement he was directing here, or advising there; now seeing to the transfer of shot, shell, or cartridge; giving his orders to this and that man or officer, as though on dress-muster; occasionally in earnest conversation with Semmes, who occupied the horse-block, glasses in hand, and leaning on the hammock-rail; at times watching earnestly the enemy, and then casting his eye about our ship, as though keeping a careful reckoning of the damage given and received. Nothing seemed to escape his active mind or eye, his commanding figure at all times towering over the heads of those around."

Aboard the *Kearsarge* Captain Winslow stood atop an arms chest on the starboard side of the quarter-deck, half of his body exposed above the rail as he overlooked his own deck while scrutinizing the enemy. He repeatedly gave the order, "Faster, sir! Faster! Four bells!" to Henry McConnell, third engineer, while holding up four fingers signifying "Full speed ahead!" He gave orders in the same manner to Quartermaster William Poole at the helm. In addition to his other duties, Winslow watched the oncoming shells, directing the men near him when to dodge them. Men would drop flat, supporting themselves on hands and toes until the shot had struck or gone "howling" by, then spring up to resume action. Drenched in sweat and covered with powder stains, they were alternately laughing, talking, and cheering. The sponger of one gun was so stained with a "thick coating of burnt powder that it was hard to tell where blue undershirt ended and skin began."

Kell's counterpart on the *Kearsarge*—Executive Officer James S. Thornton—passed from one gun to another advising the crews: "Don't fire unless you get good aim; one shot that hits is better than fifty thrown away." There was a brief pause in the action at one of the pivot guns as both vessels became enveloped in smoke. To an officer's anxious inquiry as to the cause of the delay, the gun captain replied, "Nothing is the matter, sir. She is all ready to give him a dose." "Then why in hell don't you fire?" demanded the officer. "I'll fire, sir, as soon as I get sight" came the unruffled reply. The smoke soon disappeared, and a missile from the gun struck the ocean close to the *Alabama*'s water line, sending a shower of spray into the air. There was even comic relief for the Federals. To the amusement of their shipmates, two old sailors used up a box of ammunition firing a twelve-pound howitzer boat gun.

Among the many observers on shore was Captain Sinclair. Equipped with "splendid glasses," Sinclair noted that, although the *Alabama* fired three shots for every two of her opponent, she usually fired too high. He also noticed a difference in the powder smoke of the two ships: that from the *Alabama* resembled "puffs of heavy steam," while that of the *Kearsarge* was "much lighter." It was obvious to those taking part in the action that there was a difference. As Kell later recalled, "The report from the *Kearsarge*'s battery was clear and sharp, the powder burning like thin vapor, while our guns gave out a dull report, with thick and heavy vapor." Thus was Kell proved correct in his earlier evaluation of the *Alabama*'s powder and the extent of its deterioration. The situation was far more serious than Semmes had believed when he challenged Winslow.

There was no question, moreover, as to the superiority of the gunners on the *Kearsarge*. Kell would admit that the Yankee guns were "served beautifully, being aimed with precision, and deliberate in fire." Captain Winslow noted in his official report: "The firing of the *Alabama* from the first was rapid and wild. Toward the close of the action her firing became better. An *Alabama* sailor admitted: "Our guns were too much elevated, and shot over the *Kearsarge*. The men all fought well, but the gunners did not know how to point and elevate the guns." Austin Quinby, a marine corporal on the *Kearsarge*, noted the effect of this on the Federals. He later wrote in his journal: "When the battle commenced it made our hair stick right up strait but after we had got settled down to work and saw by their rapid and haphazard fire that they were not doing us much damage we took it easy; they would fire when they were in their smoke and when we were enveloped in ours. . . ."

The corporal also observed that in their haste and excitement the *Alabama*'s gunners fired off about six of their ramrods, resembling "black meteors with their long tails." Of the more than three hundred shot and shell fired by the *Alabama* during the hour-long engagement, only twenty-eight struck the *Kearsarge*. On the Federal side, the *Kearsarge* fired 173 shot and shell (mostly shell), a large number finding their mark and accounting for the "fearful work" of destruction. No grape or canister was used, although Winslow had a large quantity on hand.

Although the shells of the *Kearsarge* were taking a heavy toll in killed and wounded, the *Alabama* remained on the offensive, her captain waiting for the lucky shot that would cripple his opponent. At length, his forward pivot-gun crew set a hundred-pound shell smashing under the counter of the *Kearsarge*, glancing along until it lodged in the rudderpost. As the *Kearsarge* trembled from the shock, the sailors on the *Alabama* cheered loudly. Here was their lucky shot. However, their cheers died when the anticipated explosion failed to occur. For Semmes and Kell, the failure was bitter. To his dying day each would believe that faulty powder or a defective fuse had prevented the shell from exploding. They were convinced that this shell alone could have sunk the *Kearsarge*. At the very least, they believed, it should have made the rudder inoperable and thus influenced the outcome, since the *Alabama* was still very much in action. Actually, however, if the shell had exploded at first contact—when it was supposed to— it would have damaged the ship's counter, some twenty feet from the sternpost.

John Bickford, a first loader at one of the *Kearsarge*'s pivot guns, had a different version of the failure of so many shells to explode: "It's true that quite a number failed to explode, but it wasn't the fault of the shells. It was the fault of the excited men who fired them." According to Bickford, almost all of the unexploded shells from the *Alabama* still had on the lead caps that should have been ripped off by the gun loaders. As he explained in articles published years later in the Boston *Journal* and the Boston *Evening Transcript*, unless the lead cap was removed to expose the fuse primer—set to explode in so many seconds—it was impossible for a shell to explode. The Yankee from Gloucester, Massachusetts—afterward awarded the Medal of Honor for "marked coolness and good conduct" during the fight—told of his experience with one such shell: "I was standing on the starboard side of the gun, with my foot directly on the planksheer, when all of a sudden I heard the whir of a shell, a Blakely, and instantly my foot got a jar that seemed to fill it with pins and needles. That . . . shell had struck the planksheer and gone way through it, at least so far that it exposed its primer, or where it should be, but I saw that the patch was still there on the shell. . . .

"Well, of course all the gun crew jumped back, looking for an explosion. I just turns round and says to 'em, 'Never mind that, boys, it won't go off, because they forgot to take the patch off.' I stayed where I was, loading the gun, and all the fellows jumped right to work again."

A shell from the *Alabama*'s Blakely gun caused the only casualties on the *Kearsarge*. It passed through the starboard bulwarks below the main rigging, exploding on the quarter-deck and injuring three sailors at the after pivot gun. William Gowin, the most seriously injured, refused assistance and dragged himself to the forward hatch, where he was helped below by the surgeon. Gowin—who had an arm amputated—died within the week, becoming the only fatality aboard the *Kearsarge*.

The twenty-eight shot and shell which struck the *Kearsarge* did no major damage. Twelve struck the hull, while eight were believed to have damaged the rigging. Two of the boats were put out of commission and one of the sails was badly torn. A shell entered the funnel of the *Kearsarge* and exploded, tearing out a space about three feet in diameter and throwing metal about the deck. A piece of the shell passed through a water dipper that a thirsty fireman had just raised to his lips. A hundred-pound shell ploughed across the roof of the engine-room skylight, coming within fourteen inches of Engineer McConnell before passing harmlessly overboard through the port rail.

During the latter part of the fight, the *Alabama* received the full effect of accurate and deadly fire. Seaman James Hart, carrying a shell to his gun, was blown to pieces. The "first serious disaster" to the ship was the destruction of her rudder. For the remainder of the action, steering could be done only by using tackles. At about the same time—forty-five minutes after the battle had commenced—an eleven-inch shell passed through the starboard side, emerging and exploding on her port side and tearing great gaps in her timbers and planking. To the delight of the *Kearsarge* sailors, it "raised the very devil." A coal-bunker bulkhead caved in, filling the fire room and almost burying the men there under coal. With only two boilers left working, the *Alabama*'s steam pressure was greatly reduced.

Filled with smoke and steam and with gaping holes in her hull, the *Alabama*—careening heavily to starboard—was in no condition to continue fighting. It was either escape, surrender, or be destroyed. The men were ordered to lie low, as it was feared that Winslow would now order a raking fire. But Semmes was not ready to surrender. He believed that by shifting the weight of his battery from starboard to port he might raise the shot holes above the water line. The ship was now five miles from the coast and with luck might make the three-mile limit. He gave the order: "Mr. Kell, as soon as our head points to the French coast in our circuit of action, shift your guns to port and make all sail for the coast."

The helm was righted, the fore trysail sheets and two jibs hoisted, and the evolution executed successfully. At the same time, the pivot guns—after being cleared of the dead—were shifted to port with only a brief pause in the action. Kell appeared at the skylight above the engine room and in a "voice of thunder" shouted to the men below: "What is the matter in the engine room? Put on steam!" Engineers William Brooks and Matt O'Brien, covered with sweat and coal dust, answered that the *Alabama* carried all the steam she could manage without blowing up. Then reconsidering, O'Brien declared, "Let her have the steam; we had better blow her to hell than to let the Yankees whip us!" But it would take more than the extra twenty-five pounds of steam to save the *Alabama*. Winslow had anticipated Semmes's intentions and steamed across his adversary's bow. He was now in a position to rake her.

Aboard the *Alabama* none could doubt the seriousness of the situation. An officer, looking out a port and seeing the water rushing into the gangway at every roll, was certain that the *Alabama*'s "last moments were close at hand." A sailor later recalled: "Our men were then very fatigued and many disabled and wounded. We still fired as well as possible from the port side, though we knew the day was lost." O'Brien came on deck to report that the rapidly rising water was almost flush with the furnace fires. He found Semmes on the horse block with a handkerchief tied around his hand to cover a painful although superficial wound. Semmes listened in silence, then ordered: "Return to your duty!" The engineers were now certain that they would go down with the ship. Engineer John Pundt said bitterly: "Well, I suppose 'Old Beeswax' has made up his mind to drown us like a lot of rats! Here, Matt! Take off my boots!" On deck there was some confusion, "though nothing like a panic, excepting on the part of one or two."

Semmes ordered Kell to find out how long the ship would float. Going below, Kell found the sight "appalling." The holes in the hull were "large enough to admit a wheel barrow." Surgeon David Llewellyn was at his post, but the wounded man on his table had been swept away by a shell. Kell returned to the deck and reported that the ship could not remain afloat for more than ten minutes. Semmes, apparently unaware that his colors had again been shot down, gave the order: "Then, sir, cease firing, shorten sail, and haul down the colors; it will never do in this nineteenth century for us to go down, and the decks covered with our gallant wounded." As there was no white flag available, a man on the spanker boom held up a makeshift one—the white portion of the Confederate ensign. The officers and men on the *Kearsarge* would later claim that when they observed the white flag and the firing of a lee gun they ceased firing, but that two more shots were then fired from the *Alabama*, one from the forward pivot gun. Unconvinced that his enemy had surrendered, Winslow cried out: "Give it to them again, boys; they are playing us a trick!" Each of his gun captains obeyed the order instantly, firing five volleys into the *Alabama*. Two 11-inch shells struck the coal bunker, throwing up coal dust as high as the yardarm. Aboard the doomed raider, Kell cried out: "Stand to your quarters, men. If we must be sunk after our colors are down, we will go to the bottom with every man at his post!" And among the sailors the word was passed, "There's no quarter for us!" But when the white flag was again raised on the spanker boom, all firing ceased. Semmes then ordered Kell: "Dispatch an officer to the *Kearsarge* and ask that they send boats to save our wounded—ours are disabled."

Finding the dinghy undamaged, Kell put Master's Mate George Fullam in charge of her with instructions to surrender the ship and request assistance. Marine officer Beckett Howell, a nonswimmer, was allowed to take an oar as one of the crew. When Kell discovered that another boat was only slightly disabled, he directed the removal of the wounded to it. Among these was Seaman James King—"Connemara"—a troublemaker who had caused Kell many a headache since shipping on the *Alabama* at Singapore. As Kell stood briefly over the mortally wounded sailor, King seized his hand and kissed it. Amazed, Kell could not help thinking of the numerous times King had been punished on his orders. Lieutenant Wilson and Surgeon Francis Galt were placed in charge of the boat and the wounded taken away, for the ship was settling fast. Winslow—who remembered how the *Hatteras* had been lured to destruction by Semmes—was apparently uncertain whether the *Alabama* was actually sinking. He continued to wait for more evidence. Only after Fullam had come aboard (after first deliberately dropping his sword over the side of the dinghy) was Winslow aware of the situation.

Fullam delivered his message; then, looking up and down the deck, he asked where the dead and wounded were. When told that only three men had been wounded, he exclaimed, "My God, and it's a slaughter house over there!" (He would later be astonished to learn that actually only nine men had been killed on the *Alabama* during the combat.) When Lieutenant Wilson came on board the *Kearsarge*, his appearance and statements seemed to confirm Fullam's account of the "slaughter": he was covered with blood from the casualties at his gun early in the fight, and he still believed that sixteen of the seventeen men of his gun crew had been killed. Wilson offered Winslow his sword, but Winslow graciously refused it.

Aboard the sinking vessel Kell gave the order to abandon ship and directed the crew to find a spar or whatever else might assist them in keeping afloat. As the men stripped to their

underwear, Kell urged them over the side. He then returned
to the stern, where Semmes, his steward Bartelli, and a few
other sailors were preparing to abandon ship. They were
almost level with the ocean. Seaman Mars assisted Semmes as
he removed his coat and boots, while the sail maker, Henry
Alcott, helped Kell to pull off his boots. Semmes still wore his
cap (turned inside out), trousers, and vest, while Kell had
stripped to his shirt and underdrawers. The Luff was able to
save only his watch, which he had tied to his waistband with a
lock of his wife's hair. Both men had unceremoniously dis-
carded their swords while undressing. Seaman Mars—one of
the best swimmers on the ship—was entrusted with Semmes's
dispatches and accounts. Unfortunately, no one knew that
Bartelli, who remained at his captain's side, could not swim.

It was now every man for himself. Wearing a life preserver, Semmes slipped into the sea, followed by Kell, who held
onto a grating for support. Kell later wrote that the water "was
like ice, and after the excitement of battle it seemed doubly
cold." The men swam off as best they could to escape the
vortex of the sinking ship. As the *Alabama* "settled stern
foremost, launching her bows high in the air," Kell turned for
a final look. Years later, in an interview for the Atlanta
Constitution, he recalled his feelings at the sight: "As the
gallant vessel, the most beautiful I ever beheld, plunged down
to her grave, I had it on my tongue to call to the men who
were struggling in the water to give three cheers for her, but
the dead that were floating around me and the deep sadness I
felt at parting with the noble ship that had been my home so
long deterred me."

Kell's grating was not adequate, and he found the waves
breaking over his head "distressingly uncomfortable." Notic-
ing a makeshift float of empty shell boxes, Kell shouted to a
sailor, a strong swimmer, to examine it. The man called out:
"It is the doctor, sir, and he is dead." Llewellyn, like Bartelli,
had been unable to swim, a fact of which his shipmates were
unaware. Eight others also drowned before help came. Even
good swimmers like Kell found it difficult to remain afloat.
Seeing his senior officer weakening, Midshipman Eugene
Maffitt began to disengage his own life preserver, gasping out,
"Mr. Kell, you are so exhausted, take this life preserver." Kell,
knowing that the boy was prepared to sacrifice himself, refused. After what seemed like hours, but actually was only

about thirty minutes, Kell heard a voice cry out, "Here's our Luff!" An *Alabama* sailor in one of the *Deerhound*'s small boats had recognized the expansive beard floating on the water. Kell was seized by the back of his neck and lifted into the boat.

Together with several of his crew, Semmes had already been rescued by the boat from Lancaster's yacht. Stretched out on the stern sheets "as pallid as death," he opened his eyes and gave his uninjured hand to Kell, who inquired, "Are you hurt?" "A little," came the answer. The hand injury was indeed slight, but he was suffering from exhaustion. They were brought immediately to the *Deerhound*, where Kell learned the identity of the yacht and its owner. To Kell's surprise, he found Fullam aboard. Winslow had allowed him to help pick up survivors, and by not returning to the *Kearsarge*, the master's mate had cheated the Federals of several prisoners, including the brother-in-law of the Confederate President. From Fullam came the report that the *Kearsarge* had been protected by "chain armor." He had seen the places where the *Alabama*'s shot had torn the cover planking away, indenting and breaking the chain beneath.

The rescued men were made comfortable. Semmes had the jacket of an English lieutenant loaned him by Lancaster, while Kell was given that gentleman's carpet slippers and a pair of his trousers. Lancaster asked Semmes to what part of France he wished to be taken. He smiled at the reply, "Oh, any part of Great Britain."

As the Confederate raider settled stern first, Lieutenant Thornton aboard the *Kearsarge* passed the word, "Silence, boys." Seaman Bickford told his gun crew that one could yell when licking a man "but not when you had him down." Meanwhile, the survivors from the *Alabama* continued to be picked up, and they were told that they were prisoners of war and would be treated humanely. One of them, mistaking Winslow for the *Kearsarge*'s steward, asked him for whiskey. Identifying himself, Winslow gave him some whiskey and added, "My man, I am sorry for you." And pointing to his colors, he said, "That is the flag you should have been under."

Suddenly, the *Deerhound* was observed to be "stealing away." Bob Strahan, captain of a thirty-two-pounder, turned his gun directly upon her. However, Winslow sent an officer to order him not to fire. As the *Deerhound* steamed away, the men waited in vain for the order to stop her. Years after the war, Executive Officer Thornton told an interviewer: "I was waiting impatiently for the order to come to fire on the English yacht which had rescued Semmes from his sinking ship. I never for a moment doubted that such an order would be given. But it was not, and I felt so indignant that I almost lost self-control. I felt for awhile that it was a barren victory and that we had spent our powder all for nothing."

Winslow later claimed he did not know the *Deerhound* was escaping; he refused at first to believe "she could be guilty of so disgraceful an act. . . ." Although there is no reason to doubt Winslow's statement, the ship's surgeon declared, "Probably not another person on board the *Kearsage* was of the same opinion. . . . Captain Winslow alone is responsible for the escape of Semmes."

Winslow was generous in victory. Calling his sailors to muster, he read them a prayer and announced: "We have won the battle without loss of life; God must have been on our side. The *Alabama*'s men have been in the water, and you are requested to give them some of your clothing and report any expense to me. These men have surrendered, and I want you to use them as brother shipmates. Your dinner will be served out to you. Share it with them." When the grog tub was brought up, all were allowed to refresh themselves.

Meanwhile, as the *Deerhound* steamed toward Southampton, the Confederates on board were grateful to have escaped death or imprisonment. When the officers tried to thank Lancaster, he merely told them, "Gentlemen, you have no need to give me any special thanks; I should have done exactly the same for the other people if they had needed it."

Semmes's career as a captain on the high seas ended with the sinking of the *Alabama*. He returned to the Confederacy early in 1865 and—promoted in rank to admiral—commanded the ironclad vessels of the small James River Squadron during the last weeks of the war. When the capture of the Confederate capital appeared imminent, he ordered his ships to be destroyed, and then—appointed a brigadier general—he led his sailors as a military unit following the evacuation of Richmond. After the war he was imprisoned by Federal authorities but was released after four months without being brought to trial. Before his death in 1877 he produced his memoirs of the war years—*Service Afloat*—intended to vindicate himself and his cause from his enemies' charges of treason and piracy.

Winslow received promotion to commodore from a government long embarrassed by its failure to apprehend and destroy the *Alabama*. The victory was the zenith of a long naval career, and it assured Winslow of his place in history. He died in 1873, three years after his promotion to admiral.

The battle off Cherbourg was refought with pen and ink—often with great vindictiveness—during the succeeding decades. Accusations and counteraccusations by the survivors would all but obscure the truth of what happened on that June day when the *Alabama* steamed out to meet the *Kearsage*—and her destiny.

—April 1972

THE BURNING
OF CHAMBERSBURG

by LIVA BAKER

It was time, said General Early, for "some act of retaliation."

Colonel William E. Peters stared at his commanding officer incredulously. Had he heard the order correctly? On whose authority was it given? he asked. Peters, thirty-five years old and a veteran of three years of fighting, had proved his bravery often enough; he had two wounds to show for it. But there were limits beyond which, even in war, he would not—or could not—go.

The general showed Peters the written order signed by his own superior. The colonel read it quickly. His response was unhesitating, calm, and resolute. No, he told the general, he would not obey. He would sooner break his sword and throw it away than make war on defenseless women and children.

July 30, 1804, was a breezeless, sultry day in Chambersburg, Pennsylvania, a fair-sized town made up mostly, during these war years, of women, children, and old men. Lying about twenty miles north of the Mason-Dixon line and never more than a night's ride from the Confederate lines as the war raged up and down the Shenandoah Valley, Chambersburg had been raided, occupied, liberated, and reoccupied since the war had begun in April 1861. Horses, wagons, and grain had been appropriated frequently and freely; warehouses holding government stores had been destroyed; merchants had had to spend a good deal of time and money shipping their goods to Philadelphia for safekeeping whenever occupation seemed imminent, then shipping them back again when the danger had passed; the town's womenfolk had nursed hundreds of wounded soldiers—both Confederate and Union—following

165

the battles of Antietam and Gettysburg; and, of course, most of the eligible young men had been taken into the Union Army.

Nevertheless, Chambersburg's involvement in the war had been superficial thus far. Hardship, yes, but not much more. The Confederate occupations had inflicted no casualties among the townspeople, and the town itself remained relatively intact. Indeed, with some rare exceptions, the soldiers' behavior on these previous occasions had been almost courtly; supplies had been requisitioned apologetically; the burning of government stores had been blamed on military necessity; the Rebel soldiers had paid for the hats, socks, and gloves they had chosen in local shops, and their officers had been entertained in the homes of prominent citizens. Confederate General Robert E. Lee himself, while camped just outside the town in Messersmith's woods on his way to Gettysburg the previous summer, had issued a general order reminding his troops that although they were in enemy country, "we make war only upon armed men" and "we cannot take vengeance for the wrongs our people have suffered without lowering ourselves in the eyes of all." Lee's order prohibited "unnecessary or wanton injury to private property" and promised arrest and summary punishment to all offenders.

But that was a year ago, a brighter day when, prior to the Battle of Gettysburg, the Confederates had marched into town triumphant, conquerors in enemy country, well able to afford magnanimity toward the conquered. Now, in the summer of 1864, that time of self-confidence and high spirits seemed dim and distant. Its resources, men, and morale almost exhausted, the Confederacy itself was only months from final defeat. In addition Lee, following his defeat at Gettysburg, had been soundly thrashed in the Southern press for not leaving the country he had invaded in ruins; an informant had advised a Chambersburg resident: ". . . if ever the Confederates come again they will plunder and destroy; and my advice to you is, if ever you hear of their coming get everything out of their way that you can."

What was to happen in Chambersburg on the next to last day of July was the culmination of a series of escalating acts of retaliation for previous atrocities. Some months before, Major General David Hunter of the Union Army, operating in Virginia, had been harassed by bushwhackers and guerrillas who plundered wagon trains and assassinated Union soldiers. Once, in Charles Town, West Virginia, six of his soldiers had been found strapped to a fence, their throats cut from ear to ear. Defenseless against the marauders, who posed as farmers and tradesmen by day and conducted their deadly forays by night, General Hunter distributed through the Valley of Virginia a circular in May 1864, threatening retribution: ". . . for every train fired upon, or soldier of the Union wounded or assassinated by bushwhackers in any neighborhood within the reach of my command, the houses and other property of every secession sympathizer residing within a circuit of five miles from the place of outrage, shall be destroyed by fire. . . ." As good as his word, by July 1864, Hunter had burned, with particular savagery, the homes of several prominent Virginians and the Virginia Military Institute. As the guerrilla tactics of the Confederates had invited Hunter's retaliation with an increase in ferocity, Hunter's own escalation evoked a similar response.

Tough, tobacco-chewing Lieutenant General Jubal Anderson Early of the Confederate Army was not one to shrink from such a task. He himself had pursued Hunter through the Valley of Virginia and had witnessed "evidence of the destruction wantonly committed by [Hunter's] troops under his orders." Camped near Martinsburg, West Virginia, following his attack on Washington itself in mid-July, Early heard details of Hunter's most recent outrages in Virginia. He decided, Early said, that "it was time to try and stop this mode of warfare by some act of retaliation."

He ordered Brigadier General John McCausland, with his own cavalry brigade plus that of Brigadier General Bradley T. Johnson and a battery of artillery, to march on Chambersburg, to demand $100,000 in gold or $500,000 in greenbacks as compensation for three specific houses that Hunter's Union troops had burned. "In default of the payment of this money," Early's written order declared, the town "is directed to be laid in ashes in retaliation for the burning of said houses, and other houses of citizens of Virginia by Federal authorities." Early had no particular grudge against Chambersburg; the town was selected, he later wrote, "because it was the only one of any consequence accessible to my troops, and *for no other reason*."

Marching day and night, snatching what little sleep they

could on horseback, General McCausland and his two cavalry brigades reached the outskirts of Chambersburg about three o'clock on the morning of Saturday, July 30. Colonel William Peters and his 21st Virginia Cavalry were among the advance forces. Resistance had been slight—a small force of Federal cavalry at Clear Spring had been driven off, another small force at Mercersburg also routed. At the fringe of Chambersburg a small unit of Union soldiers with one piece of artillery held the Confederates in check for about two hours. When daybreak disclosed the relative sizes of the two forces—twenty-six hundred Confederates to a hundred Union troops—the Northerners retreated through the town, "being careful," a Union officer reported later, "not to fire a shot within its limits in order that there should be no excuse for firing buildings or committing any barbarities upon the people."

The main part of the two Confederate brigades formed a battle line on hills commanding the town. The artillery was brought up, and three shells were fired into the town, inflicting neither casualties nor damage. When the shots were not answered, small squads of skirmishers immediately but cautiously advanced on foot through the alleys and streets of Chambersburg.

The streets clear, Colonel Peters was ordered to follow with his 21st Virginia Cavalry. Still unaware of the purpose of the raid, Peters obeyed quickly and efficiently. More cavalry detachments followed. By 6 A.M. Chambersburg had been occupied once again by the enemy, some five hundred of them, including the commanding general, John McCausland. The rest of the Confederate force remained camped outside the town.

Accounts of what happened next differ considerably in their details, because, no doubt, of the confusion, the noise, and the perspectives of the various people involved. McCausland's account is as reliable as any for the general outline of events: "I at once went into the city with my staff and requested some of the citizens to inform the city authorities that I wanted to see them. I also sent my staff through the town to locate the proper officials and inform them that I had a proclamation for their consideration. Not one could be found. I then directed the proclamation to be read to as many citizens as were near me, and asked them to hunt up their town officers, informing them I would wait until they could either find the proper authorities, or by consultation among themselves, determine what they would do. Finally, I informed them that I would wait six hours, and if they would then comply with the requirements [pay the ransom of $100,000 in gold or $500,000 in greenbacks], their town would be safe; but if not, it would be destroyed, in accordance with my orders from General Early."

McCausland's accounts omits any description of the behavior of the troops, behavior that Chambersburg residents later testified was barbarous from the moment the Confederates entered the town. According to witnesses, plunder began immediately at Mr. Paxton's shoe and hat store, followed by looting at liquor stores and in private homes. Residents were stopped on the streets at pistol point and divested of watches, purses, and clothing.

Nevertheless, the ransom was not paid. Some townspeople were willing to pay it; others were not. Some laughed at the demand, incredulous that the Southerners, whom they had known previously as the politest of enemies, would actually carry out their threat to burn the town. Some believed Federal forces were near and would protect them at the last moment—a faith that proved unfounded. Others protested that there was not that much money in the town, for upon learning of the Confederate approach the previous day, the bankers had discreetly fled, taking the money with them. Still others simply defied the invaders, saying they would not pay five cents even if they had it.

How long McCausland gave the townspeople before he ordered the town burned is a matter of dispute. The general claimed he waited the promised six hours; other reports set the firing time at two to four hours; one witness claimed the smoke was rising even while the general was negotiating with Chambersburg officials. In any case, the ransom was not forthcoming, and McCausland ordered his men to burn the town.

Colonel Peters was directed to move his men to the courthouse, arm them with torches, and fire the town. Peters, according to one Confederate military historian, was a man of "imperturbable courage. He couldn't be shaken. Earthquakes, tornadoes, electric storms couldn't move him. He would have stopped and asked, 'What next?' if the earth were opening beneath him and the mountains falling on him." He had joined the Confederate Army as a private on the day after the Virginia Convention had voted for secession and had risen to the rank of colonel. But all the ugliness he had seen over the past three years had not deprived him of civilized reaction, and he was about to show that all his courage had not been exhausted in cavalry charges.

He went to McCausland, as the general recounted the episode, and "asked me if it was being done by my orders. I showed him the order of General Early, which he refused to obey, declaring that he would break his sword and throw it away before he would obey it, as there were only defenseless women and children in Chambersburg." Upon hearing this, McCausland ordered Peters to collect his regiment and withdraw from the town, which he did. The general then had him put under arrest for insubordination.

There were other Confederates who, while not declaring outright their intent to disobey, helped civilians to escape. Some of the men obeyed only reluctantly. Most of the Confederates, however—hungry, weary, far from home, ill-equipped, badly armed, mounted on worn-out horses, and having drunk liberally from the contents of looted liquor stores—carried out their orders with abandon and, they believed, complete justification. "That it was right I never questioned, nor do I now," one participant wrote years later. "The responsibility rests on Gen'l Hunter."

A warehouse was the first to go, followed by the courthouse and town hall. General McCausland rode with an aide through the streets, pointing to all the flames and smoke, notifying the residents that his threat had not been an idle one. The main part of the town was enveloped in flames within ten minutes.

The Confederates formed into squads and fanned out from the center of town. For two hours they rushed from house to house, burst open the doors with planks and axes, rifled every room for jewelry, silverware, and money, hacked up the furniture for kindling, and put torches to bedding and bureaus or lit balls of cotton saturated with kerosene. Some people were given time to collect a few belongings before their houses were fired; others were not. Describing the scene, a Confederate captain said: "It was impossible at first to convince the people, the females particularly, that their fair city would [be] burnt; even when the torch was applied, they seemed dazed. Terror was depicted in every face, women, refined ladies and girls running through the streets wild with fright seeking some place of safety." Then he added soberly: "I hadn't bargained for this, but such it was."

One old woman was told by a Confederate squad to run, that her house was on fire. Her reply that she had not been able to walk for three years was met with curses, and one of the soldiers poured powder under her chair, saying *he* would teach her to walk. Neighbors later rescued her.

A squad of Confederates demanded their breakfast of the local schoolmaster. "Did you ever teach niggers?" asked a cavalryman.

"Yes, sir," the schoolmaster replied.

"Damn him, fire his house," came the quick command.

The widow of a Union soldier begged for mercy. In response soldiers set fire to her house and robbed her of her money.

Not all the Confederates behaved so savagely. Reminded by a woman that she had fed him during a raid in 1862 and nursed him after the Battle of Gettysburg, one soldier shrank from firing the woman's house. A Confederate surgeon wept when he saw the flames rise and spent the morning helping victims escape. Another Confederate surgeon gave his horse to a woman to carry what belongings she could out of town. When asked who his commanding officer was, he answered, "Madam, I am ashamed to say that General McCausland is my commander!" A Confederate captain put his men to work extinguishing fires in one section of town. Another officer unbuckled his sword in disgust and left it in a Chambersburg house, where it was discovered later in the ruins.

Reactions among the townspeople varied, too. Most simply fled as fast as they could with as many belongings as they could carry to the cemetery and fields around the town, where they sat and stared unbelieving at the smoke issuing from their former homes. Others were defiant; one old woman gave a soldier such a thrashing with a broom that he hastily retreated from her house. In return for promises of amnesty a few people paid small ransoms; in some cases the promises were kept, in some cases the houses were burned anyway.

And, of course, there were those who simply added another few lines to the story of retribution. A Confederate officer, isolated from his comrades by his love for plunder, was captured by a mob of angry townspeople. Fired at and wounded, he tried to hide in the cellar of a burning house. He begged for his life, but he was shot down without mercy.

Miraculously, casualties were few during the burning of Chambersburg. Flames licked the couches of invalids, but somehow all were rescued. Children ran through the streets frightened and directionless, but in the end were reunited with their families. Damage to the town itself amounted to four hundred buildings burned, 274 of them homes, at an estimated value of about $1,500,000.

The Confederates left Chambersburg by 1 P.M. A Union officer's dispatch described their departure as "going north, taking McCausland with them drunk." Within a few hours Union troops marched through the town in pursuit, and a battle followed on August 7 at Moorefield, Virginia, during which the Confederates were badly beaten by Union soldiers shouting "Remember Chambersburg! and "Surrender, you house-burning villains!"

Colonel Peters was never brought to trial for his insubordination. Under pressure of the Union troops' pursuit, he was released from arrest and at Moorefield went into battle again at the head of his regiment. General McCausland being absent, his second in command, General Bradley T. Johnson, ordered Peters to hold off the Union cavalry while he, Johnson, went to get support. But the Union cavalry could not be held off, and the force of the attack "carried off the Twenty-first Virginia like chaff before the whirlwind." Peters was shot through the chest; dispatches following the battle described him as "mortally wounded."

Following the battle at Moorefield, General Johnson described the demoralization of his men in his report: "It is due to myself and the cause I serve to remark on the outrageous conduct of the troops on this expedition. . . . Every crime in the catalogue of infamy has been committed. . . . At Chambersburg, while the town was in flames, a quartermaster, aided and directed by a field officer, exacted ransom of individuals for their houses, holding the torch in terror over the house until it was paid . . . the grand spectacle of a national retaliation was reduced to a miserable huckstering for greenbacks. After the order was given to burn the town of Chambersburg and before, drunken soldiers paraded the streets in every possible disguise and paraphernalia, pillaging and plundering and drunk. As the natural consequence, lawlessness in Pennsylvania and Maryland reproduced itself in Virginia. . . . had there been less plunder there would have been more fighting at Moorefield. . . ."

Whether or not General Early approved of his troops' behavior during this expedition, he never regretted his order to burn Chambersburg. In his memoirs Early wrote: "This was in strict accordance with the laws of war and was a just retaliation. I gave the order on my own responsibility. . . . It afforded me no pleasure to subject non-combatants to the rigors of war, but I felt that I had a duty to perform to the people for whose homes I was fighting and I endeavored to perform it, however disagreeable it might be."

As for Colonel Peters, despite his wound he survived, and after the war he returned to his peacetime profession as a teacher of Latin. He joined the University of Virginia faculty, and a school hall is named in his honor. Shortly before he retired in 1902, Peters's wife wrote: "The event I am proudest of in the long and useful life of my husband is that of his courageous refusal to make war on helpless women and children. . . . Too well he knew that obedience to the cruel edict of war against Chambersburg . . . would mean but a repetition of the dreadful scenes of looting, rapine and desolation that had followed the burning of Southern towns by the northern soldiery. Hence, as a Virginian, soldier and gentleman, he preferred the imminent personal risk of a violation of the command of his superior officer, to being made individually responsible for a fate so direful overtaking the defenceless inhabitants of the doomed city."

—August 1973

THE HIT-AND-RUN RAID

by CHARLES MORROW WILSON

St. Albans, Vermont, and the Great (or not so great) Bank Robbery.

Wednesday, October 19, 1864, began as a normally quiet day in the normally quiet county seat village of St. Albans, on Lake Champlain, in far upstate Vermont. For the most part the shopkeepers were refiling their shelves and emptying out their cash drawers following a golden Tuesday. The day before, a skirmish force of Army horse buyers had completed and paid cash for a county-wide roundup of about seven hundred Vermont Morgans, lightest, toughest, and therefore most coveted for Union cavalry horses.

The three local banks were loaded, but not with customers. Lewis Cross, St. Alban's pioneer photographer, was moderately busy, but only because he kept the Main Saloon on the side, and local horse traders were in an elbow-lifting mood. Miss Beattie's Millinery Shop was also fairly busy. Wives and daughters of the local horse traders were seeing to that.

On the whole, local manpower was in perceptibly short supply. At least forty of the relatively active males of the community had left for Montpelier, where the Vermont legislature was opening. Most of the rest of the lawyers and other "court-housers" were away at Burlington where the supreme court was in session.

It is a good bet that not one of the village absentees knew or even suspected what he was missing. As a matter of fact, he was missing one of the most astounding and audacious chapters in the whole astounding and audacious history of the Civil

War. He was missing the sight of upwards of a score of Confederate soldiers turned bank robbers in line of military duty, thereby defying the entire Union Army while aggressively invading farthest New England. Any absent citizen of St. Albans, Vermont, was also missing a front-row seat at the climax of the most unusual drama of the war.

The exceptional man shortage in St. Albans had been relieved in some small part by the quiet arrival of twenty or more normally dressed male strangers, all young (twenty-three was the average age of the group), courteous, and friendly; most of them tall, reasonably handsome, and decidedly winsome.

Plenty of strangers, including attractive young men, sojourned in St. Albans, Vermont. They still do. The lake fishing and the hunting were and still are above average. The same is true of the village restaurants and public houses, which continue to meet the needs of hunters and fishermen. Any way you take it, including by way of Lewis Cross's picture files, St. Albans of 1864 looked considerably like St. Albans of the present century. The arrival of the group of sportsmen made no particular stir.

The first three of the nice young men had drifted into St. Albans on October 10, put up at the Tremont House where the spokesman signed the register as Bennett Young, gave his age as twenty-one, and explained that he and his companions were from St. Johns, Canada, and had come for a sporting vacation. One of his companions was a strong-featured, hook-nosed youngster who gave his name as Samuel Simpson Gregg. The other was a slender, pallid young man who introduced himself as the Reverend Mr. Cameron, and promptly pulled a heavy Bible from his side-satchel valise (all of the visitors carried these rather peculiar valises on shoulder straps) and began reading to the occupants of the boarding-house parlor. The charitable lady boarders took him to be a theology student. They agreed he was a little touched.

On the same day two others registered at the American Hotel, half a block down Main Street. One was a still-beardless youngster who signed in as George Scott from Canada, and registered also for his companion, Joe McGrorty, who was in his thirties and was known to the others as "Grandpappy." The following day three more personable young men checked in at the same hotel. There was nothing unusual about them either, except that they too wore the side valises, on straps swung over the right shoulder.

All were the friendly and inquiring kind, and apparently a bit inclined toward solitude. They strolled out alone, visiting the banks, saloon, restaurant, stores, gun shops, and livery stables, shaking hands, chatting much and buying little. Oddly enough, but always in a nice way, they sought to borrow firearms—for hunting, naturally. Even when refused they were engagingly nice about it, and usually expressed a gunlover's desire to have a friendly look at the host's gun shelf. Their interest in horses was at least as ardent. All seemed reverently interested in horseflesh and local ownership thereof. This was and still is a good way to win friends and influence people in Vermont, where Justin Morgan and his neighbors had already started the only original American breed of horse. (We aren't talking of "strains"; the Vermont Morgan is still the only American-made breed of horse.)

On the busy Tuesday before the historic Wednesday, two more of the friendly young strangers came to breakfast at the Tremont. Four more joined them for lunch—dinner is the word in Vermont. On the cloudy Wednesday just mentioned, the noon train from Montreal brought in several more of the engaging male visitors. Two more arrived by hack. Altogether, there were at least twenty of them, perhaps a few more; the exact number is hard to pin down.

Bank-closing time (3 P.M.) ended the quiet for this day, and for many days to come.

At the St. Albans Bank on Main Street (all three of the town's banks were on two adjacent blocks of Main Street), Chief Teller C. N. Bishop was sitting by the front window counting and sorting the currency when five men strolled in the door. Two were unknown to him, but Bishop recognized the other three as friendly newcomers who had previously introduced themselves as Tom Collins, Marcus Spurr, and Turner Teavis. He also recognized that the latter two were leveling oversize Colt revolvers embarrassingly close to his head. He noted too (at least according to the contemporary report of Edmund Royce) that the wretches brought with them a rank atmosphere of alcoholic fumes.

Teller Bishop dashed for the directors' room, where Martin Seymour, the other clerk, was working on the books. The two tried to lock the door. But the invaders bore down on them, seized the tellers by the throats, and announced that they were Confederate soldiers, prepared to take the town and its money. While two of the Confederates held pistols against the tellers' heads, the other three went money hunting. One scooped the banknotes that Bishop had been counting on the open table into his side pocket, meanwhile overlooking the counter drawer, which held $9,000 in gold certificates. Another pulled open the bottom drawer of the counting table and lifted out a dirty canvas bag heavy with $1,500 in silver coin. The amateur lifted the bag disparagingly, commented "Too damn' heavy," scooped about a third of the contents into his side valise, and left the rest.

Another amateur noticed the front door opening and stepped forward to admit Sam Breck, a local merchant, come to pay a note and carrying $393 in his right hand. The Confederate took the money and then rushed the honest merchant into the back room. Next came youthful Morris Roach, Joe Weeks's clerk, to make the day's deposit. He made it with the fighting Confederacy and landed in the directors' room where Tom Collins, with drawn pistol, was explaining that this raid was being made to avenge the ravages inflicted on Virginia by Phil Sheridan's Union cavalry.

While this was in progress, his colleagues were doing an appallingly bad job of bank looting. Fumbling through the unlocked safe, they completely missed some $50,000 in U.S. bonds which customers had left for safekeeping, and a $50,000 block of ready-signed St. Albans Bank notes. They picked up a few hundred dollars' worth of U.S. bonds but bypassed all the gold coin, thereby exiting with about $60,000 while leaving more than twice that amount within easy reach. The robbery time was twelve minutes, most of them filled with talk.

Simultaneously another group of five youthful Confederates was carrying out a lesser looting of the Franklin County Bank, which still stands resolutely on St. Albans's Main Street. Kentuckian William H. Hutchinson, twenty-three, was in charge of this amateur theft.

Bill Hutchinson made his entry several minutes before 3 P.M. He found Marcus Beardsley, the cashier, sitting in front of the big monkey stove, chinning with the merchant Jim Saxe, and old Jackson Clark, the long-coated, stovepipe-hatted hometown woodsawyer, who carried his bucksaw wherever he went except, possibly, to bed. Hutchinson, a handsome six-footer with glistening chestnut sideburns, strolled up and inquired the price of gold. Cashier Beardsley replied that he did not handle it, but when J. R. Armington, a local moneybags, ambled in with money to deposit, Beardsley suggested that Hutchinson might be able to make a deal with him.

Hutchinson traded two gold pieces for greenbacks. Armington and Saxe took their leave. The Confederate kept up an affable conversation with the cashier until his four assistants strolled in. After a seemingly embarrassed pause, one advanced a few steps, pulled a heavy Navy revolver from his side pocket, pointed it at Beardsley's head, and stood staring at the cashier. Believing the man to be a lunatic, Beardsley could think of nothing to do but stare back. Two more of the new arrivals drew out large revolvers and silently pointed them at the speechless cashier.

Still lounging at the counter, Hutchinson broke the silence by explaining that he and these others were Confederate soldiers, here to rob the bank and burn the town. At that point Clark made a dash for the front door. Two of the Confederates blocked the way and relieved him of his bucksaw. Clark broke loose and again made for the door, whereupon the bank robbers pro tem grabbed him and heaved him into the tiny vault-room behind the teller's cage. When they sought to shut the heavy iron door, Cashier Beardsley warned that the vault was air-tight; any man would soon suffocate in it. He was now to learn that silence can be golden. Three of the Confederates converged on the cashier, dropped him into the vault-room, and banged shut the heavy door, leaving both prisoners to reflect on whether they would suffocate or be roasted by the promised firing of the town.

Again a quintet of obviously amateur robbers made a hurried and slovenly job of looting. They too left twice as much as they took (approximately $50,000) and made a sprinting exit. After their departure Armington chanced to stroll by the bank, saw the door open, and stepped inside, where he heard a muffled banging in the vault-room. The hard-used cashier shouted the combination, and after about twenty minutes Armington got the big door open. Beardsley and the sawyer staggered out in time to see the robbers mounting horses, also stolen locally. They apparently did not notice that the village's third bank, the First National, barely forty rods down Main Street, was also being robbed.

Social correctness prevailed in this instance. The head robber was Caleb McDowell Wallace, of the Kentucky Wallaces, nephew of the late John J. Crittenden, former U.S. senator from Kentucky. The door guard was Alamada Pope Bruce, a nephew of Vice-President Alexander Stephens of the Confederacy. At exactly 3 P.M. Confederate Wallace entered the bank's front door with a henchman lockstepped behind him. With his right hand he drew and cocked an oversized revolver, placed the muzzle directly below the nose of Albert Sowles, cashier and only employee present. One local citizen was there—General John Nason, Vermont's highest ranking survivor of the War of 1812—reading his newspaper near the coal stove. Being almost deaf, the aged general did not even stir when the obviously amateur holdup man (his pistol hand trembled violently) told Cashier Sowles that the bank was going to be looted.

At that point Grandpappy Joe McGrorty, Confederate States Army, dashed behind the counter and began filling his pockets with bank notes, and tossing handfuls of U.S. bonds to his colleagues. Then he pulled some coin bags out of the open safe, and demanded to know the contents. "Copper cents," murmured Cashier Sowles. The neophyte robber opened one or more of the bags, found pennies, and dumped the coins on the floor. He didn't discover that one of the bags was full of gold coin.

At that moment Bill Blaisdell, the local strongman, chanced to be strolling by and looked in to inquire what was going on. Alamada Bruce, who was guarding the door, came at him with drawn pistol. The local strong man picked up the Confederate, tossed him to the stone steps, and fell upon him. Wallace advised Bruce to shoot him, but Bruce was in no condition to obey. At that point (according to local legend) General Nason peered around the stove to admonish, "Now boys! Two on one's not fair!"

Blaisdell subsided when two revolver muzzles were turned on him, and permitted the robbers to march him across Main Street to the village green. Having pocketed and bagged a take of somewhere near $98,000, the quartet strolled out of the bank, leaving the cashier unmolested. General Nason, it is said, glanced up from his newspaper to ask, "What gentlemen were those?"

Thus a handful of Confederates, completely without criminal records or professional experience, robbed the three banks of St. Albans without firing a shot, without casualty, and with a net gain of $208,000 for the Losing Cause. Their timing and general strategy were superb; their robbery technique was almost uniformly bad. But at least it was bloodless.

That did not hold for the outside work directed by Confederate Lieutenant Bennett Young and six or eight youthful followers. The "outguards" had the tougher job.

St. Albans's Main Street has always been a broad and wide-open one. The outguards sought to keep the street free of people. For the first few minutes they accomplished this by escorting all passers-by to the shady green directly across Main Street. The escorting progressed nicely until Collings Huntington, "an eminently respectable citizen," came strolling along to fetch home his children from the local academy. As he passed the American Hotel carriageway, a youthful stranger touched his shoulder and told him to cross over to the green. When Huntington demurred, the stranger drew a revolver and fired. The ball struck Huntington on the left of his spine, followed along a rib, and came out, leaving only a flesh wound. He quietly joined the waiting group on the public green.

Meanwhile the front guards were taking up, on a better-late-than-never basis, the very necessary task of "recruiting" horses for making their getaway. Farmer Shepherd from Highgate, driving his wagon team in front of the Franklin County Bank, was deprived of his horses at the point of a revolver; two of the raiders stripped off the harness, climbed aboard the horses, and using headstalls for bridles, went gallumphing down the street. Lieutenant Young had already recruited a horse for himself. As he swung to the saddle, Leonard Bingham, a local derring-doer, made a lunge for him. That was the wrong play. At least six of the Confederates opened fire. Bingham went down with a belly wound.

Young decided that the time had come to set the town afire, a feat painstakingly prearranged. He ordered his men to begin using their glass bottles of "Greek fire," a chemical solution which was supposed to burst into flame on exposure to the air. The raiders first smashed their bottles against the front of Atwood's Store, but the stinking stuff just wouldn't burn. One raider dashed back to the American Hotel, and for reasons best known to himself treated the water closet with Greek fire. The stuff smouldered harmlessly.

At any rate the boys who had been infantry were changing into cavalry. They relieved Bedart's Saddle Shop of practically its entire stock of saddles, bridles, and blankets. They rustled seven more horses out of Fuller's Livery Stable. Edward Fuller got back just in time to ask what was going on. He soon found out. Young rode up and demanded that he hand over a pair of spurs. The liveryman was a pistol toter. He ducked behind a hitching-post, whipped out his gun, and pulled the trigger. The little Derringer snapped in futile misfire. Young guffawed: "Now you'll get me the spurs?" Apothecary L. L. Dutcher, the original historian of "The Great Raid," records that Fuller answered, "Yes, but I thought you were joking."

The livery stable proprietor dashed through Bedart's shop and sprinted back to Welding's prospective rooming house which Elinus J. Morrison from Manchester, New Hampshire, was building. Morrison shouted to his workmen to climb down and defy the invaders. The workmen did not seem to hear well. Lieutenant Young, meanwhile, was taking careful bead on Fuller. The livery stable proprietor jumped behind an elm tree. The bullet overtook Morrison as he was making a tactical withdrawal into Miss Beattie's store, struck his hand, and lodged in his abdomen. Onlookers dragged the builder to Dutcher's Apothecary Shop for first aid. Morrison died of the wound the following day, the only known fatality of the raid.

Meanwhile, the plain-clothed Confederates were Rebel-yelling, shooting, and taking horses for their escape. As they began riding out of St. Albans in columns of four, the horse dealer Wilder Gibson emerged from the saloon, rifle in hand, posted himself in front of Smith's Store, drew a careful and steady bead, and fired upon the hindmost of the gang. Reportedly one of the raiders slumped, and later died of the wound. This was never confirmed.

At any rate, the raiders were getting away, thundering down the road north. They stopped long enough to make another unsuccessful attempt to kindle a bridge with the Greek fire, and to annex another good saddle horse. Then the raiders rode into Canada, crossing the Missisquoi at Enosburg Falls.

The St. Albaners organized a pursuit party, reportedly of sixty to seventy men. This took half an hour, too long a delay to permit them to overtake the Confederates but long enough to add to the slapstick. Near Sheldon Village a farmer had been ridden down by the raiders and made victim of a forced horse trade—a badly winded nag for his fresh and buxom mare. The farmer was just standing there, recovering from his surprise, when he saw the pursuit party bearing down on him. Judging them to be more of the raiders, he ran like the wind across an open field. The St. Albaners recognized the winded horse, thought the fleeing farmer to be one of the Confederates, and took out after him shouting and whooping, until the harassed yeoman lost them in a swamp.

The pursuit became more and more ludicrous. A telegraph operator at St. Albans had keyed out a dispatch that the Rebels were sacking the town. At Burlington, Vermont, forty miles south, church bells tolled, an estimated force of 200 men assembled and armed and entrained for the north. The train broke down.

Perhaps that was just as well, for the Canadian peace officers were functioning effectively. Canadian sympathy for the Confederacy was widespread and well accredited, but the Canadian constabulary, with a good intelligence system, recognized the need for impartiality. From Montreal, some forty miles to the northeast, a sheriff's posse had ridden overland to a point near Enosburg where they waited on Canadian soil to intercept the raiders. Thirteen of the "bank robbers," including Lieutenant Young, were presently arrested and lodged in jail in Montreal. The rest of the raiders escaped temporarily.

Approximately $80,000 of the bank loot was taken from the prisoners and was held pending court action. The case was assigned to Justice Charles J. Coursol of Montreal. After weeks of consideration he ruled that his court had no proper jurisdiction or cause to hold trial and therefore ordered all the Confederates discharged from jail. The Justice further directed that Chief of Police Lamothe of Montreal restore all the money to the raiders. The freed Confederates were cheered by sympathizers on the streets of Montreal. The Canadian press, however, was cool, denouncing the raid as the work of "brigands."

Five of the raiders who had escaped were picked up by local Canadian authorities during the month of November and sent to Montreal. While court action was pending, the U.S. government demanded extradition, and the robbed banks of St. Albans forwarded a similar petition. Justice Smith of Montreal, who heard the pleas of extradition in January, ruled that "the transactions in St. Albans, Vermont, were acts of war," and held that the Confederates were not liable to extradition. He discharged them.

While in the Montreal jail Lieutenant Young and his well-treated companions seemed quite unworried. One testimony is provided by an entry dated November 22, 1864, in the diary of Judge James Davis of St. Albans: "My son, Wilbur Davis, received a letter this morning from Bennett Young, the Confederate leader, dated at Montreal jail, enclosing three dollars requesting him to send the [St. Albans] Daily Messenger to him there. He expects to be at liberty in a few days when he will be at a public house, where he wished the paper to be delivered after his release."

Lieutenant Young was not far wrong. As things turned out, he and his men were free by mid-December.

Bennett Young had had two goals in mind when he planned and executed the raid. These were to get some good cash money into the collapsing Confederate treasury, and to "stir up and unsettle" the Yankee frontier so that combat troops would be drawn away from the fighting fronts and sent to the Canadian border. In addition, Young apparently hoped that the general uproar might possibly stir up a war between the United States and Canada.

Success was only moderate. How much of the money ever got to the Confederacy is in question. Young later asserted that the entire $208,000 was delivered to the Confederate Commissioners in St. Catherine's, Ontario, but the claim is open to question. Young himself did not leave Canada until after the collapse of the Confederacy, and it is alleged that a good deal of the money was spent in Canada. And although the United States authorities did send a good many troops to the border after the raid, most of them were militia, invalided veterans, or home guards. If any of the pressure on Confederate armies in the South was thereby lessened, the effect was too slight to do Robert E. Lee any good. And far from involving the United States in a war with its northern neighbor, the raid apparently had the effect of deflating Canadian sympathy for the Confederacy.

The Canadian government behaved with dignity. Governor General Lord Monck recommended—and the Provincial Parliament passed—a bill to repay the three Vermont banks in the amount of $50,000 (Canadian) in gold—then the equivalent of the $88,000 in U.S. currency found on the persons of the captured robbers. The gold, duly delivered to the banks and divided among them in proportion to their respective losses, still left the banks with a combined loss of $120,000. All three weathered it easily. (The banks had also spent $20,000 in a futile, lawyer-enriching drive for extradition of the "robber gang.")

Canadian court records brought out and confirmed other portions of the intriguing story of Bennett Hiram Young. As he told his tale, the Louisville youth was eighteen when the Civil War began. He volunteered as a private and was assigned to the 2d Regiment of Maryland Infantry. Early in 1863 he was transferred as a cavalry replacement to the famed command of J. E. B. Stuart. He rode with Jeb into Gettysburg, where he was taken prisoner and dispatched by "cow car" to Camp Douglas, near Chicago, which the Union Army had converted to a stockade for Confederate prisoners. During April 1864, Young and five fellow prisoners, finding the camp poorly guarded, managed to make good their escape.

Without any particular difficulty the twenty-one-year-old made his way to Washington, D.C., then to Richmond, Virginia, where he presented "a bold plan" which the Confederate high command eagerly accepted. The plan was to return to Camp Douglas with a secret force of thirty volunteers, raid the gates, release most or all of the estimated 10,000 Confederates, and organize as many of them as possible in an "army-size raider force." The St. Albans story encourages one to wonder what might have happened had the bold plan succeeded.

Apparently Young, who had been rewarded with a lieutenant's commission, settled for a twenty-man force, and set out for Chicago. But when they scouted Camp Douglas, the youthful invaders found a heavily reenforced guard. They abandoned the proposed gate raid, scattered for St. Catherine's, and began planning the St. Albans raid.

After the war Bennett Young returned to his home town, Louisville, where he presently became a successful lawyer and railroad executive and promptly married a pretty girl and begot a pretty daughter. Early in July 1911, at a young sixty-eight, General Bennett Young (he had lately been elected commander in chief of Confederate Veterans) took his wife and daughter on a "memory trip" to Montreal for a luxurious week at the Ritz-Carlton, and made his presence known to St. Albaners.

The townspeople got together and appointed a four-man delegation, including the Vermont representative to Congress, the local newspaper editor, and "Old John" Branch, who personally remembered the raid ("Rebels didn't steal my Pa's hoss, on account they see it was blind"), to call on General Young.

It was a truly friendly visit, and it was lengthily recorded in the *Montreal Gazette* of July 29. General Young wore the iron-gray and gold full dress of a Confederate general, his white hair lending impressive contrast to his handsome uniform. The Kentuckian's bourbon stores were abundant. For a long evening, the Vermonters and the dignified Confederate fraternized. Toward midnight they touched glasses in a final toast. No hard feelings.

—August 1961

"WE WILL NOT DO DUTY ANY LONGER FOR SEVEN DOLLARS PER MONTH"

by OTTO FRIEDRICH

The United States had promised black soldiers that they would be paid as much as whites. Sergeant Walker believed that promise.

This is in honor of Sgt. William Walker, of the 3d South Carolina Infantry Regiment, a young black soldier who believed in the United States government's promises of equal rights. This is in honor of Sgt. William Walker, who was brave enough to act on his belief in his rights. This is in honor of Sgt. William Walker, who died in disgrace, executed by the United States government for acting on his belief in its promise of equal rights.

The main charge against him was mutiny. The specifications of the court-martial at Hilton Head, South Carolina, dated January 11, 1864, provide the basic details: "That he, Sergeant William Walker, Co. 'A,' 3d S.C. Infy, did unlawfully take command of his Company 'A,' and march the same with others of the Regiment, in front of his Commanding Officer's tent (Lt. Col. A. G. Bennett), and there ordered them to stack arms; and when his Comdg Officer Lt. Col. A. G. Bennett inquired of the Regiment what all this meant, he, the said Sergt. William Walker, replied: 'We will not do duty any longer for ($7) seven dollars per month';—and when remonstrated with, and ordered by their Comdg Officer (Lt. Col. A. G. Bennett) to take their arms and return to duty, he, the said Sergeant Walker, did order his Co. ('A') to let their arms alone and go to their quarters, which they did, thereby exciting and joining in a general mutiny."

To understand this trial, it is essential to remember that dark-skinned people had no constitutional right to equal treatment during most of the Constitution's first century. In the Dred Scott decision of 1857, the Supreme Court specifically ruled that a black who claimed to be a freedman could not argue his claim in federal court because he was by definition not a citizen. And though the Civil War was implicitly fought over the issue of slavery, neither President Lincoln nor the Congress made any great effort for a long time to free any slaves. On the contrary, the original version of the Thirteenth Amendment, passed by Congress, with Lincoln's approval, in February 1861, promised that the federal government would make no attempt to interfere with the institution of slavery. It was only the Southerner's attack on Fort Sumter two months later that nullified this remarkable amendment, and not until four years later, when the war was over and Lincoln dead, was a new Thirteenth Amendment ratified, proclaiming that "neither slavery nor involuntary servitude . . . shall exist within the United States."

A few radicals had argued that view from the beginning. "Our cry now must be emancipation and arming the slaves," wrote the young Henry Adams in November 1861. But even the most idealistic of Presidents has to make compromises with political reality, and Lincoln was probably correct in believing that any attempt to abolish slavery would inspire slaveholding states like Kentucky and Maryland to join the Southern rebellion.

Some of the men directly in charge of fighting the war were less sensitive to politicians' anxieties. Maj. Gen. John Charles Frémont, who had been the Republican candidate for the presidency in 1856 and who now commanded what was known as the Western Department of St. Louis, decided to act on his own. In a proclamation of August 30, 1861, he declared martial law throughout Missouri and the liberation of all Rebels' slaves. "The property, real and personal, of all persons in the State of Missouri who shall take up arms against the United States. . . . is declared to be confiscated to the public use, and their slaves, if any they have, are hereby declared freemen." Lincoln responded by giving the adventurous general a direct order, "in a spirit of caution, and not of censure," to go no further than Congress had authorized, and Congress had authorized nothing resembling Frémont's proclamation.

These official hesitations about freeing the slaves applied all the more to the idea of arming them. It was not only in the South that the image of black slaves acquiring weapons conjured up hideous scenes of revenge, massacres, and atrocities. But again, the men charged with waging war had to confront reality, and the reality was that the Union army needed a great many soldiers. "If it shall be found that the men who have been held by the rebels as slaves are capable of bearing arms and performing efficient military service," Secretary of War Simon Cameron said in a report issued in December 1861, the end of the first year of the war, "it is the right, and may become the duty, of this Government to arm and equip them. . . ." Lincoln was angered not only by Cameron's views but by his audacity in making such a statement public without the President's approval.

Though many Union generals regarded blacks as worthless, a few kept pressing Lincoln to make use of them. The first serious attempt to recruit and arm former slaves took place on the Sea Islands off the coast of South Carolina. There in the lovely old mansions of Beaufort, on Port Royal Island, the cotton barons of South Carolina had plotted the Southern insurrection, so it was eminently fitting that the Union navy should invade their headquarters. It sent southward an armada of seventy-four steam frigates, steam sloops, gunboats, and transports loaded with twelve thousand seasick troops. After cannonading the islands' strongholds, the invaders finally entered Beaufort in November of 1861 and found that every white inhabitant (except one man too drunk to move) had fled. Only the slaves were left.

There were about ten thousand of them, more than 80 percent of the islands' pre-war population, and their appearance dismayed some of their liberators. "Nearly all the Negroes left on the islands are in densest ignorance," wrote one arriving Northern officer, Capt. Hazard Stevens, "some of the blackest human beings ever seen, and others the most bestial in appearance. These ignorant and benighted creatures flooded into Beaufort . . . and held high carnival in the deserted mansions, smashing doors, mirrors, and furniture and appropriating all that took their fancy."

The Northerners had no idea what to do with these blacks. They were hardly slaves now, since their masters had fled, but they had not been officially freed, so they were not really people either, much less citizens. Gen. Benjamin Butler had devised a solution to this problem by insisting that escaped slaves were "contraband." The word ordinarily referred to property, and the application of this term to slaves seemed to satisfy everyone's sense of legality and propriety. So the ten thousand contraband objects on the Sea Islands, who needed, after all, to be fed and clothed and sheltered, were assigned to the United States Treasury Department. The Treasury Department appointed a bright young Boston lawyer named Edward Pierce to go to Port Royal and take charge of the contraband. He sent his charges back to the work they had always done, planting, hoeing, and picking cotton. He rewarded them, however, with something they had never seen before: cash wages.

Then came Maj. Gen. David Hunter, West Point '22, commander of the grandly named Department of the South, which actually included little more than these beautiful but swampy islands off the Carolina coast. Scarcely a month after his arrival in Port Royal in March 1862, Hunter issued a decree proclaiming that all people "heretofore held as slaves" in the three nearest coastal states—South Carolina, Georgia, and Florida—"are . . . declared forever free." On the same day on which he freed the slaves, however, Hunter ordered his subordinate officers "to send immediately to these headquarters, under a guard, all the able-bodied negroes capable of bearing arms."

Pierce of the Treasury was outraged at this autocratic conscription of his contraband cotton workers. They "were taken from the fields without being allowed to go to their houses even to get a jacket . . .," Pierce wrote to Washington. "Wives and children embraced the husband and father thus taken away, they knew not where, and whom, as they said, they should never see again." Once again Lincoln himself struck down an overzealous general. "The Government of the United States," he declared, "Had no knowledge, information, or belief of intention on the part of General Hunter to issue such a proclamation."

But though Lincoln thus disavowed Hunter, disavowed both the emancipation of slaves and the arming of slaves, he remained under pressure to do both. Edwin Stanton, who had replaced the corrupt Cameron as Secretary of War, gradually came to favor the recruitment of blacks, and Congress drifted nervously toward the same view. The Second Confiscation Act, passed in July 1862, authorized the President "to employ as many persons of African descent as he may deem necessary and proper for the suppression of this rebellion." In the Militia Act, passed the same month, the President was authorized "to receive into the service of the United States, for the purpose of constructing intrenchments, or performing camp service, or any other labor, or any military or naval service for which they may be found competent, persons of African descent. . . ." The Act also specified that persons of African descent would be paid $3 a month less than white soldiers—that is, $10 a month instead of $13—and that $3 of that pay would be deducted for clothes, whereas whites could spend or keep their $3.50 clothing allotments.

So although General Hunter was forbidden in May to emancipate or draft blacks into his forces, Gen. Rufus Saxton, the new military governor in Port Royal, was authorized on August 25 to recruit five thousand of them. And these recruits, Stanton said to Saxton on his own authority, were "to be entitled to receive the same pay and rations as are allowed by law to volunteers in the service." That declaration by the Secretary of War amounted to a pledge of equal pay and equal rights. It was understood as such not only in Port Royal but wherever Union officials undertook recruitment of black soldiers. But Congress had never authorized any such pledge, nor, when challenged, would Congress honor it.

Capt. Thomas Wentworth Higginson, who knew nothing of these complications, was having dinner with two other officers in the barracks of the 51st Massachusetts Regiment when he received a letter from General Saxton announcing that he was "organizing the First Regiment of South Carolina Volunteers" and offering him the colonelcy and command of what was to become the first Union regiment of freed slaves. Higginson was astonished. "Had an invitation reached me to take command of a regiment of Kalmuck Tartars," he recalled, "it could hardly have been more unexpected." But Saxton had heard good reports about Higginson, and they all were true.

Higginson embodied many of the characteristics that Bostonians like to consider elements in the classic Bostonian persona: courage, independence, eloquence, idealism. He was an ordained Unitarian minister, but also an ardent swimmer and football player, also an ardent abolitionist, a friend and comrade-in-arms to John Brown, also an ardent feminist, one of the signers of the call to the first National Woman's Rights Convention, and author of a celebrated polemic entitled *Ought Woman to Learn the Alphabet?* After his antislavery activities had forced him to resign from his wealthy parish in Newburyport, he declared, "An empty pulpit has often preached louder than a living Minister." And after he had discovered the reclusive Emily Dickinson, whose poems he was the first to publish, she wrote to him: "Of our greatest acts we are ignorant. You were not aware that you saved my life."

Higginson was reluctant to abandon his comrades in the 51st Massachusetts Regiment, but on making a quick trip to Port Royal, he found that he could not resist the challenge of leading "eight hundred men suddenly transformed from slaves into soldiers, and representing a race affectionate, enthusiastic, grotesque, and dramatic beyond all others." Though that may sound patronizing, Higginson soon came to love his black troops, and they loved him. One of their most extraordinary confrontations occurred on New Year's Day of 1863, when ten cattle were slaughtered and barbecued for an open-air feast to accompany the reading of Lincoln's new Emancipation Proclamation. There was the presentation of a new regimental flag. "Then followed an incident so simple, so touching, so utterly unexpected and startling, that I can scarcely believe it . . .," Higginson wrote in *Army Life in a Black Regiment.* "Just as I took and waved the flag, which now for the first time meant anything to these poor people, there suddenly arose, close beside the platform, a strong male voice . . . into which two women's voices instantly blended, singing, as if by an impulse that could no more be repressed than the morning-note of the song-sparrow—'My country, 'tis of thee,/Sweet land of liberty,/Of thee I sing.' People looked at each other, and then at us on the platform, to see whence came this interruption. . . . Firmly and irrepressibly the quavering voices sang on, verse after verse; others of the colored people joined in; some whites on the platform began, but I motioned them to silence. I never saw anything so electric; it made all other words cheap; it seemed the choked voice of a race at last unloosed."

Once Congress had authorized the recruiting of black soldiers, Secretary of War Stanton established a Bureau for Colored Troops in May 1863 and asked the War Department's solicitor, William Whiting, of Boston, to look into the vexing question of what the black recruits should be paid. Despite Stanton's promise of equal treatment, Whiting replied that the only applicable law was the Militia Act of 1862, in which Congress had specifically stated that "persons of African descent" were to be paid ten dollars per month (minus three dollars for clothing), or three dollars less than white soldiers received. "There seems to be inequality and injustice in this distinction," Stanton said in his annual report for 1863, "and an amendment authorizing the same pay and bounty as white troops receive, is recommended." Lincoln was not convinced. Since blacks "had larger motives for being soldiers than white men . . . they ought to be willing to enter the service upon any condition," the President said to Frederick Douglass, the black leader. The decision to grant them lower pay, Lincoln added, "seemed a necessary condition to smooth the way to their employment at all as soldiers." For the time being, Stanton wrote to the governor of Ohio, all blacks who had relied on his promise of equal pay "must trust to State contributions and the justice of Congress at the next session."

Colonel Higginson was furious. The refusal to grant equal pay, he declared, "has impaired discipline, has relaxed loyalty, and has begun to implant a feeling of sullen distrust in the very regiments whose early career solved the problem of the nation, created a new army, and made a peaceful emancipation possible." Col. Robert Gould Shaw, who commanded the 54th Massachusetts Infantry Regiment, the first black unit recruited in the North, was even more furious. Though the Massachusetts legislature appropriated funds to provide equal pay for Shaw's regiment, which was already stationed on the Sea Islands and ready to go into action, the regiment refused to accept any pay at all unless it was given equal pay by the federal government. These soldiers should either be "mustered out of the service or receive the full pay which was promised them," Shaw wrote to the Massachusetts governor, John Andrew. "Are we *soldiers* or are we *laborers*?" wrote one of Shaw's black soldiers, James Henry Gooding, in a letter to President Lincoln. Then, in the flowery rhetoric of his time, Gooding answered his own question: "Mr. President . . . the patient, trusting descendants of Afric's clime have dyed the ground with blood in defense of the Union and democracy."

Unpaid, the 54th Massachusetts marched into combat,

leading a hopeless charge against Fort Wagner, in Charleston Harbor. After a long but ineffective cannonading, Shaw's outnumbered troops had to charge uphill and across a deep ditch into a storm of Confederate gunfire. Colonel Shaw, who was twenty-five, led them all the way, reached the fort's parapet, and climbed it. "He stood there for a moment with uplifted sword, shouting, 'Forward, 54th!'" as William James said many years later in dedicating Saint-Gaudens's great monument on Boston Common, "and then fell headlong, with a bullet through his heart." More than half of Shaw's unpaid black troops died in that heroic charge before the remnants were finally beaten back. And after all the dead were dumped into a common trench, the Confederate commander was said to have remarked of Shaw, "We have buried him with his niggers."

It was a fact that black casualties in the Union army were far higher than white casualties. Of the approximately 180,000 black troops eventually recruited, about 37,000 died. That death rate amounted to slightly more than 20 percent, as compared with a death rate of 15.2 percent among white troops and only 8.6 percent of the regular army. The disparity occurred not because blacks were regularly used as cannon fodder but because most Civil War casualties, white and black alike, resulted from sickness. Among blacks, the remarkable statistics are that 2,870 died in combat, more than 4,000 died of unknown caused, and 29,756 are known to have died of illness. In fact, the regiment with the second-highest number of deaths in the entire Union army was the 65th U.S. Colored Infantry, which lost 755 men without ever going into combat at all.

There were a number of reasons for this. High among them were inferior food, inferior clothing, inferior medical care, inferior everything. All wars breed corruption, after all, and the Civil War, fought in the early days of freewheeling capitalism, certainly bred its share. As Thomas Beer wrote in *Hanna*, "Bayonets of polished pewter, tents of porous shoddy, coffee made of pulse and sorghum, carbines that exploded on the drill ground ... and many other versions of the wooden nutmeg were offered to the Army between 1861 and 1864.

"Often nothing could be done. The actual vendor vanished in a cloud of agents and guileless middlemen. ..." And who could be more vulnerable to this sort of swindle than the fledgling black regiments? One of their commanders, Brig. Gen. Daniel Ullman, complained to a senator about "arms almost entirely unserviceable and . . . equipment . . . of the poorest kind."

And woe to anyone who fell ill. Since black troops were supposed to be led by white officers, only eight black doctors were taken into the Army, and six of these served in Washington hospitals. White doctors generally refused to serve in black regiments, and so, according to one general's report, "In very many cases Hospital Stewards of low order of qualification were appointed to the office of Assistant Surgeon and Surgeon." There were "well-grounded objections . . .," the general went on, "against the inhumanity of subjecting the colored soldiers to medical treatment and surgical operations from such men."

One reason that blacks were so prone to sickness, though, was overwork. The black troops were used mainly to dig trenches and fortifications, to cut trees and haul supplies, to provide, for seven dollars per month, what they once provided for nothing: slave labor. "My men were . . . put into trenches and batteries, or detailed to mount guns, haul cannon and mortars, and were kept constantly and exclusively on fatigue duty of the severest kind . . . ," said Col. James Montgomery of the 2d South Carolina Volunteers. "I frequently had to take men who had been on duty from 4 o'clock in the morning until sundown to make up the detail called for, for the night, and men who had been in the trenches in the night were compelled to go on duty again at least part of the day." Or as another officer wrote, "Where white and black troops come together in the same command, the latter have to do all the work."

The maw of war kept demanding more men. At Gettysburg alone, the two sides together suffered more than fifty thousand casualties before the Union forces finally beat back Robert E. Lee's invasion of Pennsylvania. The following week in July 1983, Lincoln's draft law went into effect, and after the first names had been chosen by lottery, mobs of antidraft rioters began tearing New York City to pieces.

For four days they burned and killed, and nobody knows the final death toll, but many were black. Nobody knows, either, how much of this kind of news reached the Sea Islands off South Carolina or what impression it made on black recruits like William Walker in the 3d South Carolina Infantry Regiment.

We do not know a great deal about William Walker. For most of his short life he belonged to that large category of people on whom history keeps no records. There are only some military documents—notably a forty-eight-page hand-written transcript of his court-martial. One paper says he was born in Hilton Head; another, in Savannah. One says, "Occupation: Servant." It adds: "Name of former owner not of record." From this we can deduce that Walker had been born and reared a slave and that if anyone asked him who his master was, he probably refused to say.

He was five feet seven inches tall, according to these Army documents. Eyes black, hair black, complexion black. He was illiterate—hardly surprising since it was against the law in South Carolina to teach a slave to read, and any black found in possession of a pencil and paper was liable to flogging. He was twenty-three years old when he died.

On Walker's death certificate his occupation was given not as "servant" but as "pilot." In his last appeal for mercy, just three weeks before his execution, he said that he had served six months as pilot on an armored gunboat, the USS *Montauk*. This implies, surely, that he knew the region well; it also implies a certain intelligence, energy, and eagerness to serve the Union cause.

Walker may be the anonymous ex-slave who turned up in a report by Comdr. John L. Worden, captain of the *Montauk*, about the blockading fleet's venture up the Big Ogeechee River to attack Fort McAllister in Georgia early in 1863. "I learned through the medium of a contraband, who had been employed upon these waters as a pilot, the position of the obstructions below the fort . . . ," Worden wrote on February 2, 1863. "This information, with the aid of the contraband, whom I took on board, enabled me to take up a position nearer the fort in the next attack on it." The *Montauk* accomplished little in its exchange of gunfire with Fort McAllister, but it discovered the Confederate raider *Nashville*, a paddle-wheeled merchant steamer that had been newly outfitted with cannon, lying aground near the fort. "A few well directed shells determined the range," Worden reported on February 28, "and soon we succeeded in striking her with XI-

and XV-inch shells." The *Nashville* caught fire, then exploded. But a Confederate torpedo blew a hole in the *Montauk* and nearly sank it before its engineer could patch the leak. We know no details of Walker's role in all this, only that he proudly stated in his appeal: "I almost destroyed the rebel steamer *Nashville* in the Big Ogeeche[sic] River. . . ."

One day in April 1863 Walker got a pass to return home and visit his family—he had a wife named Rebecca—and there he heard that a third regiment of South Carolina blacks was being organized. He knew that his job as a pilot exempted him from conscription, but the cause called out to him. To join the Union infantry in combat must have seemed better than being just a river pilot. "On the promise solemnly made by some who are now officers in my regiment," he later said, "that I should receive the same pay and allowances as were given to all soldiers in the U.S. Army, [I] voluntarily entered the ranks."

Not quite. He was enrolled as a sergeant from the start, on April 23, 1863, and that also implies that he had a certain quality of self-possession, authority, leadership, some quality unusual for an illiterate ex-slave of twenty-three. It did not earn him any extra pay, however. All black recruits received the same seven dollars per month, regardless of rank. And they soon found that their white officers could be as harsh as any slavemasters. "For an account of the treatment that has been given to the men of the 3rd Regt S.C. Vols by a large majority of their officers," Walker declared at his court-martial, "nine-tenths of those now in service there will be my witness that it has been tyrannical in the extreme." Walker's judgment was corroborated, after his death, in a statement by a Col. P. P. Browne of the provost marshal's office, about some other blacks accused of taking part in Walker's "mutiny." All his interrogations, said Colonel Browne, led him to the conclusion "that during the summer and fall of 1863 . . . the regiment . . . was under bad management and in a greatly demoralized condition; . . . that several of the officers who had most to do with these men have either been dismissed [from] the service or are under charges which will cause their dismissal; . . . that being made up of South Carolina Slaves their great ignorance of their duties and responsibilities as *Soldiers* led them to commit errors which more intelligent men would have avoided; . . . that the officers of the Regiment were [more] to blame than the men."

Sergeant Walker, eager and enthusiastic, signed up for three years' service in April 1863. By that August, just four months later, he was embittered, quarrelsome, insubordinate. The indictment listed several instances of "mutinous conduct" that occurred long before the protest demonstration about equal pay. The first specification charged that on August 23 he did "join in a mutiny at Seabrook Wharf [in Hilton Head], when on detail, and go away to camp when ordered not to do so by 1st Lieut. Geo. W. Wood." The second specification charged that Walker "did use threatening language, such as 'I will shoot him,' meaning 1st Lieut. Geo. W. Wood. This he said in a loud voice, so as to be heard all over camp, having, at the same time, a gun in his hand."

Lieutenant Wood was mysteriously absent from the court-martial, but Lt. Adolph Bessie testified for the prosecution in support of this charge. In doing so, however, he made it sound as though the quarrel had been started by Wood rather than Walker. "I was sick at that time," Bessie said. "The accused came to my tent, and several others of the company. He complained of Lt. Geo. W. Wood as having maltreated him, of having threatened to shoot him, or something of that kind. I told the accused I would see about it. He left my tent, and shortly after I heard considerable noise in the company street. I went out and saw the accused with a gun in his hand, and heard him say he would 'shoot Lt. Geo. W. Wood.' He repeated it several times, in front of the tent of the Orderly. . . ."

Question, by the judge advocate (Lt. S. Alford of the 8th Maine Volunteers): What was his tone of voice when threatening to shoot Lieutenant Wood?
Answer: It was loud, and could be heard quite a distance. He seemed to be talking in a rage.

Capt. Edgar Abeel attempted to arrest Walker, according to the third specification, but Walker "did refuse to obey." Abeel testified that he had ordered Walker to go to his tent under arrest. "He refused to go in arrest," Abeel said, "and said he would not for any man. . . ."

Q: Where did he go after the order?
A: He walked up and down the street of his company, but did not go in his tent.

Q: What was the conduct of the men present at the time?
A: They seemed to uphold the sergeant. A number of them said they "would go to the provost with him."

Abeel seems to have given up his attempt to arrest Walker, and the whole quarrel died down. That was in August. In October Walker got into another angry argument, this time with a Sgt. Sussex Brown. The troops were supposed to be lined up for inspection; Sergeant Brown testified, but Walker didn't appear. "I went into Sergt. Walker's tent and two men was there playing cards," he said. "I asked them, 'What are you doing?' They told me they was 'coming out now.' Sergt. Walker said, 'Let's play on,' and I told Sergt. Walker he must fall in. He cussed and said I was a 'damned son of a bitch.' I said, if you don't fall in the ranks, I will have you arrested. . . . He told me he 'didn't care a damn' about any man. He said if I didn't mind he'd put a ball in his gun and shoot me. . . ."

Q: About how many times, if more than once, did he say he would shoot you?
A: Three times.

Walker subsequently denied most of this. He claimed that he and his comrades had each had only one more card to play and that he had said, "Play your card and get out." He further claimed "that my threat of 'putting a cartridge in my gun and blowing his brains out' was only in answer to his threat that he would 'smash my head in with the butt of his gun.'" By now, though, Walker's insubordination was almost habitual, and he resisted discipline not only for himself but for other men. Drum Maj. William Smith testified that when he tried to arrest a man named Ranty Pope for refusing to go on fatigue duty, Walker intervened. "I told him [Pope] I would tie him up," Smith said. "Sergt. Walker told me if I tied Ranty Pope up I would also have to tie him, Sergt. Walker, up."

Q: What did you then do with the said Pope?
A: I did not do anything with him.
Q: Why not?
A: The camp was in a state of excitement and I did not like the looks of Sergt. Walker at the time.
Q: You say you did not like the looks of the accused. How

did he look or act at the time?

A: He eyed me sharply. I was actually afraid of him.

Q: Did the words or looks of the accused prevent the arrest of Ranty Pope . . . ?

A: His words and looks both.

This all happened on the morning of November 19, 1863, the day of the "mutiny." The prosecution made no effort to establish any chronology, so it is not clear whether Walker's rescue of Ranty Pope came before or after the equal pay demonstration outside Colonel Bennett's tent. The prosecution also made no effort to establish any reason for the "mutiny," any background of grievances and arguments about pay or living conditions. Walter later stated that he had not received any pay at all since August, but we don't know whether his regiment was another unit rejecting unequal pay or what the reason was. Clearly Walker was in a stage of rage, and clearly he was not alone in that rage. The whole camp was described as "mutinous," but nobody at the court-martial paid much attention to the reasons. On the main charge of stacking arms and refusing to serve without equal pay, the judge advocate simply asked Colonel Bennett whether he had seen Walker that day and then asked him to "state his conduct as far as it came under your observation."

"On the morning of Nov. 19, 1863, when a portion of the command was in a state of mutiny," the colonel began, "I noticed the accused, with others of his company and regiment, stack his arms, take off his accoutrements, and hang them on the stack. I inquired what all this meant, and received no reply and again repeated the question, when the accused answered by saying, that they 'would not do duty any longer for seven dollars per month.' I then told the men the consequences of a mutiny. I told them that if they did not take their arms and return to duty, I should report the case to the Post commander and they would be shot down. While saying this, I heard the accused tell the men not to take their arms, but leave them and go to their street, which command of his they obeyed. . . ."

Q: Where was the accused at the time you told the men to take their arms, and told them the consequences if they did not?

A: He stood on the right of the line when I first saw him.

He afterwards moved to the rear, moving back and forth. . . .

Q: Do you know the object of the accused passing to and fro. . . . ?

A He was advising the men "to go back to their quarters without their arms."

But then it became apparent that the colonel had not seen or heard the complete incident.

Q: Did you hear the accused order the company ("A") to stack their arms?

A: I did not. The arms were stacked when I came out of my tent. . . .

Q: Did you hear the accused give the command to march the company back to their street . . .?

A: He did not give the command, "March." He merely told them to go.

Walker, or perhaps the defense lawyer assigned to him, Lt. J. A. Smith of the 47th New York Volunteers, attempted to dodge responsibility. The court-martial records says only:

Question by accused: Have you had any conversation with the accused since his confinement . . . ?

Answer: I have once. . . .

Q: Did you, in that conversation, say that you were satisfied, from the information you had received, that he was not the person who used the language relative to not serving any longer for $7 dollars per month . . . ?

A: No sir, I did not.

Though there was some hearsay in Colonel Bennett's testimony, the prosecution also produced an eyewitness, 2d Lt. John E. Jacobs, who said he had seen Walker lead the demonstration from the start. "The first I saw of him after roll call, he was at the head of the Company ('A'), apparently in command of it, marching up to the Colonel's quarters," Jacobs testified. "At the front of the Colonel's quarters, he gave the command, 'Stack arms.' They stacked arms. . . . The Colonel asked, 'What does all this mean?' The accused replied, they were 'not willing to be soldiers for seven dollars per month.' The Colonel first advised them to take arms, and then commanded them to take arms. Sergt. Walker then left his place at the head of the company, and walked up and down in the rear of the company, telling the men not to take their arms. He came to the left of the line, and the company left, without taking their arms. . . ."

Walker again tried to deny responsibility.

Q: Was there more than one person gave the order to "stack arms" when the men were in front of the Lt. Col's quarters . . . ?

A: I did not hear any other man give the order.

For some mysterious reason Walker never testified in his own defense. Nor did he make any attempt to argue that the demonstration for equal pay expressed a justifiable grievance. Perhaps he (or the presumably white lieutenant acting as his assigned attorney) knew that a court-martial would not sympathize with such a line of argument. All of the defense's intermittent attempts to cross-examine the prosecution witnesses were attempts to deny involvement, to spread blame, or to spread confusion. The handful of defense witnesses served much the same purpose. Pvt. James Williams, from Walker's own Company A, was asked, "Did you hear anyone say that the 'men wouldn't serve any longer for $7 a month,' and if so, who was it?" Williams testified that the only man he had heard make such a statement was a Sergeant Bullock. And so on.

Instead of testifying, Walker and his lawyer submitted to the court a long statement in which he denied everything. About the alleged dispute with Lieutenant Wood, for example, he said: "I positively declare that I had not a gun in my hands that day, neither did I threaten to shoot Lieut. Wood." More generally, Walker declared that he and his fellow blacks were "entirely ignorant" about the rules of military law and behavior. "We have been allowed to stumble along," he said, "taking verbal instructions as to the different parts of our duty, and gaining a knowledge of the services required of us as best we might. In this way many things have occurred that might have been entirely different had we known the responsibility of our position."

As for the equal-pay demonstration outside Colonel Bennett's tent, Walker could not deny his participation, but he did once again deny his responsibility. "I believe that I have proved conclusively by the testimony of the noncommissioned officers and men of my company that I did not then exercise any command over them," he said, "that I gave no word of counsel or advice to them in opposition to the request made by our commanding officer, and that, for one, I carried my arms and equipment back with me to my company street." In other words, he denied being a rebellious hero and claimed to be a docile subordinate. Perhaps that was the lesson all slaves had to learn in order to survive, or perhaps it was just the basic teaching of the army. But though Walker denied all responsibility for the demonstration that the army regarded as a mutiny, he did remind the court that the demonstrators had been "an assemblage who only contemplated a peaceful demand for the rights and benefits that had been guaranteed them."

In the signature at the end of that statement, between the names William and Walker, there is an *X*. Over and under the X are the words *his mark*.

The members of the court-martial—a lieutenant colonel from Connecticut, a major from Pennsylvania, two captains and three lieutenants—considered the accusations and the defense and then returned the verdict: on all charges, guilty. "And the court do therefore sentence him, Sergeant William Walker, Co. 'A' 3d S.C. Vol Infantry (two thirds of the members concurring) to be shot to death with musketry at such time and place as the Commanding General may direct."

The commanding general directed that the execution take place the following month, February, at the Union outpost in Jacksonville, Florida. Walker was still imprisoned at the Provost Guard House in Hilton Head early in February, when he addressed his last appeal to the provost marshal general. By now he was reduced, as many prisoners eventually are, to pleading. "I am a poor Colored soldier . . . ," he began. He was "entirely guiltless" and had "always done my duty as a soldier and a man." He had not been paid anything at all for the past six months, and he was "suffering very much in consequence of my close confinement and absence from my family who are suffering from want and destitution." If the provost marshal general would "use your influence in the proper quarter," he went on, the evidence would lead to his release and return to duty. "I assure you, Sir," he said, "I shall never give you cause to regret your kindness."

The next document is a discharge form filled out by the lieutenant who commanded the firing squad in Jacksonville. He did not even bother to cross out the inapplicable parts. With preprinted courtesy, the discharge form said that Walker, by now reduced to the rank of private, had "served HONESTLY and FAITHFULLY with his company to the present date," but then the lieutenant wrote in a flowery script that he "was shot to death for mutiny at Jacksonville, Fla., Febry. 29th, 1864. . . ."

The form then proceeded to summarize the financial relationship between the late Private Walker and his government. "The said William Walker was last paid . . . to include the 31st day of August, 1863, and has pay due him from that time to the present date," the document said. "He is entitled to pay and subsistence for travelling to place of enrollment and whatever other allowances are authorized to volunteer soldiers, or militia, so discharged." In other words, equal pay. On the other hand, the document continued, "He has received fifty-nine 6/100 dollars, advanced by the United States on account of clothing." It further said that he had "lost" one Prussian musket, one bayonet, one bayonet scabbard, one cartridge belt, and forty rounds of ammunition. Perhaps those were the weapons he had stacked in front of the colonel's tent, and denied having stacked in front of the colonel's tent. Trying to estimate their value, to be repaid by the late Private Walker to the government that had just executed him, the lieutenant could only write, "Price list has never been furnished." As for the rest of the printed form, which said, "He is indebted to———, sutler, ———dollars," and "He is indebted to——— laundress,——— dollars, the lieutenant just crossed all that out. And so the United States government declared that its account with the late William Walker was settled in full.

Three months later Congress took up once again the question of equal pay for black soldiers and once again defaulted on the government's obligations. It voted to grant equal pay to black soldiers, but not to ex-slaves like Walker, only to those who had been freedmen on the day the Civil war started. There then began a series of deceptions in which sympathetic officers like Col. Edward Hallowell, Robert Gould Shaw's successor as commander of the 54th Massachusetts, told his men, "You do solemnly swear that you owed no man unrequited labor on or before the 19th day of April,

1861. So help you God." And all the ex-slaves who felt that they owed no man unrequited labor then or at any other time chorused their agreement.

But even then Congress's laggard bill offered equal pay only retroactive to January 1, 1864, fully a year after the so-called Emancipation Proclamation had inspired the serious recruitment of black soldiers. Colonel Higginson was eloquent in his indignation. His black troops were not mercenary, he wrote to the New York *Tribune*. If they felt that Lincoln's government could not afford to pay them, he said, they "would serve it barefooted and on half-rations, and without a dollar—for a time." But when they saw white troops earning more than they earned, they felt understandably resentful. And their white officers would have to continue "to act as executioners for those soldiers who, like Sergeant Walker, refuse to fulfill their share of a contract where the Government has openly repudiated the other share." Finally, on March 3, 1865, just a month before Lee surrendered at Appomattox, Congress passed the Enrollment Act and granted retroactively equal pay to all black soldiers.

This included the late William Walker's old regiment, the 3d South Carolina Volunteers, which because of a new regulation banning state names for army units was now known as the 21st U.S. Colored Troops. They had not seen a great deal of combat, but in these last days of the crumbling Confederacy, they were the ones assigned to march triumphantly into the slaveholders' citadel of Charleston, to recapture Fort Sumter, where the first shots had been fired, and Fort Wagner, where Colonel Shaw and his brave black troops had been slaughtered. Before fleeing Charleston, the Confederate general W. J. Hardee ordered the burning of all shipyards, cotton warehouses, and anything else that might be of value to the Union forces.

Colonel Bennett, the survivor of that confrontation with the late William Walker, arrived in Charleston by rowboat from Morris Island, out in the harbor, and sent a message to the mayor to demand a surrender and to promise "every possible assistance to your well-disposed citizens in extinguishing the flames." Then into the city marched the 21st U.S. Colored and two companies of Hallowell's 54th Massachusetts. A reporter for the Boston *Journal* tried to describe the extraordinary scene. Here were ex-slaves, he wrote, "with the old flag above them, keeping step to freedom's drum beat, up the grass-grown streets, past the slave shambles, laying aside their arms, working the fire-engines to extinguish the flames, and, in the spirit of the Redeemer of man, saving that which was lost."

There is just one postscript. In 1894, thirty years after the execution of William Walker, his wife, Rebecca, filed a claim for a pension due to a widow of a veteran of the Civil War. If she was about twenty at the time of her husband's execution, she was about fifty now, in the age of President Grover Cleveland, and perhaps she thought that everybody had forgotten the case of Sergeant Walker.

But the military bureaucracy never forgets anything. On the application by Rebecca Walker for a pension deriving from the execution of her husband, a War Department examiner named J. M. Paxtero recommended "rejection on the ground that soldier's death from gun shot while resisting authority in a state of mutiny was not in line of duty."

Quite true. Sgt. William Walker did not die in the line of duty. Let us honor him for that.

—February 1988

THE ROCK OF CHICKAMAUGA

by PETER ANDREWS

Lee—Grant—Jackson—Sherman—and Thomas. Yes, George Henry Thomas belongs in that distinguished company. Unfortunately, he and Grant never really got along.

O f all the great commanders in the Civil War, the most consistently underrated and overlooked is Gen. George H. Thomas, the big Virginia cavalryman who fought for the Union. From January 1862 at Mill Springs, where he won the first major Federal victory of the war, through December 1864 at Nashville, where he destroyed the Army of Tennessee, Thomas never lost a battle when he was in command.

If ever one man altered the course of a war in a single afternoon, it was Thomas, who took scraps of units from a beaten army and pulled them together into a defensive perimeter that held the line at Chickamauga and saved the Western command. Two months later, at Chattanooga, Thomas's Army of the Cumberland put the Union in position to break the rebellion with one of the most stunning assaults in military history.

Although Thomas won many honors and promotions and there is an impressive bronze equestrian statue of him in Washington today, it is unlikely many of the motorists who drive by him on Massachusetts Avenue know who he was. His fame, one historian said, "never really caught up with his talents."

Thomas is partially to blame for this lack of recognition. He liked to go about his work quietly. He once said he would not have his life "hawked about in print for the amusement of the curious." He was one of the few field commanders in the Union army who did not write their memoirs or publish their papers. Thomas was still on active service when he died, and the task of honoring his memory and defending his record fell to eager but secondary hands.

Thomas had a soldier's instinct for being at the right spot on a battlefield, but he was often poorly placed for building a historical reputation. His victory at Mill Springs has been dismissed as a muddled affair by historians eager to write about the more classically crafted battles of the Eastern theater. Thomas went into the history books as the Rock of Chicka-mauga, but that action is often seen as only one of a number of pieces in the larger mosaic of Union disasters. The storming of Missionary Ridge was an epic war, but command of the forces to exploit that gain was given to another general. On the road to Atlanta, Thomas provided the base that allowed William Tecumseh Sherman to weave his flamboyant flank attacks, and flamboyance is always more interesting than solidity. Thomas's victories at Franklin and Nashville, among the most decisive in the war, were subsumed in the attention given to the final campaigns of Sherman and Ulysses Grant.

Finally, Grant and Thomas never got along. It was important for Grant to be comfortable with people, and Thomas made him uneasy. Thomas exhibited a vaguely aristo-cratic manner that got under Grant's skin, and sometimes Thomas ignored his chief's orders entirely. After a lifetime of service Thomas had developed his own schedule. Once he decided what was the right action to take and when was the appropriate time to take it, no one—not Grant, not Sherman, not Secretary of War Edwin Stanton, not President Lincoln himself—could make Thomas alter his agenda. Grant never admitted to any personal animosity toward Thomas, but when it came time for dividing credit up among his generals, he was particularly stingy with the Virginian.

The men serving under Thomas were more generous. Nicknames, when freely given, are generally a sign of affection. No one had more than Thomas. He was variously known as Pap, Old Slow Trot, Uncle George, and Old Reliable. His demeanor at West Point was so grave that his fellow cadet William Rosecrans called him General Washington. In some-thing of a public relations overreach, he was also called the Sledge of Nashville. But even if Thomas had never stood at

Chickamauga, he was bound to have been known as the rock of something. It was in his nature.

A six-footer weighing more than two hundred pounds, Thomas cut a heroic figure. A Chicago journalist said the general appeared "hewn out of a large square block of the best tempered material that men are made of ... square face, square shoulders, square step; blue eyes, with depths in them, withdrawn beneath a penthouse of a brow." Thomas, the reporter concluded, was "the right kind of man to tie to."

As Rosecrans's nickname for him suggested, George Henry Thomas was the kind of soldier who looks like a future general from the moment he puts on his first uniform. In 1840 he was graduated twelfth in his class at West Point, six behind Sherman, his first-year roommate. While Sherman stayed in the ranks, however, Thomas was made corporal. Promotion was sluggish at best during the mid-nineteenth century, but Thomas served for a year in the Second Seminole War, earning a brevet promotion for bravery in action. He was one of Zachary Taylor's gunners during the Mexican War and was breveted for heroism at Monterrey and Buena Vista.

After the war he pulled a tour as an artillery and cavalry instructor at West Point. Among his students were Phil Sheridan, who learned from him, and John Bell Hood, who did not. The horses Thomas had to work with were dreadful haybags. One was flat blind, and another suffered from some kind of nervous disorder and kept falling down. At the academy Thomas picked up one of his more enduring nicknames, Slow Trot, because he wouldn't let his students drive their poor mounts any faster.

Then came service in the Western frontier with the 2d Regiment of Cavalry. The American Army has never again produced so elite a troop. It was the work of Secretary of War Jefferson Davis, who wanted to create an entirely mounted unit as the showpiece of the service. Davis authorized the officers to spend top dollar for their horses, which were then color-coordinated by unit so that each troop had animals of complementary hues. The regiment armed itself with the latest weaponry, including some of the new breech-loading rifles. Most important were the officers. It was common to give command of a new regiment to a political appointee, but Davis wanted only professionals. He made Albert Sidney

Johnston the colonel. Davis had served with Johnston in the Mexican War and thought him the finest officer in America. The lieutenant colonel's slot went to Robert E. Lee. The two majors were Thomas and William J. Hardee, whose book on tactics would become a standard Army text. The junior officers included seven future generals: George Stoneman, Richard W. Johnson, and Kenner Garrard, who fought for the Union, and Hood, Earl Van Dorn, Edmund Kirby Smith, and Fitzhugh Lee, who served the Confederacy.

For West Point graduates and militiamen alike, combat was the true university of future Civil War generals. Being shot at is an experience like no other, and lessons learned under fire bite the deepest. The lessons, however, are not always the right ones. Veterans of the Mexican War, who had seen a brisk overland charge tipped with steel win the day, would find their assault troops drowning and dying in the swamps of Seven Pines two decades later.

Thomas, who had earned a reputation as a good artilleryman in Mexico and a better cavalryman in the Indian campaigns, developed his own syllabus. In Mexico he had seen battles nearly lost because of poor planning and inadequate supply. Fighting Indians in Texas, Thomas got a more personal lesson. Leading a mounted troop in pursuit of marauding Comanches, Thomas found himself opposed by a single brave. Standing with a bow and arrow, the Indian hit three soldiers and drove a shaft through Thomas's chin, into his chest. Thomas pulled the arrow out and continued to command until the Comanche was killed. It was an impressive gesture, but surely a mounted troop could figure out a way to subdue a lone, unhorsed Comanche bowman without suffering four casualties.

Thomas made himself into the most meticulous commander of the war. "The fate of an army," he once said, "may depend on a buckle." Unlike generals who prided themselves on being fighters who couldn't be bothered with bureaucracy, Thomas enjoyed paperwork and was good at it. He was careful about his files. He made sure that his correspondence was up to date before a fight and that no papers were awaiting his signature. On the morning of Nashville, Thomas stopped his staff in the street to make arrangements for fourteen bushels of coal to be delivered to a neighbor.

Thomas was a Virginian, and when the Civil War made

men choose between their country and their state, he ago-
nized more than most. For a time he entertained some
thoughts about a position with the Virginia Military Institute.
Finally, however, he wrote his wife, Frances, he was staying
with the Union. "Turn it every way he would," Mrs. Thomas
later recalled, the most important consideration for her husband was "his duty to the government of the United States."

Coming from a Confederate state and fighting for the
Union put Thomas in a difficult position. To the North he was
a Virginia slaveowner and, therefore, suspect. His Southern
heritage had helped him gain advancement when men such as
Jefferson Davis were running the War Department, but now it
worked against him. Lincoln once struck his name from a
promotions list, saying, "Let the Virginian wait." To the
South Thomas was a traitor. His property was confiscated and
his family disowned him. After the war Thomas sent money
and supplies to his financially distressed sisters in Virginia, but
the women rejected the aid, saying they had no brother.

Thomas provided the Union with one of its few victories
in the early months of 1862, when he was sent to help retrieve
eastern Kentucky from Albert Sidney Johnston. The war was
still very much of a pickup fight then, with both sides trying to
find officers who could lead troops in the field. The opening
skirmishes had been conducted by two generals who were in
over their heads: Felix Zollicoffer, a firebrand Tennessee
newspaper editor who had served in Congress, and a Union
officer with the imposing name of Albin Francisco Schoepf.
On paper Schoepf was the better man. Born in Polish Austria,
he was a graduate of the Vienna military academy and had
served in the Prussian army while Zollicoffer offered only a
passionate devotion to the Southern cause. In fact there was
little to choose between them. The autocratic Schoepf never
learned how to handle the rude soldiery of the American
volunteer army, and Zollicoffer, whose only military experience consisted of a year's service fighting the Seminoles in
1836, simply didn't know what he was doing.

They had scrabbled at each other in October at Wild Cat
Mountain. Schoepf's army first swept the Confederates
aside but later, under vigorous counterattack, fled the field in
what became known as the Wild Cat Stampede.

The high commands of both sides attempted to bring a

measure of professionalism to the tangled situation. The South installed Maj. Gen. George Bibb Crittenden, a West Point graduate, over Zollicoffer, and the North brought in Thomas as strike-force commander. Crittenden had the harder job. Zollicoffer was as prickly as he was incompetent. He disobeyed Crittenden's order to use the Cumberland as a shield and placed his troops between Thomas and the river. It was no place for a battle, but rather than risk trying to get back across the Cumberland, Crittenden decided to make a fight of it. He took his soldiers on a night march through heavy rain, hoping to surprise Thomas in his camp. It was a daring plan, and it might well have worked against a less careful adversary. But Thomas had put out an elaborate trip-wire alert system. He had picket companies patrolling the area a mile in front of his main force and mounted sentinels three-quarters of a mile in front of the pickets.

The Battle of Mill Springs, also known as Fishing Creek and Logan's Crossroads, began around dawn on January 19, when advance Confederate units struck at Thomas's pickets. The Union men fell back to a solid defensive line, and as Zollicoffer's brigade tried to sort itself out, Thomas hit hard on the flank. The Rebel line trembled, broke, and ran. Thomas kept after the Confederates for almost eight miles. By sundown Crittenden's army of four thousand men had melted away.

In tearing open the first gap in the Confederacy's western flank, Thomas demonstrated the command style that would carry him through the rest of the war. No one likes surprises on a battlefield, and Thomas did what he could to see there were as few as possible. He briefed his officers carefully so they would know what was expected of them. He saw to it that pickets were out in good order, and he stayed on the field so the men could see him. Thus Thomas exhibited three of the qualities in an officer most prized by the troops: He communicated well with them, he was careful about their safety, and he was there.

Unfortunately, Thomas was not always as popular with his peers and superior officers. He arrived at Shiloh too late to do anything but provide burial details, but he did manage to get into one of the many disputes over rank that blighted his career. Thomas was not much concerned with the trappings of high position. He often was a uniform behind and wore his colonel's coat for five months after making general. He was acutely sensitive, however, to the proprieties of rank. He complained vigorously when he received a lower commission than he felt he had earned, and twice he refused to accept higher ones he thought inappropriate. Gen. Henry Halleck, who was trying to squeeze out Grant, shoved the victor of Shiloh aside and gave command of his Army of the Mississippi to Thomas. Unwilling to be used as a source of embarrassment to a fellow officer, Thomas asked to be relieved and sent back to his Mill Springs division. It was a magnanimous gesture, but if Grant was grateful, he never said so.

This punctiliousness was bothersome to the high command, which was trying to get on with the war. Even Lincoln, normally the most solicitous of leaders, got snappish about Thomas. When Thomas complained that Rosecrans had been improperly promoted over him, Lincoln rewrote the date of Rosecrans's commission, giving him seniority. Rank didn't mean much at Chickamauga, but leadership counted for everything.

In the summer of 1863 Rosecrans, with Thomas as second-in-command, led the Army of the Cumberland into Tennessee. At first everything went off splendidly. Rosecrans deftly faked Braxton Bragg out of Chattanooga, seizing a vital stronghold in an almost bloodless campaign. Rosecrans could have regrouped his forces, but instead he committed the fundamental error of mistaking withdrawal for retreat. Convinced he had the Army of Tennessee on the run, Rosecrans plunged into the trap Bragg was setting for him. The kind of careful picket work Thomas had done at Mill Springs might have let Rosecrans know what he was getting into, but he pushed forward scarcely knowing where his own troops were. Bragg struck back a dozen miles south from Chattanooga, in the valley of Chickamauga Creek. *Chickamauga* was an old Cherokee word meaning "river of death," and for two days the river lived up to its name as both sides lost nearly a third of their men.

It was, as were all fights in this snarled Tennessee country, an unruly business. Bad luck turned difficulty into disaster. A Union division pulled out of the line just as James Longstreet and his brigades, newly arrived from Gettysburg, hit. In a moment the Union right flank evaporated. No one likes to take a beating, but to find yourself in sudden and desperate danger during a campaign you thought you were winning is particularly dispiriting. The troops broke and headed for the rear, taking much of the high command with them. Rosecrans, a devout Roman Catholic, was seen crossing himself as he rode back to Chattanooga, where he had to be helped from his horse. Assistant Secretary of War Charles Dana, who was on the field, wrote to Washington, "Bull Run had nothing more terrible than the rout of these veteran troops."

Longstreet was triumphant. "They have fought to the last man," he said, "and he is running."

But Thomas wasn't running anywhere. As a correspondent at the time wrote, "One of those crises had now arrived, rare in the history of any country, where the personal character and power of an individual become of incalculable value to the general welfare."

Thomas assembled a defense line along Horseshoe Ridge. It didn't matter what regiment or brigade the men were from as long as they could handle a gun. There were no speeches and no calls for greatness, just George Thomas riding quietly among the men. If Old Reliable was sticking around, it was probably going to be all right. The only emotion Thomas evidenced was scratching his beard more than usual. He told a colonel the men had to hold their position regardless of the cost, and the colonel replied, "We'll hold it, General, or we'll go to heaven from it."

Many of them did, but the rest held through the day until Thomas retired in good order. Chickamauga was a bloody defeat, but Thomas had saved the Army of the Cumberland.

In Washington President Lincoln, who began the conflict knowing so little about war he took books out of the library to read up on military tactics, had developed the strategic sense that comes with understanding what is really important. The army was beaten, but it still held Chattanooga. If it could stay there, the President noted, "the Rebellion must dwindle and die."

First Rosecrans had to go. In Lincoln's harsh but accurate evaluation, he was "confused and stunned like a duck hit on the head." Lincoln gave Thomas command of the Army of the Cumberland with orders to hold on to Chattanooga until Grant could come and rescue the Tennessee campaign.

When Grant arrived, there occurred one of those social mischances that should not matter in so serious an enterprise as war but do. Grant, wet and hungry after a long ride in the rain, got to Thomas's headquarters around nine o'clock at night. Preoccupied, Thomas seemed not to notice that Grant was sitting by the fire with water puddling out of his uniform. Only after one of Grant's staff asked did Thomas offer his commander quarters, fresh clothing, and food. Grant never put on any great airs, but he did not like being made to feel cheap.

Grant largely ignored Thomas in planning the battle to regain the initiative at Chattanooga. Grant also wrote off the Army of the Cumberland as an attacking force. It had been used up at Chickamauga. He wanted Sherman.

Chattanooga was yet another Civil War battle that did not go even faintly the way it was supposed to. Missionary Ridge, a six-hundred-foot escarpment defended by rifle pits at the bottom and Bragg's marksmen with sixty pieces of artillery at the top, confronted the Federal army. Grant had in mind something very grand, a massive double end run around the ridge. Sherman would swing wide to the left and deliver the main attack on Bragg's flank at dawn, while Joe Hooker swept in from the right to cut off the Rebel retreat. Thomas and his weary Cumberland Army, positioned in the center at the base of Missionary Ridge, were not to move until Hooker was in sight.

Grant's plan went off the rails almost at once. On November 23 Thomas occupied Orchard Knob, high ground before Missionary Ridge, and, the day after, Hooker's men handily drove the Confederate defenders from Lookout Mountain. But the main battle had to be postponed for a day so Sherman could get his men in place to assault the Confederate position at Tunnel Hill. Sherman moved at sunrise but, even outnumbering his opponents almost six to one, he could make no headway. By three in the afternoon Sherman was still bogged down on the left, and Hooker, who had lost five hours repairing a bridge, was nowhere to be seen on the right.

From his command post at Orchard Knob, Grant could see the battle was getting away from him. "We must do something for Sherman," he said. Hoping a demonstration at the center would make Bragg draw troops away from Tunnel Hill, he ordered Thomas to advance on the rifle pits at the base of Missionary Ridge. The first part was easy. The Rebel riflemen, reasonably enough, retreated in the face of an approaching army. Once the Cumberland men got the pits, however, they were on their own. They had no fire support on either side. They had no orders to advance and none to retreat. Staying put was a death warrant for the troops; they were being torn apart by short-range artillery and musket fire from the summit. And so eighteen thousand men of the Army of the Cumberland did what only trained professional soldiers can do. They advanced toward the firing.

An astonished Grant watched the men scramble up the slope "like a swarm of bees." Sharply he asked Thomas who had ordered the charge. Thomas said he didn't know, but Gordon Granger, commander of the IV Corps, allowed that "when those fellows get started all hell can't stop them."

Whether an accident or a miracle—and it was called both—the charge was a blow the Army of Tennessee could not survive. Bragg lost control of his men as they poured off the field in panic. By the time Hooker played his part in Grant's plan, there was no interdicting the Southern retreat. The Union army didn't own horses that fast.

Grant was hailed as the hero of the West, and properly so. His battle had not gone according to plan. Battles rarely do. But he had kept his head and altered his tactics to suit changing conditions. When something didn't work, he tried something that did. That was good enough for Lincoln, who summoned Grant to Washington to take overall command of the Union army. Grant was free to choose his successor in the West.

If generalships were awarded like civil service positions, on the basis of test scores and previous experience, Thomas would have gotten the job. His record in the field was without blemish. He had brought the Union victory at Mill Springs. He saved the day at Chickamauga and won it at Chattanooga. Thomas could not be faulted on any account save one: He and Grant didn't like each other very much. Grant kept Thomas as commander of the Army of the Cumberland but gave the top assignment to his friend, Sherman, whose record up until then had been spotty. Two years before, Sherman had been removed from the field under suspicion of being insane. He was not a tidy keeper of a battlefield. Grant had been surprised at Shiloh largely because Sherman had not put out a proper picket line, and Sherman had failed utterly at Chattanooga. But Grant had liked the fiery redhead since Paducah, when

Sherman, who was senior to Grant at the time, offered to waive any consideration of rank to keep Grant supplied.

Grant was putting together a new command structure, and he knew he could work with Sherman. He wasn't so sure about Thomas. Grant may also have been betting not so much on what Sherman had been but on what he could become given the wider responsibilities of theater command. Whatever Grant's reasons, the success of the Western armies makes it difficult to argue with his decision.

There was never a more mismatched pair than Thomas and Sherman. Thomas slept long and deeply of a night. Sherman never seemed to sleep at all and was forever prowling about his camp at night in his undershirt, smoking cigars. Thomas talked very little and measured his words carefully when he did. Sherman was an exhausting talker with a freely expressed opinion on everything. Nothing was more exciting than having Sherman enter a room, one officer said, and nothing was more relaxing than having him leave it.

They had only one thing in common: Each, in his own way, was a superb commander. Thomas was a craftsman of war who put every element in its proper place before committing himself. Sherman was an artist, sloppy about details, who dealt in visions. As they moved toward Atlanta, Thomas saw enfilades, sally ports, and vedettes. Sherman saw a giant slash cutting the Confederacy in half. Together they complemented each other and made a great, if not always harmonious, team. As Sherman said of Thomas, "He's my off-wheel horse and knows how to pull with me, though he doesn't pull in the same way."

Cumberland Army soldiers on the road to Atlanta might complain, and some did, that they did the fighting while Sherman got the glory. But those were the assigned roles. Thomas and the Army of the Cumberland crowded Johnston's Tennessee troops belly to belly in the center, keeping them pinned and restricting their response to Sherman's left- and right-wing sallies.

There was some friction between the two. Sherman believed in moving fast and traveling light. He hated baggage trains and ordered them kept as small as possible. Thomas, who had wrenched his back in a train accident before the war, liked to take care of himself and his staff. Each night he set up an elaborate outlay of officers' tents. Sherman knew when he was licked. If he couldn't command his old roommate in this matter, however, he could needle him. Sherman liked to ride up to the Cumberland Army camp as if he had come upon a construction site in the Georgia countryside and ask a sentry what it was. When told it was General Thomas's command, Sherman would reply, "Oh, yes, Thomastown. A very pretty place indeed. It appears to be growing rapidly."

Sometimes, disturbed by Thomas's deliberateness, Sherman took a more querulous turn. During the campaign Sherman wrote Grant: "My chief source of trouble is with the Army of the Cumberland, which is dreadfully slow. A fresh furrow in a plowed field will stop the whole column and all begin to intrench [*sic*]."

Certainly mistakes were made. Sherman missed his chance to bag Johnston's army at Resaca, Georgia. If he had used Thomas's heavy striking force to slam the door on Johnston's line of withdrawal instead of a light, insufficiently horsed detachment that pulled up short, he might have done so. Against the advice of Thomas, Sherman ordered up a bloody and needless battle at Kenesaw Mountain. Thomas lost more than nineteen hundred men trying to storm a position that was taken easily by maneuver a few days later.

Nevertheless, the Georgia campaign was a dazzling success. When Sherman announced in September 1864 that Atlanta had been fairly won, the Union, at last, had the Confederacy by the throat. The question was how to end the campaign.

His original orders were to hound the Army of Tennessee to its death, but Sherman was starting to think about salt water. In propounding his idea for a march to the sea, Sherman elevated military strategy to a higher level. "If we can march a well appointed army right through this territory," he wrote Grant, "it is a demonstration to the world foreign and domestic, that we have a power which [Jefferson] Davis can not resist. This is not war, but rather statesmanship."

Grant didn't like the idea at first. The Army of Tennessee, now under the command of John Bell Hood, was still in the field. But Grant acquiesced when Sherman promised both to sweep to the Atlantic shore and to have Thomas take care of Hood.

The conventional wisdom has it that Sherman was delighted when Davis sacked Joseph E. Johnston and replaced

217

him with Hood late in the Atlanta campaign. Hood was a gallant officer who had left a leg at Chickamauga, but he was known to be an impetuous commander, given to bold and ill-considered action. The memoirs of several Union officers relate how delighted they were at the prospect of a blunderer's appearing at their front. Most of these sentiments, however, were written well after the war was safely won, and it is possible Sherman may have been made uneasy by the change of command. Joe Johnston had always been Sherman's patsy. Johnston was a classicist well versed in the history and the art of war. He knew the rules. He knew what was possible and what was not. Johnston understood that Sherman held the whip hand. While looking for just the right opportunity to hit back, which he never seemed to find, Johnston danced to Sherman's tune. John Bell Hood, on the other hand, was tone-deaf. He did not know the rules and usages of war, and it is unlikely he would have abided by them if he had. He was a dangerous man. He attacked when there was no prospect of victory and didn't mind running up a big butcher's bill. Sherman could beat Hood, but it might be expensive. After Kenesaw Mountain, Sherman had become the most parsimonious of field commanders, shunning big battles and direct assaults whenever he could.

Sherman's decision to split forces was a brilliant one in that it allowed both generals to do what they did best. Sherman, rid of Thomas's circus tents, could really fly, while Thomas, whose specialty was the calculated sledgehammer blow, could pound the life out of John Hood.

Sherman stripped the Virginian of some of his best troops and headed for the ocean while Thomas turned to face Hood. Thomas might have been well advised if, like Sherman, he had cut off all communication lines with Washington before he started.

After going over some of the same ground they covered on the way to Atlanta, Thomas and Hood met in earnest on the frozen turf outside Nashville. It was a terrible business.

The string was running out for Hood. His battered army was getting hard to hold together, and he was tired of maneuvering to no effect. It was time to say the hell with it and fight. Hood was a gambler, and he decided to trust to what Albert Sidney Johnston had called "the iron dice of battle." He brought his army to attack Thomas at Franklin. Hood waved aside Nathan Bedford Forrest's advice to try turning the Union flank and ordered a frontal assault. It was a sad thing to do. At Gettysburg George Pickett had led a charge following an extended artillery bombardment and lost 1,354 men trying to cover one mile. Hood proposed to send his men twice that far with no artillery preparation at all.

"I don't like the looks of this fight," said the Confederate general Benjamin Franklin Cheatham. A veteran of the Mexican War who had fought at Belmont, Shiloh, Perryville, Stones River, Chickamauga, and Chattanooga, Cheatham had seen more combat than most men, but he had never seen anything like the afternoon of November 30, 1864, when the Army of Tennessee rose and threw itself on the Union lines at Franklin. For a moment it looked as if the Rebels might pull it off. They ripped into the Union outer defenses, scattering two brigades and capturing eight guns. But it was no go. In a textbook demonstration of how to commit reserves, the Union brigade commander, Emerson Opdycke, without waiting for orders, plugged the gap in a melee of hand-to-hand fighting. Hood kept at it for almost six hours, finally calling off the attack at nine in the evening. More than six thousand Confederate troops, including five generals, had gone down.

After his shattering victory Thomas retired to Nashville to prepare the final knockout. Incredibly, the high command wanted more. Grant, in his Virginia headquarters, did not realize how completely Thomas had control of the situation and was afraid Hood might get loose. He badgered Thomas to attack. But Thomas was having none of it. The weather was too bad and the ground had iced over, making attack difficult. Besides, there were horses to look after and men to equip before fighting again.

"I thought," Thomas said, "after what I had done in the war, that I ought to be trusted to decide when the battle should be fought. I thought I knew better when it should be fought than anyone could know as far off as City Point, Virginia."

Thomas went carefully about his business while his superiors fumed. Not being entirely helpful, Sherman wrote to Grant on December 16: "I know full well that General Thomas is slow in mind and in action but he is judicious and brave, and the troops feel great confidence in him. I still hope he will out-maneuver and destroy Hood." On the day Sherman wrote, destroying Hood was precisely what Thomas was doing.

The problem between Grant and Thomas was that each had a different idea of what was important. Grant was thinking about his final campaign to defeat the Confederacy, and Thomas, with his eternal fussing about details, was putting the campaign at risk. Grant was willing to accept a partial victory as long as it kept Hood from upsetting his plans. Thomas, who had a more limited area of responsibility, was thinking about an individual action. Why go into battle if he couldn't give Hood a thorough whipping? After all, that had been Grant's original order to the Western army.

Grant grew so upset that in six days he scribbled out three separate orders relieving Thomas. Deciding to take personal command in the field, Grant gave the last relief order to a telegraph operator and went to his hotel to pack. The operator, on his own responsibility, decided to hold off sending the telegram until he received the regular night traffic from Nashville. The wires started clacking at about eleven, and when the code clerks deciphered the messages, it was all over. Thomas had struck Nashville on December 15, smashing one corps and, on the following day, two more. The Army of Tennessee, the bravest, unluckiest, and most poorly led military force in American history, had ceased to exist.

Sherman, fresh from his capture of Savannah, sent Thomas a wonderfully self-congratulatory Christmas Day message saying that "had any misfortune befallen you I should have reproached myself for taking away so large a proportion of the army and leaving you too weak to cope with Hood. But as the events have turned out my judgment has been sustained."

Grant found Thomas's pursuit of Hood inadequate. You were always on safe ground criticizing pursuit in the Civil War. Nobody, including Grant, did it well. But Grant's charge was particularly churlish in this case. Thomas had already seen to it there wasn't much left to pursue. After Thomas retired to winter quarters, Grant split up the Army of the Cumberland and doled it out to other units until it was essentially reduced to the IV Corps. As an army commander Thomas was out of business.

The War Department was in a giving mood that December, and Stanton asked Grant about rewarding Thomas with the three stars of a major general. Grant started to block the promotion but later relented. On Christmas Day Thomas found his name was on a promotions list being sent to the Senate for confirmation. He was ranked behind Sherman, George Meade, and Phil Sheridan. His unit surgeon, George Cooper, looked at the slate and allowed that "it is better late than never."

"It is too late to be appreciated," Thomas replied. "I earned this at Chickamauga."

And then he started to cry.

In May 1865, after Lee and Johnston had stacked arms and sent their men home, the Union army put on the greatest parade ever staged on this continent. On the day given to Sherman and his armies of the West, somehow there was no room for George Thomas in the parade. He watched from the reviewing stand. As units of the old Army of the Cumberland rolled by in their insolent western gait, Thomas whispered to no one in particular, "They made me."

After the war Thomas found himself briefly caught up in the turbulent politics of the Reconstruction. Andrew Johnson tried to exploit Thomas by offering to make him commanding general in place of Grant. Thomas wouldn't bite. He frostily refused, saying the promotion was too late a reward for his war service and not justified by anything he had done since.

Thomas was assigned to the command of the Division of the Pacific in 1869, with headquarters in San Francisco. A detail man to the last, he sat at his desk on March 28, 1870, to write a letter to a newspaper correcting an erroneous article concerning his handling of the Nashville campaign. Several pages into the letter he was writing, "This was a very brilliant battle, most disastrous to the enemy, and as the writer in the Tribune says, no doubt contributed materially to the crowning success at Nashville. . . ." Suddenly the bold penmanship quavered. Thomas suffered a massive stroke and collapsed. He died that evening.

—March 1990

GENERAL GRANT'S GALLANT LAST BATTLE

by *ROBERT LINCOLN REYNOLDS*

It was a race with death, and he had a book to write.

On the porch of a little summer cottage at Mount McGregor, New York, in the foothills of the Adirondack Mountains, a man sits in a wicker armchair, writing on a pad of yellow scratch paper. It is July and the sun is warm, but his feet and legs are covered by a shawl, he wears a brown woolen stocking cap, and a scarf is drawn about his throat. Walking slowly along the lane outside the cottage is a small but steady stream of people. Though obviously they have come to see the man on the porch, they are strangely quiet and make no attempt to attract his attention; for his part, he seems almost unaware of their presence, so preoccupied is he with the pencil and the yellow pad.

The man is not really old—on this midsummer afternoon in 1885 he is just past sixty-three—but his hair and beard are quite gray, his once-portly figure has shrunk, and in his face lines of suffering are deeply etched. Ulysses S. Grant, conqueror of the Confederacy and former President of the United States, is dying of cancer of the tongue.

For some time past he has been aware of another staggering fact, too: he is flat broke, having been swindled out his modest fortune by a clever con man. These facts explain the pad and the swiftly moving pencil. Grant is trying, in the only way he can think of, to provide for his wife, his children, and his grandchildren: he is writing his memoirs of the Civil War, and the task has developed into a grim race with death.

The events that led General Grant to this poignant

moment began a little more than a year before. On Sunday morning, May 4, 1884, a caller rang the bell of the general's town house at 3 East 66th Street in Manhattan. The caller was a flashy young man named Ferdinand D. Ward, who with Ulysses S. Grant, Jr., was a partner in thè brokerage firm of Grant & Ward. Everyone in Wall Street knew that Ward was just a promoter and young "Buck" Grant only a figurehead; the firm's real prestige lay in the renown of its silent senior partner.

Ward bore distressing news. The Marine National Bank of Brooklyn, in which their firm's assets were deposited, was in trouble. An unusually large withdrawal was expected on Monday morning, and unless the general could raise $150,000 to help cover it, the bank would fail—and drag Grant & Ward down with it.

Hurriedly, the general called for his carriage and drove the few blocks down Fifth Avenue to the home of William H. Vanderbilt, the railroad tycoon. There, hat in hand, apologizing for disturbing his old friend on Sunday, an embarrassed Grant asked if he might borrow the money. Vanderbilt knew his way around Wall Street, and what he knew about Ferdinand D. Ward he didn't like. Nevertheless, he reached for his checkbook, saying to Grant: "I'm not doing this for the Marine Bank or the firm of Grant & Ward, but for you, General, personally."

That check, promptly turned over to Ward, should have taken care of Monday's emergency. Yet when General Grant arrived at his office on Tuesday, he was met by Buck, his face drained of color. "Father," he said, "you'd better go home. The bank has failed." Ward had simply cashed Vanderbilt's check and pocketed the money. Now he had vanished, leaving the Grants, father and son, to face the consequences.

That afternoon the firm's cashier found the general at his desk with his head in his hands. Beside him was a pad on which he had scribbled the names of relatives and friends who on the strength of his reputation had invested all they had and now faced ruin. Besides Buck there were Grant's other sons, Fred and Jesse, and their families, as well as his widowed sister, his nieces, and several old Army comrades. The general himself had put up all his liquid capital, about $100,000. Even the little hoard of $20 gold pieces he had received as token payments for attendance at various boards-of-directors meetings had vanished.

When Ward and James D. Fish, president of the Marine Bank, were eventually brought to trial, it was discovered that Ward had been juggling two sets of books; the genuine ones showed liabilities of nearly $17 million, assets of less than $68,000. Ward professed not to know what had become of the money: he had simply "lost" it. "I have made it the rule of my life," General Grant said sadly, "to trust a man long after other people gave him up; but I don't see how I can ever trust any human being again."

Ward and Fish went to jail, but the Grants were exonerated as innocent dupes. That did not ease their shame—or improve the family's fortunes. The general was almost literally penniless: at a family conference he emptied his wallet and counted a total of $80 in cash; his wife, Julia, had another $130 around the house. Checks outstanding with the butcher and the grocer—drawn, of course, on the Marine Bank—were sure to bounce. Only an unsolicited loan from their friend the Mexican ambassador, and another from a total stranger who evidently learned of their plight from the newspapers, enabled them to face the immediate future.

And then the pain in the general's throat began.

He noticed it for the first time in June, when he bit into a peach, but he did nothing about it until October, when the pain became so severe that he consulted Dr. John Hancock Douglas, the city's leading throat specialist. Douglas's face turned grave as he noted the intensity of the inflammation, and Grant asked bluntly, "Is it cancer?"

"I was cautious in my reply," Douglas said later, but when Mrs. Grant and Fred came to see him he told them he feared Grant's dire suspicion was correct. Still, though the doctor had never known such a cancer to be cured, he thought it might possibly be arrested. This slender hope the family grasped eagerly. What Grant believed he kept to himself. At any rate, treatment was begun at once.

Meanwhile, Grant had been making strenuous efforts to put his financial affairs in order. William Vanderbilt was not pressing him for payment; on the contrary, he wanted to wipe out the $150,000 debt altogether. But Grant considered it a debt of honor, and now he and Julia offered to turn over to Vanderbilt every tangible asset they had, including even Grant's military souvenirs and the valuable collection of gifts they had received from heads of state during their trip around the world after leaving the White House. Gallantly, Vanderbilt refused; the Grants insisted; finally, Vanderbilt yielded. But he would not keep the souvenirs and gifts, he said: those were a national trust and should be given eventually to the Smithsonian Institution in Washington.

There remained an essential problem: where were the Grants going to get enough money to live on?

For some time the editors of the *Century* magazine had been after General Grant to contribute to a series of memoirs by the leading military and naval leaders of the Civil War. Suddenly their offer of $500 each for four articles looked very good indeed. Enlisting the research assistance of his son Fred, an army colonel, and that of a former military aide, General Adam Badeau, Grant set to work.

His first article, on the Battle of Shiloh, was disappointingly dry and brief, like an official military report. Robert Underwood Johnson, the *Century* editor in charge of the series, went to see Grant and in a leisurely conversation began drawing out of him the little human details that would put flesh and blood on the dry bones. Where, for example, had the general rested after the first day's hard fighting? Well, it had started to pour down rain, Grant remembered, and he had sought shelter in a hospital tent. "But I couldn't stand the amputations," said the gentle man whom his enemies had called "The Butcher," "and had to go out in the rain and sit for the most of the night under a tree."

That was just the sort of detail that would fascinate his readers, Johnson said eagerly, and at his urging Grant agreed to try again. Soon he was writing to the editor: "Why, I am positively enjoying the work. I am keeping at it every day and night, and Sundays." The results were so good that the magazine voluntarily doubled its fee, and meanwhile drew up a contract for a book-length memoir of Grant's entire military career.

His good friend Mark Twain, who often dropped in to share a cigar and an hour of talk with the general, got wind of the proposal. What kind of royalties had the Century Company offered? Twain wanted to know. Ten percent? Absurd. Twain's own publishing firm, Charles L. Webster and Company, would do much better than that. Eventually it was agreed that the general should receive 70 percent of Twain and

Webster's profits on the book, and he set to work on *The Personal Memoirs of U. S. Grant.*

But as 1884 drew to a close his enthusiasm faltered. He was seeing the doctors almost every day now, yet his throat was getting no better. General Badeau, who had joined the household in October, watched in silent anguish at mealtimes as Grant, at one end of the table, sought to hide his pain from his wife, at the other. "He no longer carved or helped the family," Badeau noted, "and at last was often obliged to leave the table before the meal was over, pacing the hall or the adjoining library in his agony." For a while it seemed Grant was losing his will to live. He did not want to write or even talk, but would sit for hours staring at a blank wall, "like a man gazing into his open grave." When Grant told Badeau he did not wish to live if he could not recover, Badeau became alarmed and Grant felt obliged to assure him, "I am not going to commit suicide."

Gradually the general took himself in hand and got back to the *Memoirs* again, seeming to find solace in them. He would work from ten or eleven in the morning until two or three in the afternoon and again, when he felt up to it, later in the day, dictating to a stenographer or writing in longhand himself. He composed deliberately and seldom changed anything once he had committed it to paper.

And now a strange thing began to happen. This man who all his life had been either a rough soldier or a rough-and-ready politician was becoming a writer. Afraid that his battle descriptions might be too technical, he would read them aloud to his family in the evenings, and then ask, "Is that plain to you?" Though his memory was extraordinarily accurate, he insisted that everything he wrote be checked against official war records. And he began to take pride in his literary style. Too shy to come right out and ask Twain how he liked what had been written so far, Grant put the question to him through a member of the family. "I was as much surprised as Columbus' cook would have been to learn that Columbus wanted his opinion [on] his navigating," Twain was later to write modestly. But he said what he truly believed: that the *Memoirs* compared favorably with one of the best military articles ever written, Caesar's *Commentaries.* Grant was pleased and encouraged.

The work progressed, but so did the cancer at the base

of the general's tongue. In mid-February, 1885, Dr. Douglas and the family physician, Dr. Fordyce Barker, called in two specialists for consultation. Each in turn examined the patient, then each gave his opinion. There was no possibility of error: the affliction was definitely cancer; moreover, it was inoperable.

Apparently the gloomy prognosis—it amounted, of course, to a sentence of death—was never given directly to the Grants. But somehow a truthful account of the consultation found its way into a newspaper, where Grant saw it. Thereafter, Badeau said, "He acted like a condemned man." To a friend Julia Grant wrote: "My tears blind me. Genl. is very very ill. I cannot write how ill."

"General Grant is dying," said the New York *World* on March 1. As the news flashed around the country, an extraordinary wave of affection washed back upon the doorstep at 3 East 66th Street. Jefferson Davis, once the President of the Confederacy, and the sons of Robert E. Lee sent messages of sympathy. Former President Rutherford B. Hayes came to call, as did a number of Grant's former Cabinet officers and old Army comrades, especially his favorites, William Tecumseh Sherman and Phil Sheridan. And on March 4 Congress passed a law restoring Grant to his former rank—General of the Army—on the retired list. As the roll call ended in the House, a great cheer swept the chamber; and mixed with the Yankee hurrahs were a number of enthusiastic Rebel yells: in some unfathomable way a common sympathy for Grant in his gallant struggle with death was helping to draw North and South together again.

Though he knew now that he was doomed, Grant refused to be beaten. "General Grant was a sick man," Twain was to note, "but he wrought upon his memoirs like a well one and made steady and sure progress." Before winter was over he had finished Volume I, 180,000 words in all. It was an astonishing body of work under the circumstances, for the pain was increasing steadily. Larger and larger doses of cocaine and morphine were required, and sometimes the drugs would cause hallucinations. On one occasion the general suddenly rose to his feet, looked about the room with haunted eyes, and whispered, "The cannon did it! The cannon did it!" His frightened family watched as he clutched his throat, then fell back into his chair.

On April 1 came a crisis so fearful that a minister was called in to baptize him. But thereafter the patient seemed to rally. By April 27, his birthday, he was able to stand in an upstairs window and acknowledge the tribute of New York's Seventh Regiment as it paraded by in his honor, its band blaring bravely away. Afterward he joined the family in a festive dinner. There was a cake with sixty-three candles, and the house was full of flowers.

The weeks of May and early June were good ones for General Grant. He had considerable remission from pain and was able to get a good deal of writing done. On May 5 Mark Twain wrote to a friend, "In two days General Grant has dictated 50 pages of foolscap." As the warm weather approached, Dr. Douglas wished to move his patient to a high, dry climate, and when the Philadelphia financier Joseph W. Drexel offered the Grants the use of his cottage at Mount McGregor, they accepted gratefully.

They made the journey northward on the New York Central in a special train, in the private car of William Vanderbilt, the Central's president. A reporter aboard the train watched Grant's face as the general looked out upon the crowds that waved and cheered at the stations along the way. His features betrayed no emotion. But once the train came to an unscheduled stop near a signalman's shanty, and when the signalman came out his eyes met Grant's. Immediately he flung both arms upward in salute. One of them was a stump. As the train started to move again he called up to the window: "Thank God I see you alive, General Grant." And indicating the missing hand he added: "I lost that with you at the Wilderness . . . an' I'd give th'other one to make you well." That was too much even for the impassive Grant. His lips tightened, his eyes filled, and awkwardly he lifted his hat in salute to his old comrade in arms.

The trip to Mount McGregor was made on June 16. By that time Grant's voice was very near gone. Thereafter, except for an occasional hoarse whisper, he communicated with his doctors and his family by means of handwritten notes. Some of them have survived.

The day after the general arrived at the cottage he wrote to Dr. Douglas: "I can feel plainly that my system is preparing for dissolution in three ways: one by hemorrhages, one by strangulation, and the third by exhaustion. . . . I have fallen off in weight and strength very rapidly for the last two weeks. There can not be a hope of going far beyond this time. . . ."

On June 23, after overtaxing himself in whispered dictation, he wrote: "I said I had been adding to my book and to my coffin. I presume every strain of the mind or body is one more nail in the coffin."

At about the same time he wrote: "I have tried to study the question of the use of cocaine as impartially as possible . . . When the medicine is being applied the tendency is to take more than is necessary, and oftener. . . . I will try to limit its use. This latter you know how hard it is to do."

Nevertheless, for two or three days at the end of June he tried manfully to do without the cocaine entirely. His agony was fierce, and he scribbled: "A verb is anything that signifies to be; to do; or to suffer. I signify all three." The cocaine was resumed, and though it brought blessed relief, the general knew his time was running out. "I gain in strength some days," he wrote to Dr. Douglas on July 2, "but when I do go back it is beyond where I started to improve. . . . Under these circumstances life is not worth living. . . . I would therefore say to you and your colleagues, to make me as comfortable as you can. . . ."

On July 10 his West Point classmate General Simon Bolivar Buckner, who had fought with the Confederacy and had surrendered Fort Donelson to Grant during the war, made a special trip to Mount McGregor to visit him. The reunion overjoyed the dying man as further evidence that the old enmities were fading. He had another reason to rejoice that day: the page proofs of Volume I arrived from the printer; Volume II, he knew, was about ready to be set in type. By July 16, except for checking over some final proofs, Grant had won his race. Gratefully he wrote: ". . . I first wanted so many days to work on my book . . . it was graciously granted to me . . . There is nothing more I should do to it now, and therefore I am not likely to be more ready to go than at this moment."

A week later, as evening neared, he asked to be put to bed. Everyone about him knew he was giving up the struggle, for he had slept in a chair for weeks, fearful that if he lay down he would choke to death. At 8:10 next morning—it was July 23, 1885—Ulysses S. Grant passed peacefully away in his sleep.

His book—1,231 pages and 295,000 words—is his monument. It is easily the best of the many Civil War memoirs, and may be one of the finest military autobiographies ever published: straightforward but dramatic and occasionally eloquent, generous to friend and foe alike, a modest and unadorned mirror of the man himself. His countrymen bought 300,000 copies within two years after Grant's death, and the financial security of Julia and the family was assured: the royalties came to $450,000.

At Grant's funeral in New York, Generals Sherman and Sheridan walked together as pallbearers with Buckner and Joseph E. Johnston, the last Rebel commander to lay down his arms. Two former Presidents of the United States, Hayes and Chester A. Arthur, and the incumbent President, Grover Cleveland, came to do him honor, and the press was full of eulogies. But the tribute Grant would have appreciated most came from his old friend Sherman. Two days before the funeral, talking quietly with Mark Twain over a drink at the Lotos Club, Uncle Billy had said it all: "He was a *man*—all over—rounded and complete."

—Unpublished

THE BIG PARADE

by THOMAS FLEMING

Once the South was beaten, Eastern and Western troops of the Union army resented each other violently. Then the tension disappeared in one happy stroke that gave the United States its grandest pageant—and General Sherman the proudest moment of his life.

When the Civil War sputtered out early in May 1865, there were two huge Union armies within a few days' march of Washington, D.C. One was the Army of the Potomac, winner of the war in the East, commanded by Maj. Gen. George Gordon Meade. The other was the Army of the Tennessee, or the Western Army, the men who had marched through Georgia to the sea, commanded by Maj. Gen. William Tecumseh Sherman. What to do with these two very different bodies of men was a problem that vexed politicians in Washington.

The sheer logistics of getting vast numbers of men off the payroll was problem enough. But Sherman's Western Army was more than a problem; it was a threat. The men around the volatile Secretary of War Edwin Stanton suspected Sherman and his men of contemplating the overthrow of the federal government. Lincoln was dead, and Stanton was the de facto ruler of the country, as Andrew Johnson groped to comprehend the situation with the usual bewilderment of Vice Presidents suddenly catapulted from superfluity to power. With furious intensity Stanton was prosecuting the band that had conspired with John Wilkes Booth in the plot to assassinate Lincoln. Driven by political ambition and his own punitive instincts, Stanton was trying to convict the entire South of murder. The trial, conducted before a military tribunal at the Arsenal Penitentiary, added to the tension in the jittery capital.

Undoubtedly Stanton's attitude toward Sherman was not improved by Sherman's brother-in-law, the former Maj. Gen. Tom Ewing, who was defending three of the alleged Lincoln conspirators—Dr. Samuel Mudd, Samuel Arnold, and Edward Spangler—and doing a very good job of it. But the larger reason for Stanton's attitude was the treaty of peace Sherman had negotiated with Joseph E. Johnston, commander of one of the last Confederate armies in being.

T wo weeks after Appomattox, in Raleigh, North Carolina, Sherman had sat down with his fellow West Pointer and signed a document that endorsed the legitimacy of Southern state governments as soon as they took an oath of allegiance to the United States. It also guaranteed political rights to the ex-Rebels as well as "rights of person and property." Sherman thought he was following Lincoln's policy of reconciliation, but to vengeful minds he sounded as if he were reconstituting the Old South, complete with slavery. Stanton and the Radical Republicans were outraged—and frightened. Calling in reporters, Stanton accused Sherman of insubordination, stupidity, and treason. Headlines across the country echoed the Secretary's condemnation.

Not too surprisingly, Sherman's soldiers took a dim view of anyone who said such distressing things about "Uncle Billy." In Raleigh they burned a collection of Northern newspapers someone had brought into the town. The implication was clear that they would just as cheerfully burn the newspaper offices. Some people in Washington had little difficulty imagining that these Westerners, who had denounced New England abolitionists and Southern ultras with equal fervor before the war, might decide to take charge of the country. They had just torn the South apart, and it was not completely illogical to imagine them doing the same thing to the East.

What to do? Someone, his name lost to history, came up with a brilliant idea. The government would give both armies a "grand review." They would march separately, on successive days. It not only defused the political mine that was fizzling under the government's feet—it turned out to be the greatest parade in American history.

But this happy result was by no means immediately apparent. The behavior of Sherman and his men as they marched toward Washington was not reassuring. When they camped outside Richmond, they were annoyed to discover that the Union general in charge of the Confederate capital, Henry Halleck, had issued orders barring them from the city, while Southerners were being permitted to go and come without so much as a pass. Tempers flared, fistfights and small riots erupted, and only with difficulty were the Westerners restrained from shooting up Army of the Potomac units guarding the routes into the Confederate capital.

When General Halleck, who was chief of staff and in theory the second-in-command of the entire Union Army, invited Sherman to parade one of his army's corps as a symbolic gesture through Richmond by way of testifying to their martial prowess, Sherman told him to go to hell. Sherman had found out that Halleck was siding with Stanton and had sent telegrams to Western subordinates, such as George Thomas in Nashville, telling them to disregard any and all orders from Sherman.

Sherman, "outraged beyond measure," said only a direct order from the Union general in chief, Ulysses S. Grant, would change his mind about parading through Richmond. Grant was doing everything in his power to contain the crisis. He had rushed to Raleigh and helped Sherman revise the surrender terms, ignoring an order from Stanton to relieve him from command. Grant now suggested it might be a good idea for Sherman to march his army through Richmond. It would give his troops a look at the city and remove the sting of Halleck's refusal to let them in as tourists.

Sherman stiffly complied, first warning Halleck to stay out of sight, lest he be insulted by his angry cadres. The comments of the Army of the Potomac spectators were not complimentary. They sneered at "Sherman's Greasers" and said they looked like Mexicans, "dark with pitchpine smoke." For their part, the Westerners, having examined the city's defenses, said they could have taken Richmond in a week. When they marched past Halleck's headquarters, they expressed their opinion of him, Western style. One of them broke ranks, sauntered up to the immaculate sentry at the door, and shot a stream of tobacco juice all over his highly polished shoes.

The Westerners' performance did not improve as they approached Washington. The first to arrive were a pair of bummers, loaded with loot, riding magnificent horses. Asked how they could be part of Sherman's army, most of which was still departing from Richmond, they explained that they always made it their business to keep to the front. Roaring protests, they were thrown in the guardhouse. They were released when their comrades reached the city and undoubtedly joined those who crowded the capital's saloons and demanded "three groans for the Secretary of War."

The nervous War Department ordered the Westerners to camp on the southern side of the Potomac, hoping a river between the two armies would reduce the friction. They could not keep Sherman there, however. He stormed into the capital, but another talk with Grant and a conference with his brother, Sen. John Sherman of Ohio, calmed him down. Whether he could calm his soldiers was not so certain.

Officially, Washington, D.C., was still in mourning for the slain Lincoln. Many hotels and offices and private homes were draped in black. Nevertheless, the government launched an all-out effort to create a celebratory atmosphere. For five days before the march, teams of workers decked every public building with blue-and-white bunting. Arches of spring flowers soared above Pennsylvania Avenue.

In front of the White House sweating carpenters hammered together a covered pavilion, decorated with flags and flowers and evergreens. On the roof were scrolled the names of the great battles: Antietam, Gettysburg, Shiloh. Opposite this presidential reviewing stand was another covered platform for state governors, members of Congress, and Supreme Court justices. Other stands for guests and Army and Navy officers, the press, and convalescent soldiers stretched along both sides of the broad street.

Enormous crowds surged into the capital from Maryland and more distant states. Henry Adams's future wife was one of a group of young Massachusetts women who arrived to find every hotel and boardinghouse room in the city taken. They settled for a single attic room near Willard's Hotel. The day before the review, they hired carriages and rode out to the camps of the various Eastern regiments, where we may be sure they were cordially entertained.

May twenty-third dawned oppressively hot and dry. Clouds of choking dust filled every street as chaises and carriages and wagons carried spectators to Pennsylvania Avenue. At nine o'clock a signal gun boomed, and the Army of the Potomac headed down the wide street. It was inevitable that they would be given the privilege of marching first. This was Washington's own army, the men who had defended the city from the oncoming Confederates in a score of desperate battles. Their commanders and many of their lesser officers were well known to every Washingtonian.

Not a few politicians and generals hoped the Easterners would shame Sherman's marauders with the precision of their marching and the magnificence of their uniforms. The first impression tended to fulfill this expectation. "The swaying of their bodies and the swinging of their arms were as measured as the vibrations of a pendulum," wrote one eyewitness. "Their muskets shone like a wall of steel."

Uniforms were spotless, shoes gleamed, and every man gripped his musket with a white-gloved hand. They came down the avenue in formation, twelve men to a file, while two elaborate bands, each the size of a symphony orchestra, played "When Johnnie Comes Marching Home," "Tramp Tramp Tramp, the Boys Are Marching," and "The Battle Hymn of the Republic."

At the head of the column rode the army's commander, Major General Meade, the hero of Gettysburg. Cheers rang out, and people pushed forward to deck garlands around the neck of his horse. Meade, known to his men as the Old Snapping Turtle, managed a frosty smile. He had had the difficult task of commanding this great army in the shadow of Gen. Ulysses S. Grant, who was its real director in the convulsive, costly battles of 1864 that had loosened Robert E. Lee's grip on Richmond.

Although Meade was hailed with affection, the crowd was baffled by Grant's absence. Where was the Quiet Man? Why wasn't he at the head of the column?

Grant had solved a difficult political problem in his

usual unassuming, almost offhand way. Theoretically he could have led both armies. He was the commander in chief of both, and he had commanded in the battles that broke the Confederacy in the West in 1863. Instead, he decided to let Meade and Sherman have the cheers. In the same simple uniform he had worn in the field, without a trace of gold braid, he had slipped through the White House grounds and taken his place on the presidential reviewing stand without the slightest fanfare.

After General Meade and his staff came the cavalry. Spectators searched for another hero, Maj. Gen. Philip Sheridan, but in vain; he was on the Rio Grande warning the emperor Maximilian and his French backers to get out of Mexico. Even so, there was more than enough cavalry to satisfy the most fanatic devotee—no less than seven miles of it. The numbers testified to Little Phil's contribution to the war—the idea that cavalry could and should operate independently as a strike force capable of tearing up the enemy's rear and destroying his cavalry in head-on battle. It took the horsemen a full hour to pass any given point in the line of march.

In Sheridan's absence, the star of the men on horseback was the twenty-five-year-old Maj. Gen. George Armstrong Custer. A New York *World* reporter noted his "sunrise of golden hair which ripples down upon his blue shoulders." Ignoring regulations as usual, Custer wore a crimson necktie and buckskin breeches. As he neared the reviewing stand in front of the White House, a woman rushed out of the crowd and threw a wreath of flowers to him. He lunged forward to catch it, and his horse bolted—or seemed to. Custer's hat blew off, and he went hurtling past the reviewing stand, hair streaming out a foot behind him "like the charge of a Sioux chieftain."

After the cavalry came some of the more colorful regiments of the Army of the Potomac: Zouaves in gaudy blue and red, Irish outfits with sprigs of green in their hats. Then came the artillery, the arm that had made the crucial difference for the Easterners in many of their struggles with Lee. The gunners sat stiffly on caissons behind their weapons.

For the spectators the most moving sight in the long line of march was the battle flags. Bullet-riddled, some of them bloodstained, many in shreds, they were the rallying points around which brave men had died on so many hard-fought fields. On this day they were hung with ribbons and garlands, and many people rushed into the street to press their lips against the torn folds.

It took seven hours for the Army of the Potomac to pass the reviewing stand. Everyone agreed the troops had given a splendid military performance. Even before the parade began, the reporter for *The New York Times*, which had been savagely critical of Sherman's treaty with Johnston, assumed Meade's men would win the popularity contest. He predicted thin crowds for the next day's march. Most people would be "indifferent" about watching another column of men trudge past for seven or eight more hours in the hot sun.

Not everyone on the presidential reviewing stand admired the Army of the Potomac's performance, however. William Tecumseh Sherman thought the Easterners marched poorly—too many "turned their eyes around like country gawks to look at the big people on the stand"—and he disparaged the "pampered and well-fed bands that are taught to play the latest operas."

Sherman did not express this admittedly prejudiced opinion publicly. To Meade, who eventually joined him on the reviewing stand, Sherman apologized in advance for his "poor tatterdemalion corps." Meade assured him that the people would make allowances, and the bandmaster offered to bring his two regiments of opera players back for the Westerners. Sherman politely declined. He would depend on his regimental bands because the men were more used to marching with them.

This was something less than the truth. The Army of the Tennessee had not done any parading for the better part of a year. Uneasily aware that his wild men might disgrace themselves, Sherman nevertheless went to work. That night he summoned his top officers to a conference on the next day's march. "Be careful about your intervals and your tactics," he said. "I will give plenty of time to go to the Capitol and see everything afterward, but let them keep their eyes fifteen feet to the front and march by in the old customary way."

Maj. Gen. William Hazen, thinking he was pleasing Sherman, asked his help to get the men of the XV Corps to cut their hair. Sherman refused, telling Hazen he wanted the spectators to see the army as it had looked on the march through the South. Nevertheless, many generals with friends in the commissary department managed to get some new uniforms to issue to their men. They also ordered those who were in rags to be barred from the parade. But a New York *World* reporter noted that still left plenty of bare feet.

Precisely at 9:00 A.M. the Army of the Tennessee rounded the corner of the Capitol and headed down Pennsylvania Avenue. The weather was not quite as warm as the day before. As for the spectators, their numbers had, if anything, grown. *The New York Times* man ruefully estimated them at two hundred thousand, glumly noting that "thousands left the city after the first day but their places were taken by newcomers."

The pundits and politicians were finding out that however much they might deprecate Sherman and his soldiers, to the public they were the supermen who had somehow marched undefeated and unsupplied through the heart of the South. The Army of the Potomac had earned their affectionate admiration. But the Army of the Tennessee had an aura that virtually compelled people to come see it.

Sherman rode at the head of the column, wreaths of roses around his horse's neck. His old slouch hat was in his hand, and his red hair glistened in the bright sun. Behind him came the plowboys from Ohio, Wisconsin, Illinois, Michigan. They took furtive, astonished glances at the signs arched over the avenue: HAIL TO THE WESTERN HEROES. HAIL, CHAMPIONS OF SHILOH, VICKSBURG, CHATTANOOGA, ATLANTA, SAVANNAH, PRIDE OF THE NATION.

The Westerners marched with a rolling, springy stride, perhaps two to four inches longer than that of the men of the East. They were "nothing but bone and muscle and skin under their tattered battle-flags," said Brig. Gen. Carl Schurz, who had marched with them. Another man thought they marched "like the lords of the world." The New York *Tribune* reporter believed their faces were "more intelligent, self-reliant and determined" than those of the Army of the Potomac. The New York *World*'s man found them "hardier, knottier, weirder."

Within minutes the Westerners had won their last victory. The spectators went wild. Sobbing women held up babies;

others simultaneously praised God and wept. Thousands of white handkerchiefs waved from the sidelines. Rooftops, windows, even the trees were full of cheering civilians.

For some regiments the excitement was almost unbearable. Wild cheers burst from their throats. Hearing those yells, Sherman rode in an agony of uncertainty. He could not break his own order and look back. He could only pray his legions had not become the undisciplined mob that the Army of the Potomac considered them. Finally, as his bay horse mounted the slope before the Treasury Building, Uncle Billy could stand the suspense no longer. They were only minutes from the presidential reviewing stand. He whirled in his saddle as he reached the crest of the rise.

What he saw made that "the happiest and most satisfactory moment" of his life. Every man was obeying the order to keep his eyes rigidly to the front. They all were marching to the same beat. "The column was compact," he wrote in his memoirs, "and the glittering muskets looked like a solid mass of steel. . . ."

As Sherman passed the presidential reviewing stand, he raised his sword in salute. The New York *World* reporter said the acclamation was "without precedent." Every man, woman, and child in the crowd shouted his lungs out "as if he had been the personal friend of each and every one of them. . . . Sherman was the idol of the day." This was the same man newspapers had called a traitor only ten days before.

Behind Sherman his massed bands burst into "Marching through Georgia." Flowers poured down like raindrops from the roofs and trees, until the street was ankle-deep in blossoms. As the XV Corps passed the reviewing stand, the officers shouted an order. They whipped off their hats and bellowed a cheer for the President. But their eyes remained locked to the front.

For the Westerners, saluting a new President was the hardest part of the march. A boy from the 12th Wisconsin said: "We couldn't look at the reviewing stand." Had Lincoln been there, he added, "our line would have broken up."

Sherman swung his horse into the White House grounds, dismounted, and joined the dignitaries on the reviewing stand. He embraced his wife and son for the first time in eighteen months and shook hands with his father-in-law, Thomas Ewing, and with President Johnson and General

Grant. Next in line was Secretary of War Stanton, who gamely put out his hand. An eyewitness said Sherman's face turned scarlet and his red hair all but stood on end. He ignored the outstretched hand. "I declined it publicly," he wrote with grim satisfaction, "and the fact was universally noticed." Then he sat down to watch his men.

The Army of the Tennessee continued its triumphant progress along Pennsylvania Avenue. Not only the rolling stride and the resolute frontward gaze hypnotized the spectators; equally interesting were the accouterments the men had carried with them through the South. The New York *World*'s reporter was intrigued by the signalmen carrying sixteen-foot staffs with mysterious flags like "talismanic banners." Behind almost every company was a captured horse or mule loaded with cooking utensils, captured chickens, and an occasional pig on a rope. Here was the explanation of how they had marched through Georgia unsupplied except, in Grant's words, by "sweet potatoes sprung up from the ground."

Behind each division came living evidence of why they fought, proof that the war had been, as Lincoln had hoped, "a new birth of freedom." A pioneer corps of black men marched in double ranks, with picks, staves, and axes slung across their brawny shoulders. Behind them came six horse-drawn ambulances for each division, their bloodstained stretchers strapped to their sides. At the sight of them the cheers died away and a hush fell on the nearest spectators.

To complete the unorthodox aura, riding sidesaddle beside the ambulances was the angel of the army, sunbonneted Mother Mary Anne Bickerdyke. More than once she had taken on Sherman himself to demand better food and more medicine for the wounded.

On the reviewing stand, as the first divisions passed, the German ambassador reportedly said, "An army like that could whip all Europe." A half-hour later he gasped, "An army like that could whip the world." An hour later: "An army like that could whip the devil."

For seven and a half hours the men of the West strode down Pennsylvania Avenue on those sinewy young legs that had carried them farther than most armies had marched in the history of warfare. In the end the cheering spectators realized the aura of invincibility came from something invisible, intangible, something profoundly connected to the idea of freedom. Lincoln had summoned these grandsons of the pioneers from the nation's heartland to settle the ancient issue between the founding sections. More than one spectator sensed it was the martyred President himself in his Western prime they saw striding past them on May 24, 1865.

Within a month this exotic host—and its less glamorous brothers in the Army of the Potomac—had vanished like its creator, "melted back," in the words of one newspaperman, "into the heart of the people from whence it came."

—March 1990

CONTRIBUTORS

SCARRITT ADAMS is a retired U.S. Navy captain and has lectured in American history at the University of Maryland.

PETER ANDREWS is a contributing editor of *American Heritage* and is working on a biography of William Tecumseh Sherman.

LIVA BAKER is an education historian and author of a biography of Felix Frankfurter.

BRUCE CATTON was founding editor of *American Heritage* and the author of *A Stillness at Appomattox,* for which he was awarded the Pulitzer Prize.

CARL DEGLER is Margaret Byrne Professor of American History Emeritus at Stanford University. His most recent book is *In Search of Human Nature.*

NORMAN DELANEY taught history at Del Mar College in Corpus Christi, Texas.

THOMAS FLEMING is a novelist and historian whose works include *Time and Tide.*

OTTO FRIEDRICH is a senior editor at *Time.* His latest collection of essays is entitled *The Grave of Alice B. Toklas and Other Reports from the Past.*

JAMES M. MCPHERSON is the Edwards Professor of American History at Princeton University. His most recent book is *Abraham Lincoln and the Second American Revolution.*

ALLAN NEVINS was professor of history at Columbia University and one of the founders of *American Heritage.*

STEPHEN B. OATES is the author of biographies of Nat Turner, John Brown, Abraham Lincoln, and Martin Luther King, Jr. ROBERT LINCOLN REYNOLDS is a former associate editor of *American Heritage*.

STEPHEN W. SEARS is a former Book Division editor at American Heritage. Among his books are *Landscape Turned Red: The Battle of Antietam* and *George B. McClellan: The Young Napoleon*.

RICHARD SNOW is the editor of *American Heritage* and the author of several books about American history.

CHARLES MORROW WILSON was an assignment editor for *Reader's Digest* and a Vermont historian.